Lecture Notes in Artificial Intelligence 10093

Subseries of Lecture Notes in Computer Science

More information about this series at http://www.springer.com/series/1244

Matteo Baldoni · Jörg P. Müller
Ingrid Nunes · Rym Zalila-Wenkstern (Eds.)

Engineering Multi-Agent Systems

4th International Workshop, EMAS 2016
Singapore, Singapore, May 9–10, 2016
Revised, Selected, and Invited Papers

 Springer

Editors
Matteo Baldoni
Università degli Studi di Torino
Turin
Italy

Jörg P. Müller
TU Clausthal
Clausthal-Zellerfeld, Niedersachsen
Germany

Ingrid Nunes
Universidade Federal do Rio Grande do Sul
Porto Alegre, Rio Grande do Sul
Brazil

Rym Zalila-Wenkstern
University of Texas at Dallas
Richardson, TX
USA

ISSN 0302-9743   ISSN 1611-3349   (electronic)
Lecture Notes in Artificial Intelligence
ISBN 978-3-319-50982-2   ISBN 978-3-319-50983-9   (eBook)
DOI 10.1007/978-3-319-50983-9

Library of Congress Control Number: 2016960290

LNCS Sublibrary: SL7 – Artificial Intelligence

Printed on acid-free paper

This Springer imprint is published by Springer Nature
The registered company is Springer International Publishing AG
The registered company address is: Gewerbestrasse 11, 6330 Cham, Switzerland

Preface

The engineering of multi-agent systems (MAS) is a multi-faceted, complex task. These systems consist of multiple, autonomous, and heterogeneous agents, and their global behavior emerges from the cooperation and interactions among the agents. MAS have been widely studied and implemented in academia, but their full adoption in industry is still hampered by the unavailability of comprehensive solutions for conceiving, engineering, and implementing these systems.

Although much progress has been made in the development of MAS, the systematic engineering of large-scale MAS still poses many challenges. Even though various models, techniques and methodologies have been proposed in the literature, researchers and developers are still faced with the common questions:

- Which architectures are suitable for MAS?
- How do we specify, design, implement, validate and verify, and evolve our systems?
- Which notations, models, and programming languages are appropriate?
- Which development tools and frameworks are available?
- Which processes and methodologies can integrate all of the above and provide a disciplined approach to the rapid development of high-quality MAS?

Existing approaches address the use of common software engineering solutions for the conception of MAS, the use of MAS for improving common software engineering tasks, and also the blending of the two disciplines to conceive MAS-centric development processes.

The International Workshop on Engineering Multi-Agent Systems (EMAS) provides a comprehensive venue where software engineering, MAS, and artificial intelligence researchers can meet, discuss different viewpoints and findings, and share them with industry. EMAS was created in 2013 as a merger of three separate workshops (with overlapping communities) that focused on the software engineering aspects (AOSE), the programming aspects (ProMAS), and the application of declarative techniques to design, program, and verify MAS (DALT). The workshop is traditionally co-located with AAMAS (International Conference on Autonomous Agents and Multiagent Systems) which in 2016 took place in Singapore. The previous editions were held in St. Paul (LNAI 8245), in Paris (LNAI 8758), and in Istanbul (LNAI 9318).

This year the EMAS workshop was held as a one-and-a-half-day event. Fourteen papers were submitted to the workshop and after a double review process, ten papers were selected for inclusion in this volume. All the contributions were revised by taking into account the comments received and the discussions at the workshop. Among them, the paper "How Testable Are BDI Agents? An Analysis of Branch Coverage" by Michael Winikoff, also appears in LNAI 10002 [N. Osman and C. Sierra (Eds.), AAMAS 2016 Ws Best Papers, LNAI 10002, pp. 90–106, 2016, DOI: 10.1007/978-3-319-46882-2_6], since it was selected as the best paper of the workshop, while the paper "Augmenting Agent Computational Environments with Quantitative Reasoning Modules and Customizable Bridge Rules" by Stefania Costantini and Andrea Formisanom also appears in LNAI 10003 [N. Osman and C. Sierra (Eds.), AAMAS 2016 Ws Visionary Papers, LNAI 10003, pp. 104–121, 2016, DOI: 10.1007/978-3-319-46840-2_7], because it was selected as the most visionary paper of the workshop. The volume includes two extended versions from the AAMAS 2016 demonstration abstracts, namely, "PriGuardTool: A Web-Based Tool to Detect Privacy Violations Semantically," by Nadin Kokciyan and Pinar Yolum, and "Using Automatic Failure Detection for Cognitive Agents in Eclipse," by Vincent Jaco Koeman, Koen Victor Hindriks, and Catholijn Maria Jonker.

We would like to thank the members of the Program Committee for their excellent work during the reviewing phase. We also acknowledge the EasyChair conference management system that –as usual– provided support for the workshop organization process. Moreover, we would like to thank the members of the Steering Committee of EMAS for their valuable suggestions and support.

November 2016

Matteo Baldoni
Jörg P. Müller
Ingrid Nunes
Rym Zalila-Wenkstern

Organization

Workshop Organizers

Matteo Baldoni	University of Turin, Italy
Jörg P. Müller	TU Clausthal, Germany
Ingrid Nunes	UFRGS, Brazil
Rym Zalila-Wenkstern	University of Texas at Dallas, USA

Program Committee

Natasha Alechina	University of Nottingham, UK
Matteo Baldoni	University of Turin, Italy
Luciano Baresi	Politecnico di Milano, Italy
Cristina Baroglio	University of Turin, Italy
Jeremy Baxter	QinetiQ, UK
Ana L.C. Bazzan	Universidade Federal do Rio Grande do Sul, Brazil
Olivier Boissier	ENS Mines Saint-Etienne, France
Rafael H. Bordini	FACIN-PUCRS, Brazil
Lars Braubach	University of Hamburg, Germany
Nil Bulling	TU Delft, The Netherlands
Rem Collier	University College Dublin, Ireland
Massimo Cossentino	National Research Council, Italy
Fabiano Dalpiaz	Utrecht University, The Netherlands
Mehdi Dastani	Utrecht University, The Netherlands
Louise Dennis	University of Liverpool, UK
Virginia Dignum	TU Delft, The Netherlands
Juergen Dix	Clausthal University of Technology, Germany
Amal El Fallah Seghrouchni	LIP6 - University of Pierre and Marie Curie, France
Baldoino Fonseca	Federal University of Alagoas, Brazil
Aditya Ghose	University of Wollongong, Australia
Adriana Giret	Technical University of Valencia, Spain
Jorge Gomez-Sanz	Universidad Complutense de Madrid, Spain
Sam Guinea	Politecnico di Milano, Italy
Christian Guttmann	Institute of Value Based Reimbursement System (IVBAR), Sweden
James Harland	RMIT University, Australia
Vincent Hilaire	UTBM/IRTES-SET, France
Koen Hindriks	TU Delft, The Netherlands
Benjamin Hirsch	EBTIC/Khalifa University, UAE
Tom Holvoet	K.U. Leuven, Belgium

Jomi Fred Hubner	Federal University of Santa Catarina, Brazil
Michael Huhns	University of South Carolina, USA
Franziska Klügl	Örebro University, Sweden
Joao Leite	Universidade Nova de Lisboa, Portugal
Yves Lespérance	York University, Canada
Brian Logan	University of Nottingham, UK
Viviana Mascardi	University of Genoa, Italy
Philippe Mathieu	University of Lille 1, France
John-Jules Meyer	Utrecht University, The Netherlands
Frederic Migeon	IRIT, France
Ambra Molesini	Università di Bologna, Italy
Pavlos Moraitis	Paris Descartes University, France
Haralambos Mouratidis	University of Brighton, UK
Jörg P. Müller	TU Clausthal, Germany
Ingrid Nunes	UFRGS, Brazil
Juan Pavón	Universidad Complutense de Madrid, Spain
Alexander Pokahr	University of Hamburg, Germany
Enrico Pontelli	New Mexico State University, USA
Alessandro Ricci	Università di Bologna, Italy
Ralph Ronnquist	Intendico Pty Ltd, Australia
Sebastian Sardina	RMIT University, Australia
Valeria Seidita	University of Palermo, Italy
Onn Shehory	IBM Haifa Research Lab, Israel
Viviane Silva	IBM Research, Brazil
Guillermo Simari	Universidad Nacional del Sur in Bahia Blanca, Brazil
Munindar P. Singh	North Carolina State University, USA
Tran Cao Son	New Mexico State University, USA
Pankaj Telang	North Carolina State University, USA
Wamberto Vasconcelos	University of Aberdeen, UK
Jørgen Villadsen	Technical University of Denmark, Denmark
Gerhard Weiss	University Maastricht, The Netherlands
Michael Winikoff	University of Otago, New Zealand
Wayne Wobcke	University of New South Wales, UK
Pinar Yolum	Bogazici University Turkey
Neil Yorke-Smith	American University of Beirut, Lebanon
Rym Zalila-Wenkstern	University of Texas at Dallas, USA

Steering Committee

Matteo Baldoni	University of Turin, Italy
Rafael H. Bordini	FACIN-PUCRS, Brazil
Mehdi Dastani	Utrecht University, The Netherlands
Juergen Dix	Clausthal University of Technology, Germany
Amal El Fallah Seghrouchni	LIP6 - University of Pierre and Marie Curie, France
Paolo Giorgini	University of Trento, Italy
Jörg P. Müller	TU Clausthal, Germany

Contents

nDrites: Enabling Laboratory Resource Multi-agent Systems

Katie Atkinson[1], Frans Coenen[1], Phil Goddard[2],
Terry R. Payne[1], and Luke Riley[1,2(✉)]

[1] Department of Computer Science, University of Liverpool, Liverpool L69 3BX, UK
{atkinson,coenen,payne,l.j.riley}@liverpool.ac.uk
[2] CSols Ltd., The Heath Business & Technical Park,
Runcorn, Cheshire WA7 4QX, UK
{phil.goddard,luke.riley}@csols.com

Abstract. The notion of the multi-agent interconnected scientific laboratory has long appealed to scientists and laboratory managers alike. However, the challenge has been the nature of the laboratory resources to be interconnected, which typically do not feature any kind of agent capability. The solution presented in this paper is that of nDrites, smart agent enablers that are integrated with laboratory resources. The unique feature of nDrites, other than that they are shipped with individual instrument types, is that they poses a generic interface at the "agent end" (with a bespoke interface at the "resource end"). As such, nDrites enable the required inter-connectivity for a Laboratory Resource Multi Agent Systems (LR-MAS). The nDrite concept is both formally defined and illustrated using two case studies, that of analytical monitoring and instrument failure prediction.

1 Introduction

Analytical laboratories form a substantial industry segment directed at chemical analysis of all kinds (clinical, environmental, chemical, pharmaceutical, water, food etc.). Supplying this marketplace is a \$100B per annum industry. Laboratory instruments come in many forms but are broadly designed to undertake a particular type of chemical analysis. Examples of laboratory instrument types include: inductively coupled plasma mass spectrometers (to determine metal concentrations) and Chromatography systems (to determine organic concentrations). Such laboratory instruments, although usually "front-ended" by a computer resource of some kind, typically operate in isolation. This is because the interfaces used are specific to individual instrument types (of which there are thousands) and individual manufacturers. The industry acknowledges that there are significant benefits to be gained if instruments, of all kinds, could "talk" to each other and to other devices [12,25]; an ability to support remote monitoring/managing of instruments would on its own be of significant benefit. A potential solution is the adoption of a Multi-Agent Systems (MAS) approach

© Springer International Publishing AG 2016
M. Baldoni et al. (Eds.): EMAS 2016, LNAI 10093, pp. 1–21, 2016.
DOI: 10.1007/978-3-319-50983-9_1

to laboratory resource interconnectivity: a Laboratory Resource Multi Agent System (LR-MAS).

However, at present, there is no simple way whereby the LR-MAS vision can be realised. This is not only because of the multiplicity of different interfaces for different models, but also the complex mappings, translations and manipulations that have to be undertaken in order to achieve the desired interconnectivity. Even when just considering specific laboratory instruments, rather than the wider range of laboratory resources, there are many thousands of models being sold at any one time and a huge variety of legacy systems still in routine use. The limited connectivity that exists is largely focused on what are known as Laboratory Instrument Management Systems (LIMS); systems that receive and store data from instruments (for later transmission to laboratory clients) and manage wider laboratory activities. Some software does exist to facilitate connectivity, for example the L4L (Links for LIMS) software package produced by CSols Ltd[1] (a provider of analytical laboratory instrument software); but this still requires expensive on-site visits by specialist engineers to determine the desired functionality and the nature of the bespoke interfacing. All this serves to prevent the adoption of MAS capabilities within the analytical laboratory industry, despite the general acknowledgement that large scale MAS connectivity will bring many desirable benefits [12,25].

The technical solution presented here is that of "smart agent enablers" called *nDrites*; an idea developed as part of a collaboration between CSols Ltd and a research team at the University of Liverpool, directed at finding a solution to allow the realisation of the LR-MAS vision. The nDrite concept is illustrated in Fig. 1. As shown in the figure, nDrites interact, at the "resource end", in whatever specific way is required by the laboratory resource type in question; whilst at the other end nDrites provide generic interaction. Note that in the figure, for ease of understanding, the nDrite is shown as being separated from the laboratory resource (also in Fig. 2), in practice however nDrites are integrated with laboratory resources. Thus nDrites provide system wide communications so as to allow agents to interact with laboratory resources to (say): (i) determine the current state of an entire laboratory system, (ii) determine all past states of the system (system history) or (iii) exert control on the laboratory resources operating within a given laboratory framework. Thus, in general terms, nDrites are a form of intelligent middleware that facilitate LR-MAS operation. The main advantage offered is that of cost. The idea is to build up a bank of nDrites, one per instrument type, that are integrated and shipped with the individual instruments in question. This will then alleviate the need for expensive on-site visits and provide the desired LR-MAS connectivity. The research team already have nDrites in operation with respect to two instrument types (a plasma autosampler and an inductively coupled plasma mass spectrometer (ICP-MS)[2]).

---

[1] http://www.csols.com/wordpress/.

[2] The autosampler is manufactured by Teledyne CETAC Technologies, http://www.cetac.com, while the ICP-MS is manufactured by Perkin-Elmer, http://www.perkinelmer.com/.

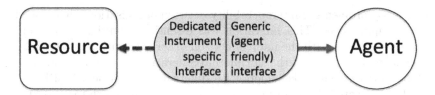

Fig. 1. nDrite smart agent enabler

The main contributions of this paper are thus: (i) the concept of nDrite smart agent enablers that facilitate multi-agent laboratory resource interconnectivity, (ii) the associated formalism that provides for the generic operation of nDrites, and (iii) two case studies illustrating the utility of the nDrite concept (the first currently in production, the second under development). The rest of this paper is organized as follows. In Sect. 2 some related work to that presented in this paper is considered. The proposed Laboratory Resource Multi-Agent System (LR-MAS) framework, including the nDrite concept, is presented in Sect. 3. In Sect. 4, we detail how the different parts of the LR-MAS link together, including how the nDrites handle the communication aspects of the system and how agents are viewed within LR-MAS. The operation of the framework is then illustrated using two case studies describing particular nDrite applications. The first (Sect. 5) is an analytical monitoring case study agent, the second (Sect. 6) is a resource monitoring application agent that operates using a data stream classifier. The paper concludes with some discussion in Sect. 7.

2   Previous Work

The notion of the pervasive, service rich and interconnected scientific laboratory has long appealed to scientists and laboratory managers of all kinds [12,25]. Many scientific laboratory processes have traditionally involved using a number of separate, but interconnected tasks, performed by different systems and services (often bespoke) with little support for automated interoperation or holistic management at the laboratory level. To facilitate this interconnectivity, early work was directed at service oriented infrastructures using *Grid* (and later, *Cloud*) computing [10,11,17,27], whereby laboratory equipment, high-performance processing arrays, data warehouses, and *in-silico* scientific modelling was wrapped, and managed, by a service-oriented client [10,11]. The main focus was that of a "service marketplace" used to discover different services [32] and to schedule or provision their use, as well as to provide support for tasks such as: security [3], notification [19], and scheduling [27]. The need for intelligent, autonomous support for such Grid infrastructures has been well documented [10,11,16,21,27, inter alia].

The Grid Computing based laboratory infrastructure idea has now been superseded by the emergence, and wide-scale adoption, of Web Services, and consequently MAS, which exploit many of the standards used for the web, and resolved many problems of interoperability between organisations that can effect grid based approaches. This migration was essential to mitigate some of the pragmatic challenges with the interconnection of services within an Open Agent Environment [33]; however, the flexible interoperation of systems and services (developed by different stakeholders with different assumptions) is still a challenge. This motivated the adoption of a wrapper-based approach to support wide spread usability within the nDrite concept.

The laboratory instrument MAS vision thus provides for the automation of process models and workflows [31,32]; sequences of processes that can occur both serially and in parallel to achieve a more complex task. The laboratory workflow concept has been extensively researched. The fundamental idea is that of a collection of software services, whereby each service is either a process (often semantically annotated [10,16,32]), or manages and controls some laboratory resource. Such workflows are typically orchestrated using editors or AI-based planning tools [32], resulting in either an instantiated workflow (one where the specific service instances are identified and used) or in an abstract workflow (one where the instantiation of the services themselves is delayed until execution time). Stein et al. [27,28] explored the use of an agent-based approach to automatically discover possible service providers where abstract services are defined within a workflow, by using probabilistic performance information about providers to reason about service uncertainty and its impact on the overall workflow. The idea was that by coordinating their behaviours, agents could "re-plan" if the providers of other services discovered problems in their provision, such as failure, or unavailability. An interesting aspect of this workflow planning approach was the use of autonomously requesting redundant services for particularly critical or failure-prone tasks (thus increasing the probability of success). However, to facilitate the notion of autonomous control, the services themselves need to be endowed with the necessary capabilities to be self monitoring (and thus self aware), discoverable, and communicable [23].

The notion of agents supporting the management of laboratory services through interoperation and workflow (either defined a-priori or dynamically at runtime) is only possible if the agents describe and publish their capabilities, using some discovery mechanism [9]. Although many formalisms (such as UDDI, JINI, etc.) have been proposed to support *white* and *yellow* page discovery systems, the discovery of agent-based capabilities based on knowledge-based formalisms describing inputs, outputs, preconditions and effects was pioneered by Sycara et. al. in the work on LARKS [29], and later with the *Profile Model* within OWL-S [1] and the machinery required to discover them [24]. However, before these descriptions and their underlying semantics can be defined, a formal model of the agent capabilities, and their properties should be modelled.

In the above previous work on the automation of process models and workflows using MAS technology, it was assumed that communication services would either be provided by some common or standardised interfaces or through some kind of mediator [30]. However, as noted in the introduction to this paper, there is no agreed communication standard currently in existence, nor is there likely to be so; whilst currently available mediators are limited to bespoke systems such as CSols' L4L system. Hence the nDrite concept as proposed in this paper.

There have been other studies directed at connecting agents to environments, although not necessarily in the context of the laboratory instrument setting proposed here, where the interfaces are integral to, and shipped with, individual laboratory instruments. The instruments thus have a built in agent connectivity potential. For example, in [4] a generic environment interface standard is proposed that is founded on an interface intermediate language that has a number of similar properties to those characterised by the nDrite concept proposed in this paper. They illustrate their interface with respect to Multi-Agent Based Simulation (MABS). In [2], the properties for large-scale "open" multi-agent systems is also emphasised, and the requirements for such systems identified. The THOMAS abstract architecture is described, whose usage is illustrated using a travel agency MAS example. In [22], the focus is on the notion of the "artefacts" for MAS such that the ad-hoc engineering of "agent societies" can be realised. All of these systems [2,4,22] are presented at a higher level of abstraction to the work described in this paper, and thus, whilst they all share a level of generality, it is difficult to draw direct comparisons with the multi-agent interconnected scientific laboratory at which the work presented in this paper is directed. Also, unlike the nDrite concept, the proposed systems do not appear to have been used in a commercial setting; whereas the work presented in this paper is very much commercially focused. The proposers adopted a bottom-up approach whereby we started with two instruments that we wish to connect and built up from there. The result is a commercial product that at time of writing was already being shipped within laboratory instruments. A similar bottom-up approach was adopted in [20], in the domain of automated negotiation, where the observation was made that many automated negotiators are intended for a specific domain of application. To address this issue, and instead of adopting a high level generic approach as suggested in [2,4,22], an alternative generic mechanism is proposed, GENIUS (*General Environment for Negotiation with Intelligent multi-purpose Usage Simulation*), directed specifically at the domain of automated negotiation.

3   The Laboratory Resource Multi-agent System (LR-MAS) Framework

A high level view of the proposed nDrite facilitated Laboratory Resource Multi-Agent System (LR-MAS) framework is presented in Fig. 2. Referring to this figure we have a number of laboratory resources, all connected to nDrites (dashed lines). The resources shown in the figure include: (i) two laboratory instruments (such as auto-samplers, laser ablation systems, mass spectrometers, and so on), (ii) a Laboratory Instrument Management System (LIMS) and (iii) a "links for LIMS" system (CSols' legacy mechanism for achieving instrument connectivity to LIMS, but still in operation as indicated by the dotted line). The figure also shows two users and a number of agents. Four of these agents are connected

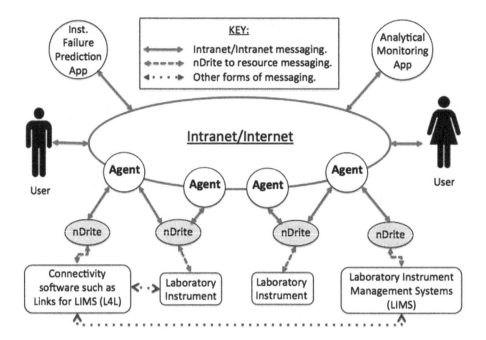

Fig. 2. nDrite facilitated Laboratory Resource Multi-Agent System (LR-MAS) configuration

directly to one or more nDrites; two provide linkages between pairs of laboratory resources while two others are simply "front ends" to resources. The two remaining agents are application agents, not directly connected to nDrites, one is an Instrument Failure prediction agent and the other an Analytical Monitoring agent. We introduce Ag to denote the set of all possible agents in a LR-MAS, where $Ag = \{ag_1, ag_2, \ldots, ag_n\}$. It should also be noted that the vision presented in Fig. 2 is a high level one, in practice the connectivity/operation will be more restrictive for reasons of data confidentiality and business efficacy.

As noted in the introduction to this paper the interconnectivity between agents and laboratory resources in our LR-MAS is facilitated by the nDrite smart agent enablers (see Figs. 1 and 2). The nDrites can be considered to be wrappers for laboratory resources in the sense that they "wrap" around a laboratory resource to make the laboratory resource universally accessible within the context of a MAS (LR-MAS). As such, nDrites can be viewed as being both the agent actuators and sensors for the laboratory resources with which they may be paired. This section provides detail of the nature of nDrites. More specifically, a formalism is presented to enable the LR-MAS vision given above. Subsect. 3.1 presents the formalism with respect to laboratory resources while Subsect. 3.2 presents the nDrite formalism both from a sensor and actuator perspective.

3.1   The Laboratory Resources Multi Agent System Model

As already noted, individual laboratories comprise a number of laboratory resources. We introduce the set of laboratory resources as $L = \{L_1, L_2, \ldots, L_n\}$. Each laboratory resource has a set of one or more actions that the laboratory resource can perform. The complete set of possible actions that laboratory resources can perform is denoted by $Ac = \{\alpha_1, \alpha_2, \ldots, \alpha_n\}$. To find the set of actions an individual resource L_i can perform we use the partial action function LRact: $L \mapsto 2^{Ac}$. Given that there are many different types of laboratory resources (laboratory instruments, robots, data systems, and so on) resources can be grouped into a set of categories $T = \{T_1, T_2, \ldots, T_n\}$, where each T_i is some subset of L ($T_j = \{L_p, L_q, \ldots, L_z\}$). Each category is referred to as a *laboratory resource type*. Thus $\forall T_j \in T$, $T_j \subseteq L$ and $\forall L_i \in T_j$, $L_i \in L$. The intersection of the actions of all laboratory resources of a particular laboratory resource type are called the *critical actions* for that type, denoted $Ac^{\cap T_j}$ where for type T_j: $\bigcap_{\forall L_i \in T_j}$ LRact$(L_i) = Ac^{\cap T_j}$. Note that individual resources can feature other individual actions that are not shared through the critical action set.

3.2   nDrites

The principal function of nDrites is to provide MAS connectivity without exposing the detailed operation of individual laboratory resources of many different kinds and the many different data formats. Recall that laboratory instruments are produced by many different vendors each using proprietary data formats; there are no standardised language or communication protocols for these different resources. Therefore, as noted previously, nDrites are used as wrappers for laboratory resources so as to create a standardised method for retrieving data from, and exerting control over, every *nDrite enhanced* laboratory resource. As such, nDrites can be viewed as both actuators and sensors. A formal definition of the operation of nDrites is presented in the remainder of this sub-section; firstly in the context of nDrites as actuators and secondly in the context of nDrites as sensors.

nDrites as Actuators. The set of nDrites are denoted as $Den = \{D_1, D_2, \ldots, D_n\}$. The set of possible nDrite actions that the complete set of nDrites Den can expose is $Dc = \{\delta_1, \delta_2, \ldots, \delta_n\}$. The following partial nDrite *action function* defines the set of nDrite actions that a given nDrite can expose DenAct: $Den \mapsto 2^{Dc}$. Some nDrite actions may only be possible with respect to particular laboratory resources, others will be *critical actions* shared across a single laboratory resource type or a number of types. To find the set of laboratory resource types to which an nDrite action may be applied we use the function pos: $Dc \mapsto 2^T$. Note also that actions may be sequenced, by an agent, so as to define workflows.

Each nDrite action δ_i requires a corresponding *action object*, which details all the necessary parameters for δ_i to operate successfully. The set of nDrite action objects (that are provided to functions that perform actions) is $Oa = \{oa_1, oa_2, \ldots, oa_n\}$. Each nDrite action object has a class type in the sense that each object belongs to a class which in turn defines the nature of the object. The set of nDrite object class types is given by $Ot = \{ot_1, ot_2, \ldots, ot_n\}$. The class type of each nDrite action object is found by the following function type: $Oa \mapsto Ot$. To find out which class type is required for each nDrite action δ_i, we use the object requirement function req: $Dc \mapsto Ot$ (we assume only one object type is required for each nDrite action).

Recall that individual laboratory resources are likely to perform individual actions in different ways. Hence, at the resource end, nDrites have bespoke interfaces (see Fig. 1). As such, nDrites are paired with individual laboratory resources (recall Fig. 2). An nDrite D_j and a laboratory resource L_i that are connected together are thought of as an *agent enabling pair*: $AEP_k = (L_i, D_j)$. The set of all agent enabling pairs is defined as $AEP = \{AEP_1, AEP_2, \ldots, AEP_n\}$.

Consequently, given an nDrite-laboratory resource pairing, the nDrite functionality can be mapped onto the resource functionality. Additionally, note that an nDrite action δ_i for an nDrite may also include additional software only actions. A software only action is an operation performed internally to the nDrite itself with no engagement with its paired laboratory resource (for example "return the nDrite identification number"). The set of software only actions are $S = \{s_1, s_2, \ldots, s_n\}$. Therefore nDrite actions map onto zero, one or many laboratory resource actions and zero, one or many software only actions[3]. To find the set of laboratory resource and/or software only actions that occur when an nDrite action is called, we use the partial nDrite exposure function exp: $Aep \times Dc \mapsto 2^{Ac} \cup 2^S$. Given $L_i \in T_k$ then $\forall \delta_k$ where $T_k \notin \text{pos}(\delta_k)$, the following holds: $\text{exp}((L_i, D_j), \delta_k) = \emptyset$. That is, zero laboratory resource and software only actions occur when an nDrite action δ_k is attempted to be invoked on an nDrite that cannot perform it. Should an nDrite D_j want to perform an action $ac \in Ac$ on its paired laboratory resource L_i, then it calls the function Perform(ac, L_i). Should an nDrite D_j want to perform an action $ac \in S$ on itself, then it calls the function Perform(ac, D_j). In both cases a Boolean is returned to indicate whether the action was successful (true) or not (false). We do not describe in detail what occurs in the Perform function due to the bespoke interface with the laboratory resource.

This completes the discussion on nDrites as actuators for agent based software. In summary, nDrites can expose all possible actions that a laboratory resource can provide, as well as expose more software only actions. Additionally, nDrites can lower the computational burden for associated agents by exposing sequences of software and laboratory resource actions. In this manner, nDrites *enhance* the capabilities of the laboratory resources that they are attached to. Of course, for agents to trigger nDrites to perform functions, the agents must know what nDrite actions each nDrite provides.

---

[3] Note that the number of exposed nDrite actions can therefore be greater than the number of instrument actions.

Inspired by [6], the LR-MAS is divided into containers where each container has three services that allow for agents to find out: (a) what nDrites there are; (b) how to communicate with each nDrite; and (c) what each nDrite can do. The three services are the following (which are not shown in Fig. 2):

(a) *White pages service*: Manages the container by registering and deregistering nDrites and agents from it. Provides unique identifiers to each registered component. Also can provides information about the name and ID of each agent/nDrite, where an agent/nDrite is located and what type each nDrite is (e.g. autosampler, ICP-MS instrument, etc.). Therefore agents can request information regarding a specific nDrite or multiple nDrites of the same type.
(b) *Message processing service*: Handles the internal and external messaging of the container. An agent/nDrite needs to know the location of this service to connect to the container (who will then inform the white pages that a new component would like to be connected). The external messaging functionality depends on the specific implementation of the service but can be email, SMS, service to service communication, etc.
(c) *Yellow pages service*: Records the functionality that each nDrite of the container wants to advertise. Agents can therefore access this yellow pages to search for a specific capability within the container.

nDrites as Sensors. For agents to work correctly with nDrites (and therefore the laboratory resources they are connected to), nDrites need to not only be actuators but also sensors. Therefore nDrites map laboratory resource actions into objects that can be understood in our LR-MAS. Previously we mentioned that nDrites, in their actuator role, receive nDrite action objects, which are required for nDrites to perform actions. Concurrently nDrites act as sensors and produce *nDrite sensor objects*. The set of nDrite sensor objects are $Os = \{os_1, os_2, \ldots, os_n\}$. Each object has a class type, where the set of object class types are defined as $Ot = \{ot_1, ot_2, \ldots, ot_n\}$ (note that this is the same definition as object types for nDrite action objects). The type of each sensor object is found by the following function type: $Os \mapsto Ot$. The set of sensor objects that an nDrite maps a set of laboratory resource actions onto, is found using the function Sen: $2^{Ac} \times \mathbb{N} \mapsto 2^{Os}$, where the natural number represents the current time point.

Every nDrite D_j collects the nDrite sensor objects it generates in an associated nDrite sensor database (SDB_j)[4] that grows monotonically over time (time-point $t = 1$ occurs when the nDrite is turned on). Depending on the end users needs, nDrite sensor databases can be local to the nDrite itself, sit on a laboratory server, or be in the cloud. The sensor database is defined as:

Definition 1. nDrite Sensor database: *The database SDB_j for an agent enabling pair (L_i, D_j) holds a set of nDrite objects Osi (where $Osi \subseteq Os$), that*

---

[4] Additionally there exists an nDrite action database for an nDrite D_j, denoted ADB_j, which holds nDrite action objects.

have been generated by D_j because L_i has performed the actions LAc (where $LAc \subseteq Ac$).

$$SDB_i^t = \begin{cases} \emptyset & \text{iff } t = 0, \\ SDB_i^{t-1} \cup Sen(LAc, t) & \text{iff } t > 0 \text{ and } Sen(LAc, t) \neq \emptyset, \end{cases}$$

For nDrites to be sensors for agents, an agent needs to be able to access the objects in the nDrites database. Therefore, included in the software only actions of each nDrite are the following database access functions:

- `GetObjectsByOccurances`$_i(2^{Ag} \times 2^{Ot} \times \mathbb{N}) \mapsto 2^{Os}$. Returns to the given agent, the most recent n objects of the given object types that occurred in the SDB_i where $n \in \mathbb{N}$.
- `SubscribeToObjects`$_i(2^{Ag} \times 2^{Ot} \times \mathbb{N})$. Causes $ag \in Ag$ to subscribe to receiving automatic updates concerning sensor objects, saved by nDrite D_i in its database SDB_i, which are of the desired object types. This subscription occurs until the given timepoint $n \in \mathbb{N}$.
- `UnSubscribeFromObjects`$_i(2^{Ag} \times 2^{Ot} \times \mathbb{N})$. Causes $ag \in Ag$ to unsubscribe to receiving automatic updates concerning sensor objects, saved by nDrite D_i in its database SDB_i, which have the desired object types. This subscription occurs until the given time point $n \in \mathbb{N}$. If $n = 0$, then the agent is completely unsubscribed.

Additional functions required for the nDrites to operate successfully as agent sensors are as follows:

- `GetSubscribers`$_i(2^{Ot}) \mapsto 2^{Ag}$. Receives a set of object types and returns the set of agents that have subscribed to these object types.
- `GetNextAction`$(L \times \mathbb{N}) \mapsto Ac$. Receives a single laboratory resource and a time limit $n \in \mathbb{N}$, and returns the next laboratory action that occurs before the timelimit. If the laboratory resource performs no recognised action within the time limit then *null* is returned.
- `Connected`$(2^{Ac} \times 2^{Ac}) \mapsto \{true, false\}$. Returns whether the first set of laboratory resource actions are connected to the second set of laboratory resource actions (*true*) or not (*false*). The two sets are connected if: (i) they form a series that can be converted into an nDrite sensor object; or (ii) they form a series that, when further nDrite sensor objects are added, can be converted into an nDrite sensor object. Also, *true* is returned if the first set of laboratory resource actions are the empty set. *False* is returned if the second set of laboratory resource actions are the empty set or if both sets are empty.
- `nDriteAdvertisingObjects`$_i(2^{Ot}) \rightarrow \{true, false\}$. Returns whether D_i is advertising that it can update the agents on the given set of object types (*true*) or not (*false*). Again, it is assumed that this advertisement is performed using a yellow pages agent.
- `CollectSensorObjects`$_i(\mathbb{N}) \rightarrow 2^{Os}$. Returns the objects from the database SDB_i that have occurred since the time point $n \in \mathbb{N}$.

4   The Laboratory Resource Multi Agent System Implementation

In the previous section, the formalism of the laboratory resource multi agent system (LR-MAS) was detailed. This section concentrates on how the different sections of LR-MAS link together. Subsect. 4.1 details the messages that are sent between the nDrites and agents. Subsects. 4.2 and 4.3 builds on the formalism to show: (i) how nDrites, in their role of agent actuators, handle incoming messages; and (ii) how nDrites, in their role as agent sensors, produce messages that get sent to agents. The section is then completed with Subsect. 4.4 which gives a brief definition for LR-MAS agents.

4.1   Communications

So far we have shown that nDrites have the available functionality to be agent actuators and sensors. As nDrites are separate software entities to agents, there needs to be a communication mechanism available for the agents to utilise the actuator and sensor capabilities of the nDrites. In this section we detail the message syntax between nDrites and agents. Note that the associated message syntax for agent to agent communication is considered to be out of scope with respect to this paper, however this can clearly be achieved using a FIPA compliant Agent Communication Language (ACL).

The LR-MAS given in Fig. 2 features a set of communicating entities (agent-nDrite pairs). Messages are sent between these entities, from the set of possible messages, denoted by $M = \{m_1, m_2, \ldots, m_n\}$. Each message contains:

(a) *meta deta*, denoted by MD;
(b) A set of *nDrite actions and nDrite action objects pairs*[5], denoted $NAOP$, where a single pair is indicated by the tuple $\langle \delta_i, oa_k \rangle$;
(c) A set of *nDrite sensor objects* (NSO).

We assume that the meta data must include two functions `Sender` and `Receiver` that returns an entity in either the set of nDrites Den or the set of agents Ag.

Definition 2. *An **nDrite system message** is a tuple denoted $m_i = \langle MD, NAOP, NSO \rangle$ where the following holds:*

1. *`Receiver`(MD) $\in Ag \cup Den$*
2. *`Sender`(MD) $\in Ag \cup Den$*
3. *If `Receiver`(MD) $\in Ag$ then `Sender`(MD) $\in Den$*
4. *If `Receiver`(MD) $\in Den$ then `Sender`(MD) $\in Ag$*
5. *If $NAOP \neq \emptyset$ then $\forall \langle \delta_i, oa_k \rangle \in NAOP$ the following holds:*
   (a) *$\delta_i \in Dc$;*   (b) *$oa_k \in Oa$;*   (c) *$oa_k \in req(\delta_i)$*
6. *$NSO \subseteq Os$*

---

[5] nDrite action object pairs are the objects that are saved in the nDrite action database (ADB).

Thus an nDrite system message must have a designated receiver and sender (conditions 1 and 2). One out of the sender and receiver must be an agent, while the other must be an nDrite (conditions 3 and 4). For each nDrite action object pair ($NAOP$), the nDrite action called for must be valid (condition 5(a)), the paired nDrite action object must be valid (condition 5(b)) and the paired nDrite action object must be required by the nDrite action they are paired with (condition 5(c)). Finally, the nDrite sensor objects NSO that are provided must be part of the sensor object set Os (condition 6). This completes our discussion of the communication model of our LR-MAS. In the following two sub-sections we discuss how both nDrites and agents operationalise these messages.

4.2   Sending Messages to nDrites

In the context of nDrite's as agent actuators, the nDrites will have to deal with many incoming messages from agents. In Algorithm 1, we present our general nDrite procedure for dealing with an incoming message. The algorithm starts with the message being unpacked (line 5). Then two sets are initialised, one for the set of nDrite actions that complete successful (line 6) and another for the nDrite actions that do not complete successfully (line 7). As nDrites are providing wrappers for laboratory resources (instruments, LIMS, etc.), an nDrite action can fail through no fault of the nDrite software. For example, a laboratory instrument's hardware could be faulty, or the server that hosts a LIMS could fail. Therefore each nDrite records which actions have succeeded and which have failed (so as to help the error recovery process for the agents within our LR-MAS).

The first thing an nDrite should check when a message is received, is whether it was the intended receiver (line 13 in Algorithm 1). If it was not the intended receiver the message is ignored (line 14), otherwise the message is processed (line 16 onwards). When processing the message, the nDrite takes one nDrite Action-object Pair ($\langle \delta, oa_k \rangle$) at a time (line 17). If this nDrite can perform the required nDrite action δ, and the required nDrite action object has been received (line 18), then δ is processed. Whenever an nDrite action object pair is to be processed, this is saved into the nDrite action database, denoted ADB (line 20), so that a record of the system history is available. The nDrite processes δ by converting it into a sequence of laboratory resource and software actions via the exp function (line 22). If the next action ac_q is a software action, then it is performed on the nDrite (line 24), otherwise it is performed on the laboratory resource (line 26). The boolean *complete* stores details on whether ac_p completed successfully. Therefore this Perform function neatly hides any limitations/constraints of the resources. That is, if the instrument is currently fully functional and idle, the action ac_p will be performed successfully and *true* will be returned. If the instrument is busy, then the Perform function will return *false*. If the instrument is faulty, then the Perform function will also return *false*, and so on.

If any of the actions from the exp function are unsuccessful, then the original nDrite action δ and information on the error (i.e. if the instrument is busy or

---

Algorithm 1. The nDriteReceive algorithm that handles an incoming message for the nDrite D_j that is paired with the laboratory resource L_i.

```
 1: function nDriteReceive(m_i)
 2: Input: ⟨m_i⟩; where m_i is the received message.
 3:
 4: begin;
 5:   m_i = ⟨MD_i, NAOP_i, ∅⟩;      // Unpack the message. No sensor objects from agents
 6:   succ = ∅;                    // Set of successful actions
 7:   fail = ∅;                    // Set of failed actions
 8:   p = 0;                       // Integer count variable for nDrite actions
 9:   t = 0;                       // Current timestamp that automatically updates
10:   complete = false;            // Boolean that notes whether the last action completed or not
11:   os_j ⊂ Os;                   // nDrite sensor object defined
12:
13:   if Receiver(MD_i) ≠ D_j then
14:     return null;               // If this nDrite is not the intended recipient then quit
15:   end if
16:   while p < |NAOP| do
17:     ⟨δ, oa_k⟩_p ∈ NAOP;
18:     if δ ∈ DenAct(D_j) and (oa_k = req(δ)) then
19:       q = 0;                   // Integer count variable for individual actions
20:       ADB_j^t = ADB_j^{t-1} ∪ ⟨δ, oa_k⟩_p;
21:       while q < |exp((L_i, D_j), δ)| do
22:         ac_q ∈ exp((L_i, D_j), δ);
23:         if ac_q ∈ S then
24:           complete = Perform(ac_q, D_j);    // I.e. ac_q is a software only action
25:         else
26:           complete = Perform(ac_q, L_i);    // I.e. ac_q is a laboratory resource action
27:         end if
28:         if complete = true then
29:           ⟨δ_i, error information⟩ ∈ fail;
30:         else
31:           ⟨δ, success information⟩ ∈ succ;
32:         end if
33:         q + +;
34:       end while
35:     else
36:       ⟨δ_i, error information⟩ ∈ fail;
37:     end if
38:     p + +;
39:   end while
40:   fail, succ ∈ os_j;           // Add the success and fail information to an nDrite sensor object
41:   m_j = ⟨MD_j, ∅, {os_j}⟩;                  // Add sensor object to return message
42:   Receiver(MD_j) = Sender(MD_i);
43:   Sender(MD_j) = Receiver(MD_i);
44:   Send m_j;
45: end;
```

---

unresponsive or faulty etc.) is added to the list of nDrite actions that failed (line 29). Otherwise the original nDrite action δ is added to the list of nDrite actions that succeeded (line 31). This process continues until all the nDrite actions in the $NAOP$ set have been dealt with (line 16).

Finally, the nDrite builds and sends a message m_j to inform the agent of what actions succeeded and what failed (lines 40 to 44). Note that these messages are automatically sent, so an agent does not have to subscribe to these nDrite sensor objects.

4.3   Sending Messages to Agents

In the context of nDrites operating as sensors for agents, Algorithm 2 presents the general nDrite sensor algorithm. The algorithm takes as input the laboratory resource L_i that is pared with the nDrite D_j. Therefore the agent-enabling pair is set as (L_i, D_j). The algorithm begins by launching a database monitoring thread (line 9), the purpose of which is to monitor this nDrite's sensor database and send updates to the subscribing agents once sensor objects of the correct type appear in the database (this thread is described in more detail later). The main function then processes series of laboratory resource actions until termination (line 10). The Φ variable holds the current laboratory resource action series that is being recorded[6]. This action series is initially set to empty (line 8).

When processing an action series the first laboratory resource action is added to the current action series, as the Connected function always returns true when the current series is empty (line 12 and 13). Next the nDrite checks whether it advertises that it can update agents on the nDrite sensor objects that would appear from the conversion of the current action series (line 23). If this is the case, then these converted objects are added to the nDrite's sensor database (line 24), which is monitored through the nDriteMonitorDB function. Next the nDrites waits until *timelimit* for the next laboratory resource action in the series to occur (line 11). If non occurs before *timelimit* then the laboratory resource action will be set to *null* (the current action series has been completed), so Connected will return *false* (line 12) and the action series will be broken (line 20 and 21). Conversely if another laboratory action is found within the time limit (line 11), then if Connected returns true, the new action α_p is added to the series Φ and the process continues (lines 13 and 14). If Connected returns false, then α_p is not added to the current series, which completes (line 16), and instead, α_p becomes the first action of a new series (lines 17 and 18).

The nDriteMonitorDB thread continues to run until the nDrite terminates. The first part of the continuous loop, collects nDrite sensor objects into Γ, which have occurred in this nDrite's database since the last time it checked (line 33). The last check time is then updated (line 34). For every nDrite sensor object os_i found (line 35), and for each agent ag_j that subscribes to updates concerning the objects of the type type(os_i) (line 36), a message is sent to each agent ag_j to inform it of the update (lines 37 to 39).

Algorithms 1 and 2 both reside within the nDrite but they do not necessarily have to be connected, that is the agents do not necessarily have to perform an action through the nDriteReceive algorithm and then observe the results through the nDriteMonitor algorithm. For example a results monitoring agent may only be interesting in receiving updates when more samples

---

[6] A laboratory resource action series can be processed by the nDrite as a collection. An example is sample analysis by a laboratory instrument. Single instrument actions can be: move to the next sample; send this sample for analysis; record sample results; move to next sample; etc. These basic actions maybe useful to some agents who want real time updates but other agents maybe "satisfied" to just have information on the collection of actions, once the sample analysis is complete.

Algorithm 2. The nDriteMonitor algorithm allows the nDrite D_j to monitor the laboratory resource L_i and convert any laboratory resource actions into LR-MAS understandable nDrite sensor objects. Once converted, the nDrite will update any agents that have subscribed to these nDrite sensor object types.

```
 1: function nDriteMonitor(Lᵢ)
 2: Input: ⟨Lᵢ⟩; where Lᵢ is the Laboratory resource to monitor.
 3:
 4: begin;
 5: p = 0;                    // Integer count variable for nDrite action
 6: t = 0;                    // Current timestamp that automatically updates
 7: timelimit                 // A predefined integer to wait for the next lab resource action
 8: Φ = ∅;                    // Laboratory action series initialised
 9: start nDriteMonitorDB() in new thread
10: while nDrite not terminated do
11:    αₚ = GetNextAction(Lᵢ, timelimit)
12:    if Connected(Φ, {αₚ}) then
13:       Φₚ = αₚ;            // Action is added to action series
14:       p + +;
15:    else if αₚ ≠ null then
16:       Φ = ∅;             // This action series has ended
17:       Φ₀ = αₚ;           // A new action series is initialised with the last action
18:       p = 1;
19:    else
20:       Φ = ∅;             // This action series has ended
21:       p = 0;
22:    end if
23:    if nDriteAdvertisingObjects(type(Sen(Φ, t))) then
24:       SDBⱼᵗ = SDBⱼᵗ⁻¹ ∪ Sen(Φ, t);
25:    end if
26: end while
27: end;
28:
29: function nDriteMonitorDB()
30: begin;
31: Integer s = 0;                                // Last timestamp checked
32: while nDrite not terminated do
33:    Γ = CollectObjects(s);
34:    s = current time;
35:    for each osᵢ ∈ Γ do
36:       for each agⱼ ∈ Subscribers(type(osᵢ)) do
37:          mₖ = ⟨MD, ∅, {osᵢ}⟩;
38:          Sender(MD) = Dⱼ; Receiver(MD) = agⱼ;
39:          send mₖ;
40:       end for
41:    end for
42: end while
43: end;
```

have been analysed by an instrument and may not be interested in scheduling these samples itself. In this case the agent would subscribe to the results objects of the instrument nDrite through the `SubscribeToObjects` function detailed previously. Then the nDrites's `nDriteMonitor` algorithm would update the agent on new sample results when they occur.

4.4   Definition of LR-MAS Agents

From the foregoing it is clear that the possibilities for LR-MAS agents are extensive. Consequently no assumptions regrading the structure of a LR-MAS agent are made here. At a highlevel, LR-MAS agents are structured as follows:

Definition 3. *An* **LR-MAS agent** *is an autonomous software component that:*

– *Takes as input messages of the form* $\langle MD, NAOP, NSO \rangle$
– *Sends messages of the form* $\langle MD, NAOP, NSO \rangle$

It is assumed that agents have an interpretation function that will map incoming messages to zero or more agent actions. Additionally why an agent would build an nDrite action object is entirely up to them, be it because of a trigger from a user's input or a trigger from a incoming message. Individual agents can perform a variety of tasks that are only limited by the nDrite actions implemented. The current classes of agent focused on for production are:

1. *System Configuration Agents*: This type of agent seeks to configure and connect laboratory resources with a minimal assistance from an installer or laboratory personal. For instance, this type of agent could smoothly connect two previously unconnectable resources and/or perform automatic ontological mapping between laboratory resources.
2. *Analytical Monitoring Agents*: This type of agent monitors results from the analysis of samples in the LR-MAS and notes how they were obtained. Issues discovered can be attempted to be rectified automatically or the approriate lab personnel can be contacted.
3. *Instrument Monitoring Agents*: This type of agent monitors data related to failures of the laboratory resource and records each failure's resolution. Over time this will allow learning algorithms within the agent to accurately predict the issues that tend to lead to failures, the failure types that might occur and on what timescale they are likely to occur.

In the following two sections, we give two real world examples (case studies) of nDrite usage (the two App agents shown in Fig. 2).

5   The Analytical Monitoring Case Study

The analytical monitoring case study is focused on the "AutoDil agent" currently in operation. The AutoDil agent uses two nDrites: (i) an Inductively Coupled

Plasma Mass Spectrometer (ICP-MS) instrument nDrite, denoted by D_{icp}, and (ii) an autosampler nDrite[7], denoted by D_{as}.

Teledyne CETAC technologies[8] have produced an autosampler named the ASX-560 that has a new automatic dilution hardware extension named the SDX. The problem is that many ICP-MS instruments do not recognise the SDX and so these ICP-MS instruments cannot communicate with the SDX to make use of it. By wrapping the ASX-560 and the SDX with an autosampler nDrite D_{as} and wrapping a variety of ICP-MS instruments with an ICP-MS instrument nDrite D_{icp}, the SDX hardware for automatic dilution can now be used with ICP-MS instruments that have no knowledge of it. This is possible through the AutoDil agent that connects the two nDrites D_{as} and D_{icp}, and monitors the interaction between them.

The main purpose of the AutoDil agent is to make sure any samples from the ASX-560 autosampler that are found to be "over-range" by the ICP-MS instrument are rediluted automatically by the SDX and sent for reanalysis to the ICP-MS via the ASX-560.

An ICP-MS analyses many samples one after the other. A collection of samples is know as a run. When a run has been completed many laboratory resource actions have been performed, which are converted by the ICP-MS nDrite D_{icp} (through D_{icp}'s nDriteMonitor function), into a results run nDrite sensor object of the type ot_{rr}.

For the AutoDil agent ag_{ad} to do its job, it must subscribe to nDrite sensor objects of the type ot_{rr} from the ICP-MS instrument nDrite D_{icp}. Note that D_{icp} will have advertised that it can update agents with respect to objects of the type ot_{rr}, thus nDriteAdvertisingObjects($\{ot_{rr}\}$) = $true$. When ag_{ad} receives an nDrite sensor object os_{rx} of type ot_{rr}, then it should analyse os_{rx} to see if any samples in the results run need redilution. Whenever ag_{ad} finds samples that require redilution, it:

1. Builds an nDrite action object oa_x that includes information on the dilution amounts for each sample and calls the AddDilutions nDrite action in D_{as} by constructing the message $m_p = \langle MD, \langle \text{AddDilutions}, oa_x \rangle, \emptyset \rangle$, where Receiver($m_p$) = D_{as} and Sender(m_p) = Ag_{ad}.
2. Builds an nDrite action object oa_y that includes information on which samples to be reanalysed and calls the SetupRun nDrite action in D_{icp} by constructing the message $m_p = \langle MD, \langle \text{SetupRun}, oa_j \rangle, \emptyset \rangle$, where Receiver($m_p$) = D_{icp} and Sender(m_p) = Ag_{ad}.

After performing both (1) and (2), the ag_{ad} waits for new objects from the ICP-MS nDrite, which may include information on samples that required further dilution.

The nDrites will deal with messages (1) and (2) through their nDriteReceive function. The nDrite D_{as} will convert the nDrite action AddDilutions through the exp function, to actions that its paired ASX-560

---

[7] An autosampler automatically feeds a liquid sample into an ICP-MS instrument.
[8] http://www.teledynecetac.com/.

autosampler can understand. The purpose of these converted actions will be to tell the ASX-560 autosampler and the SDX which samples require what level of dilution. The nDrite D_{icp} will convert the nDrite action SetupRun, again through the exp function, to actions that its paired ICP-MS instrument can understand. The purpose of these actions will be to tell the ICP-MS instrument what samples it should load from the autosampler (and therefore what data it will be collecting). The nDrites will then report to ag_{ad} what actions were successful. If all were successful then the autoDil agent knows that it should soon expect another results run nDrite sensor object os_{ry} of type ot_{rr}, which will hold information on the diluted samples.

6   The Instrument Failure Prediction Case Study

The second case study is an instrument failure prediction scenario where a dedicated instrument monitoring agent (see Fig. 2) is used to predict instrument failure using a data stream classifier trained for this purpose (as proposed in [5]). This agent is currently under development. This agent will have the capability to connect to many nDrites, including the nDrites that the AutoDil agent connects to.

Instrument failure within scientific and analytic laboratories can lead to costly delays and compromise complex scientific workflows [26]. Many such failures can be predicted by learning a failure prediction model using some form of data stream mining. Data stream mining is concerned with the effective, real time, capture of useful information from data flows [13–15]. A common application of data stream mining is the analysis of instrument (sensor) data with respect to some target objective [7,8]. There is little work concerning the idea of using data stream mining to predict the failure of the instruments (sensors) themselves other than [5] which describes a mechanism whereby data stream mining can be applied to learn a classifier with which to predict instrument failure. In our LR-MAS, an instrument failure prediction app agent implements the mechanism of [5] by communicating with other agents, which are in turn connected to nDrites (referred to as Dendrites in [5]).

7   Conclusions

This paper has described a mechanism whereby the well documented benefits of MAS can be realised in the context of analytical laboratories where laboratory resources are not readily compatible with the technical requirements of MAS. The proposed solution is the concept of nDrites, "smart agent enablers", that at one end feature bespoke laboratory resource connectivity while at the other end feature a generic interface usable by agents of all kinds. The vision is that of a Laboratory Resource MAS (LR-MAS). The operation of nDrites was fully described in the context of: laboratory resources, nDrites as agent actuators, nDrites as sensors, the adopted communication mechanisms and the associated agents. The utility of nDrites was illustrated using two case studies: (i) an analytical monitoring case study with respect to an "AutoDil agent" currently in operation; and (ii) an instrument failure prediction case study, featuring an instrument monitoring agent, that is currently under development. The nDrite concept, as presented in this paper, has now been fully implemented. A subsidiary company has been created, DendriteLabs, whose core business is the production of nDrites. To date, over 200 licenses for nDrite enabled "auto samplers" and "inductively coupled plasma mass spectrometry" instruments have been sold.

Acknowledgements. The work described in this paper was conducted as part of the "Dendrites: Enabling Instrumentation Connectivity" Innovate UK funded knowledge transfer partnership project (KTP009603).

References

1. Ankolekar, A., et al.: DAML-S: web service description for the semantic web. In: Horrocks, I., Hendler, J. (eds.) ISWC 2002. LNCS, vol. 2342, pp. 348–363. Springer, Heidelberg (2002). doi:10.1007/3-540-48005-6_27
2. Argente, E., Botti, V., Carrascosa, C., Giret, A., Julian, V., Rebollo, M.: An abstract architecture for virtual organizations: the THOMAS approach. J. Knowl. Inf. Syst. 29(2), 379–403
3. Ashri, R., Payne, T.R., Luck, M., Surridge, M., Sierra, C., Aguilar, J.A.R., Noriega, P.: Using electronic institutions to secure grid environments. In: Klusch, M., Rovatsos, M., Payne, T.R. (eds.) CIA 2006. LNCS (LNAI), vol. 4149, pp. 461–475. Springer, Heidelberg (2006). doi:10.1007/11839354_33
4. Behrens, T., Hindriks, K.V., Bordini, R.H., Braubach, L., Dastani, M., Dix, J., Hübner, J.F., Pokahr, A.: An interface for agent-environment interaction. In: Collier, R., Dix, J., Novák, P. (eds.) ProMAS 2010. LNCS (LNAI), vol. 6599, pp. 139–158. Springer, Heidelberg (2012). doi:10.1007/978-3-642-28939-2_8
5. Atkinson, K., Coenen, F., Goddard, P., Payne, T., Riley, L.: Data stream mining with limited validation opportunity: towards instrument failure prediction. In: Madria, S., Hara, T. (eds.) DaWaK 2015. LNCS, vol. 9263, pp. 283–295. Springer International Publishing, Cham (2015). doi:10.1007/978-3-319-22729-0_22
6. Bellifemine, F.L., Caire, G., Greenwood, D.: Developing Multi-Agent Systems with JADE. Wiley Series in Agent Technology. Wiley, New York (2007)
7. Cohen, I., Goldszmidt, M., Kelly, T., Symons, J., Chase, J.S.: Correlating instrumentation data to system states: a building block for automated diagnosis and control. In: Proceedings 6th Symposium on Operating Systems Design and Implementation, pp. 231–244 (2004)
8. Cohen, L., Avrahami-Bakish, G., Last, M., Kandel, A., Kipersztok, O.: Real time data mining-based intrusion detection. Inf. Fusion (Spec. Issue Distrib. Sens. Netw.) 9(3), 344–354 (2008)
9. Decker, K., Sycara, K., Williamson, M.: Middle-agents for the internet. In: Proceedings 15th International Joint Conference on Artificial Intelligence (IJCAI 1997), pp. 578–583 (1997)
10. De Roure, D., Jennings, N.R., Shadbolt, N.: The Semantic Grid: A Future e-Science Infrastructure. Grid Computing-Making the Global Infrastructure a Reality, pp. 437–470 (2003)

11. Foster, I., Jennings, N.R., Kesselman, C.: Brain meets Brawn: why Grid and Agents need each other. In: Proceedings 3rd International Conference on Autonomous Agents and Multi-Agent Systems, New York, USA, pp. 8–15 (2004)
12. Frey, J.G., De Roure, D., schraefel, M.C., Mills, H., Fu, H., Peppe, S., Hughes, G., Smith, G., Payne, T.R.: Context slicing the chemical aether. In: Proceedings 1st International Workshop on Hypermedia and the Semantic Web, Nottingham, UK (2003)
13. Gaber, M.M., Zaslavsky, A., Krishnaswamy, S.: Mining data streams: a review. ACM SIGMOD Record **34**(2), 18–26 (2005)
14. Gaber, M.M., Gama, J., Krishnaswamy, S., Gomes, J.B., Stahl, F.: Data stream mining in ubiquitous environments: state-of-the-art and current directions. Wiley Interdisc. Rev. Data Min. Knowl. Discovery **4**(2), 116–138 (2014)
15. Gama, J.: Knowledge Discovery from Data Streams. Chapman and Hall, Boca Raton (2010)
16. Gil, Y.: From data to knowledge to discoveries: Artificial intelligence and scientific workflows. Sci. Program. **17**(3), 231–246 (2009)
17. Hamdaqa, M., Tahvildari, L.: Cloud computing uncovered: a research landscape. Adv. Comput. **86**, 41–85 (2012)
18. Jacyno, M., Bullock, S., Geard, N., Payne, T.R., Luck, M.: Self-organising agent communities for autonomic resource management. Adapt. Behav. J. **21**(1), 3–28 (2013)
19. Lawley, R., Luck, M., Decker, K., Payne, T.R., Moreau, L.: Automated negotiation between publishers and consumers of grid notifications. Parallel Process. Lett. **13**(4), 537–548 (2003)
20. Lin, R., Kraus, S., Baarslag, T., Tykhonov, D., Hindriks, K., Jonker, C.M.: GENIus: an integrated environment for supporting the design of generic automated negotiators. Int. J. Comput. Intell. **30**(1), 48–70 (2012)
21. Merelli, E., Armano, G., Cannata, N., Corradini, F., d'Inverno, M., Doms, A., Lord, P., Martin, A., Milanesi, L., Moller, S., Schroeder, M., Luck, M.: Agents in bioinformatics, computational and systems biology. Briefings Bioinform. **8**(1), 45–59 (2007)
22. Omicini, A., Ricci, A., Virol, M.: Artifacts in the A&A meta-model for multi-agent systems. Auton. Agents Multi-Agent Syst. **17**(3), 432–456 (2008)
23. Payne, T.R.: Web services from an agent perspective. IEEE Intell. Syst. **23**(2), 12–14 (2008)
24. Paolucci, M., Kawamura, T., Payne, T.R., Sycara, K.: Semantic matching of web services capabilities. In: Horrocks, I., Hendler, J. (eds.) ISWC 2002. LNCS, vol. 2342, pp. 333–347. Springer, Heidelberg (2002). doi:10.1007/3-540-48005-6_26
25. Schraefel, M.C., Hughes, G., Mills, H., Smith, G., Payne, T., Frey, J.: Breaking the book: translating the chemistry lab book into a pervasive computing lab environment. In: Proceedings SIGCHI Conference on Human Factors in Computing Systems, 24–29 April, Vienna, Austria (2004)
26. Stein, S., Payne, T.R., Jennings, N.R.: Flexible QoS-based service selection and provisioning in large-scale grids. In: Proceedings of UK e-Science All Hands Meeting, HPC Grids of Continental Scope (2008)
27. Stein, S., Payne, T.R., Jennings, N.R.: Flexible selection of heterogeneous and unreliable services in large-scale grids. Philos. Trans. Royal Soc. A: Math. Phys. Eng. Sci. **367**(1897), 2483–2494 (2009)
28. Stein, S., Payne, T.R., Jennings, N.R.: Robust execution of service workflows using redundancy and advance reservations. IEEE Trans. Serv. Comput. **4**(2), 125–139 (2011)

29. Sycara, K., Widoff, S., Klusch, M., Lu, J.: LARKS: dynamic matchmaking among heterogeneous software agents in cyberspace. Auton. Agents Multi-Agent Syst. 5(2), 173–203 (2002)
30. Szomszor, M., Payne, T.R., Moreau, L.: Automated syntactic medation for web service integration. In: Proceedings IEEE International Conference on Web Services, Chicago, USA (2006)
31. Wassink, I., Rauwerda, H., Vet, P., Breit, T., Nijholt, A.: E-BioFlow: different perspectives on scientific workflows. In: Elloumi, M., Küng, J., Linial, M., Murphy, R.F., Schneider, K., Toma, C. (eds.) BIRD 2008. CCIS, vol. 13, pp. 243–257. Springer, Heidelberg (2008). doi:10.1007/978-3-540-70600-7_19
32. Oinn, T., Greenwood, M., Addis, M., Alpdemir, M.N., Ferris, J., Glover, K., Goble, C., Goderis, A., Hull, D., Marvin, D., Li, P., Lord, P., Pocock, M.R., Senger, M., Stevens, R., Wipat, A., Wroe, C.: Taverna: lessons in creating a workflow environment for the life sciences. Concurrency Comput. Pract. Experience 18(10), 1067–1100 (2006)
33. Weyns, D., Michel, F.: Agent environments for multi-agent systems – a research roadmap. In: Weyns, D., Michel, F. (eds.) E4MAS 2014. LNCS (LNAI), vol. 9068, pp. 3–21. Springer, cham (2015). doi:10.1007/978-3-319-23850-0_1

Towards Data- and Norm-Aware Multiagent Systems

Matteo Baldoni[1(✉)], Cristina Baroglio[1], Diego Calvanese[2], Roberto Micalizio[1], and Marco Montali[2]

[1] Dipartimento di Informatica, Università degli Studi di Torino, c.so Svizzera 185, 10149 Torino, Italy
{matteo.baldoni,cristina.baroglio,roberto.micalizio}@unito.it
[2] KRDB Research Centre, Free University of Bozen-Bolzano, Piazza Domenicani 3, 39100 Bolzano, Italy
{calvanese,montali}@inf.unibz.it

Abstract. We recall the key abstractions and models on which the major approaches to software specification rely, using Meyer's forces of computation as dimensions of comparison. Based on the identified strengths and lacks, we introduce data-awareness and of norm-awareness as recommended properties, explaining the advantages they bring about. We show that multiagent systems are a good candidate for the development of a data- and norm-aware programming, tracing directions for the realization of multiagent systems that are data and norm-aware. Finally, we report and comment some proposals from the multiagent systems literature that, though developed independently and not inserted in an organic framework, already face specific aspects that are relevant to bring about norm and data-awareness.

1 Introduction

One of the key characteristics of agents is their situatedness [41,50,51], i.e. the fact that an agent is immersed in an environment, be it social or physical, that it perceives, senses, and acts upon. Despite the centrality of situatedness, most studies in the research area on multiagent systems are focussed only on features of agents, while those that put forward the need of representing the environment either (1) disregard the plurality of data, thus typically relying on a propositional representation, as explained in [36], or (2) do not provide a representation of the process by which data evolve in a form that can be reasoned about, as we underline in this work.

We advocate that, in order for agents to be capable of dealing with richer data representations that go beyond the propositional case, it is necessary to rely on an information system through which data can, for instance, be aggregated or information can be extracted (*data awareness*). The environment, for what concerns its being used by the agents, should be specified on top of building blocks that amount to semantically meaningful chunks of data, which evolve as a consequence of the agents' actions. The description of how data evolve should

M. Baldoni et al. (Eds.): EMAS 2016, LNAI 10093, pp. 22–38, 2016.
DOI: 10.1007/978-3-319-50983-9_2

be provided by the environment to its agents as a body of norms. This would allow agents to deliberate how to act and which goals to pursue also in terms of expectations about the evolution of the environment (*norm awareness*). Gathering from proposals like [6,18], we propose to describe the environment in terms of data information models and data lifecycles, that are to be made available to the agents in their deliberation process. A data information model specifies the structure of the information, a data lifecycle, instead, specifies data state transitions. Finally, it is capitol that data-awareness and norm-awareness are realized in a way that does not compromise the agents' deliberative capabilities. Problems may, in fact, arise when no bound is placed on the number of tuples that can be added to database relations as the computation goes on [5,36].

Let us make a couple of examples. In a propositional setting, it is common to consider an order as pertaining to an interaction session. Combining different orders of a same client into a single shipping procedure would be positive in various respects (to reduce pollution, to save money, to make the client happy by receiving everything in one box), but the exhibition of such a behavior requires to distill information from the data specifying the different orders, to associate the orders to the single client, and to know that all orders follow a same evolution, whose description should be available to the agents in a form that can be reasoned about. Only such kind of awareness would provide the agents the means to adapt their behavior to the cases which are captured by the actual data. Similarly, in a warehouse that received various orders concerning items of a same kind, and that will undergo some packaging process, it would be more efficient to first pick all the items up (probably they will be on the same shelf) and only after start to pack them up. Instead, in a propositional setting the pick-and-pack can only occur one item at a time, introducing a considerable waste of time. Of course, it is always possible to hard-code some optimization procedure in the agents' behaviors but the interesting thing would be that the agents adapted autonomously, after reasoning on data, without any hard-coding.

To explain our point, we start the paper by recalling the key abstractions and models on which the major approaches to software specification rely, including both the ones developed by the research area on multiagent systems and those proposed by other research communities. We provide an organic view by relying on Meyer's three forces of computation [33] as reference dimensions, along which all the considered proposals are positioned. To this aim, Sect. 2 introduces Meyer's forces of computation, while Sect. 3 overviews approaches to software specification, ranging from functional decomposition to multiagent systems.

Based on the strengths and lacks emerged in this part of the paper, Sect. 4 introduces data-awareness and norm-awareness as recommended properties, showing that multiagent systems are a good candidate for the development of a data- and norm-aware programming. It explains the advantages brought about by this vision, tracing directions to the realization of multiagent systems that are data and norm-aware. Section 5, then, reports and comments some proposals in the multiagent systems literature that, though developed independently and not inserted in an organic framework, face specific aspects that are relevant to bring about norm and data-awareness. Conclusions end the paper.

2   Meyer's Forces: Processor, Action and Object

We decided to use *Meyer's forces of computation* as a common ground for comparing the different proposals because they provide a neutral touchstone, unrelated to any specific programming approach or modularization mechanism. According to Meyer, three forces are at play when we use software to perform some computations (see Fig. 1): *processors*, *actions*, and *objects*. A processor can be a *process* or a *thread* (in the paper we use both the terms processor and process to refer to this force); actions are the *operations* that make the computation; objects are the *data* to which actions are applied.

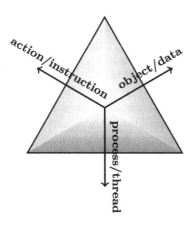

Fig. 1. Meyer's three forces of computation [33, Chap. 5, p. 101].

A software system, in order to execute, uses processes to apply certain actions to certain objects. The form of the actions depends on the considered level of granularity: they can be instructions of the programming language as well as they can be major steps of a complex algorithm. Moreover, the form of actions conditions the way in which processes operate on objects. Some objects are built by a computation for its own needs and exist only while the computation proceeds; others (e.g., files or databases) are external and may outlive individual computations. In the following we analyse the most important proposals concerning software modularization, showing how they (sometimes implicitly) give more or less strength to Meyer's forces, and the drawbacks that follow.

3   From Functional Decomposition to MAS

It becomes apparent that processor and object are the two principal forces along which most approaches to software modularization have been developed so far, while the action force remained subsidiary to one or another.

Functional Decomposition. The top-down *functional decomposition* is probably the earliest approach to building modularized software; it relies on a model that puts at the center the notion of process; namely, the implementation of a given function is based only on a set of actions made of instructions, provided by the programming language at hand, possibly in combination with previously defined functions [33]. Top-down functional decomposition builds a system by stepwise refinement, starting with the definition of its abstract function. Each refinement step decreases the abstraction of the specification. With reference to Fig. 1, the approach disregards objects/data, just considered as data structures that are instrumental to the function specification and internal to processes. Actions are defined only in terms of the instructions provided by the programming language and of other functions built on top of them (subroutines), into which a process is structured. All in all, this approach is intuitive and suitable to the development of individual *algorithms*, in turn aimed at solving some specific *task*, but does not scale up equally well when *data are shared among concurrent processes* because it lacks abstractions to explicitly account for such data and their corresponding management mechanisms.

Object-Orientation. The *Object-Oriented* approach to modularization results from an effort aimed at showing the limits of the functional approach [33]. Objects (data) often have a life on their own, independent from the processes that use them. Objects become, then, the fundamental notion of the model. They provide the actions by which (and only by which) it is possible to operate on them (*data operations*). This approach, however, disregards processes and their modularization both internally and externally to objects. Internally, because objects provide actions but have a *static nature*, and are inherently passive: actions are invoked on objects, but the decision of which operations to invoke so as to evolve such objects is taken by external processes. This also implies that there is no decoupling between the *use of an object* and the *management of that object*. Externally, because the model does not supply conceptual notions for composing the actions provided by objects into processes, and there is no conceptual support to the specification of tasks, in particular when concurrency is involved.

Actor Model, Active Objects. The key concept in the *actor model* [30] (to which *active objects* are largely inspired) is that *everything is an actor*. Interaction between actors occurs only through *direct asynchronous message passing*, with no restriction on the order in which messages are received. An actor is a computational entity that, in response to an incoming message, can: (1) send a finite number of messages to other actors; (2) create a finite number of new actors; (3) designate the behavior to be used in response to the next incoming message. These three steps can be executed in any order, possibly in parallel. Recipients of messages are identified by opaque addresses. Interestingly, in [30] Hewitt et al. state that "We use the ACTOR metaphor to emphasize the inseparability of control and data flow in our model. Data structures, functions, semaphores, monitors, [...] and data bases can all be shown to be special cases of actors.

All of the above are objects with certain useful modes of behavior." The actor model *decouples* the sender of a message from the communications sent, and this makes it possible to tackle asynchronous communication and to define control structures as patterns of passing messages.

Many authors, such as [34,37,46], noted that the actor model does not address the issue of *coordination*. Coordination requires the possibility for an actor to have expectations on another actor's behavior, but the mere asynchronous message passing gives no means to foresee how a message receiver will behave. For example, in the object-paradigm methods return the computed results to their callers. In the actor model this is not granted because this simple pattern requires the exchange of two messages; however, no way for specifying patterns of message exchanges between actors is provided. The lack of such mechanisms hinders the verification of properties of a system of interacting actors. Similar problems are well-known also in the area that studies enterprise application integration [1] and service-oriented computing [45], that can be considered as heirs of the actor model and where once again interaction relies on asynchronous message passing. There are in the literature proposals to overcome these limits. For instance for what concerns the actor model. [37] proposes to use Scribble protocols and their relation to finite state machines for specification and runtime verification of actor interactions. Instead, in the case of service-oriented approaches, there are proposals of languages that allow capturing complex business processes as service compositions, either in the form of orchestrations (e.g. BPEL) or of choreographies (e.g. WS-CDL).

The above problem can better be understood by referring to Meyer's forces. The actor model supports the realization of object/data management processes (these are the internal behaviors of the actors, that rule how the actor evolves), but it does not support the design and the modularization of processes that perform the object use, which would be *external* to the actors. As a consequence, generalizing what [14] states about service-oriented approaches, the modularization supplied by the actor model, while favoring component reuse, does not address the need of connecting the data to the organizational processes: data remains hidden inside systems.

Business Processes. *Business processes* have been increasingly adopted by enterprises and organizations to conceptually describe their dynamics, and those of the socio-technical systems they live in. Modern enterprises [13] are complex, distributed, and aleatory systems: complex and distributed because they involve offices, activities, actors, resources, often heterogeneous and geographically distributed; aleatory because they are affected by unpredictable events like new laws, market trends, but also resignations, incidents, and so on. In this light, *business processes* help to create an explicit representation of how an enterprise works towards the accomplishments of its tasks and goals. More specifically, a business process describes how a set of interrelated activities can lead to a precise and measurable result (a product or a service) in response to an *external event* (e.g., a new order) [49]. Business processes developed for understanding how an enterprise work can then be refined and used as the basis for developing software systems that the enterprise will adopt to concretely support the execution of its procedures [13, 24]. In this light, business processes become *workflows* that connect and coordinate different people, offices, organizations, and software in a compound flow of execution [1]. Among the main advantages of this process-centric view, the fact that it enables analysis of an enterprise functioning, it enables comparison of business processes, it enables the study of compliance to norms (e.g. [27]), and also to identify critical points like bottlenecks by way of simulations (e.g., see iGrafx Process[1] for Six Sigma). The adoption of a service-oriented approach and of web services helps implementing workflows that span across multiple organizations, whose infrastructures may well be heterogeneous and little integrated [1, 45].

On the negative side, business processes, by being an expression of the process force, show the same limits of the functional decomposition approach. Specifically, they are typically represented in an activity-centric way, i.e., by emphasizing which flows of activities are acceptable, without providing adequate abstractions to capture the data that are manipulated along such flows. Data are subsidiary to processes.

Artifact-centric Process Management. The *artifact-centric approach* [6, 14, 18] counterposes a data-centric vision to the activity-centric vision described above. *Artifacts* are concrete, identifiable, self-describing chunks of information, the basic building blocks by which business models and operations are described. They are business-relevant objects that are created and evolve as they pass through business operations. They include an *information model* of the data, and a *lifecycle model*, that contains the key states through which the data evolve, together with their transitions (triggered by the execution of corresponding tasks). A change to an artifact can trigger changes to other artifacts, possibly of a different type. The lifecycle model is not only used at runtime to track the evolution of artifacts, but also at design time to understand who is responsible of which transitions.

On the negative side, like in the case of the actor model, business artifacts disregard the design and the modularization of those processes that operate on them. Moreover, verification problems are much harder to tackle than in the case where only the control-flow perspective is considered. In fact, the explicit presence of data, together with the possibility of incorporating new data from the external environment, makes these systems infinite-state in general [14].

Agents and Multiagent Systems. In [41, 51], *agents* are defined as entities that observe their environment and act upon it so as to achieve their own goals. Two fundamental characteristics of agents are *autonomy* and *situatedness*. Agents are autonomous in the sense that they have a sense-plan-act deliberative cycle, which gives them control of their internal state and behavior; autonomy, in turn, implies proactivity, i.e., the ability of an agent to take action towards the achievement of its (delegated) objectives, without being solicited to do so. Agents are situated

---

[1] http://www.igrafx.com/.

because they can sense, perceive, and manipulate the environment in which operate. The environment could be physical or virtual, and is understood by agents in terms of (relevant) data. From a programming perspective, it is natural to compare agents to objects. Agent-oriented programming was introduced by Shoham as "a specialization of *object-oriented programming*" [42]. The difference between agents and static objects is clear. Citing Wooldridge [51, Sect. 2.2]: (1) objects do not have control over their own behavior[2], (2) objects do not exhibit flexibility in their behavior, and (3) in standard object models there is a single thread of control, while agents are inherently multi-threaded. Similar comments are reported also by other authors, like Jennings [31]. However, when comparing agents to actors, the behavioral dimension is not sufficient: [51, p. 30] reduces the difference between agents and active objects, which encompass an own thread of control, to the fact that "active objects are essentially agents that do not necessarily have the ability to exhibit *flexible* autonomous behavior". In order to understand the difference between the agent paradigm and objects it is necessary to rely on both the abstractions introduced by the agent paradigm, that are that of agent and that of environment [50]. Such a dichotomy does not find correspondence in the other models and gives a first-class role to both Meyer's process and object force (see Fig. 2). Processes realize algorithms aimed at achieving objectives, and this is exactly the gist of the agent abstraction and the rationale behind its proactivity: agents exploit their deliberative cycle (as control flow), possibly together with the key abstractions of belief, desire, and intention (as logic), so as to realize algorithms, i.e., processes, for acting in their environment to pursue their goals[3]. Contrariwise, active objects and actors do not have goals nor purposes, even though their specification includes a process. As we said, they are a manifestation of the object force. In the agent paradigm the manifestation of the object force is the environment abstraction. The environment does not exhibit the kind of autonomy explained for agents even when its definition includes a process. Its being reactive rather than active makes the environment more similar to an actor whose behavior is triggered by the messages it receives, that are all served indistinctly.

The A&A meta-model. Despite the centrality of situatedness in the definition of agents, most of the research in multiagent systems typically focuses on the abstraction of agent only, completely abstracting away from the notion of environment. Proposals like [22,50] overcome this limit by introducing first-class abstractions for the environment, to be captured alongside agents themselves. In particular, [50] states that "the environment is a first-class abstraction that provides the surrounding conditions for agents to exist and that mediates both the interaction among agents and the access to resources." This proposal brought to important evolutions like the A&A meta-model [38] and its implementation CArtAgO [39].

---

[2] This is summarized by the well-known motto "Objects do it for free; agents do it because they want it".

[3] Summarizing, objects "do it" for free because they are data, agents are processes and "do it" because it is functional to their objectives.

Normative Multiagent Systems. A fundamental step towards raising the value of the action force is brought by *normative multiagent systems* [8, 32], which take inspiration from mechanisms that are typical of human communities, and have been widely studied in the research area on multiagent systems. According to [8] a normative multiagent system is: "a multiagent system together with normative systems in which agents on the one hand can decide whether to follow the explicitly represented norms, and on the other the normative systems specify how and in which extent the agents can modify the norms". Initially the focus was posed mainly on *regulative norms* that, through obligations, permissions, and prohibitions, specify the patterns of actions and interactions agents should adhere to, even though deviations can still occur and have to be properly considered [32]. More recently, regulative norms have been combined with *constitutive norms* [7, 15, 19], which support the creation of institutional realities by defining institutional actions that make sense only within the institutions they belong to. A typical example is that of "raising a hand", which counts as "make a bid" in the context of an auction. Institutional actions allow agents to operate within an institution. Citing [19], the impact on the agent's deliberative cycle is that agents can "reason about the social consequences of their actions". In this light, going back to Meyer's forces, if agents are abstractions for processes and environments for objects, then *norms* are abstractions of the *action force* (see Fig. 2) because norms model actions and, thus, condition the way in which processes operate on objects. In fact, norms specify either institutional actions, or the conditions for the use of such actions, consequently regulating the acceptable behavior of the agents in a system. This view is also supported by the fact that norms concern "doing the right thing" rather than "doing what leads to a goal" [48].

4   Need of Data and Norm Awareness

Reality is complex even in simple settings because it involves data, and data are related and compose semantically meaningful chunks of information. The realization of systems where a set of autonomous and heterogeneous parties can interact effectively, leveraging the richness of the data they create and manipulate through their actions, requires, on the one hand, data-awareness and, on the other hand, a specification of the rules by which data evolve, that agents should take into account to decide if and how to act (norm-awareness). These two kinds of awareness should be seamlessly integrated in the system through appropriate abstractions.

Of the many approaches to the specification and modularization of software that we have discussed, multiagent systems are particularly promising. One key aspect in this respect is the fact that, differently than in the other approaches, the action force is not ancillary to the process force nor to the object force. Actions are the capabilities agents have to modify their environment. The process force is mapped onto a cycle in which the agent observes the world (updating its beliefs), deliberates which intentions to achieve, plans how to achieve them, and finally executes the plan [11]. Beliefs and intentions are those components of the process

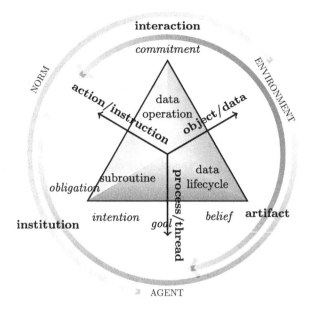

Fig. 2. Rereading Meyer's forces.

abstraction that, with reference to Fig. 2, create a bridge respectively towards the object/data force (i.e., the environment) and the action force. Beliefs concern the environment. Intentions lead to action [51], meaning that if an agent has an intention, then the expectation is that it will make a reasonable attempt to achieve it. In this sense, intentions play a central role in the selection and the execution of action. This independence of the action force from the other two is what enables the use of norms as an abstraction of the action force and, so, to model the specification of data lifecycles by way of norms. Note that, even though in general data-awareness and norm-awareness are orthogonal to BDI notions, it is natural to think of agents as BDI agents for a seamless integration of all the aspects of deliberation, including the awareness of data and of their lifecycles.

While in functional decomposition actions are produced by refining a given goal through a top-down strategy, intentions are a means by which the action force is put in relation to the process force. Thus, while in other approaches actions are hard-coded, so to say, in the process, an agent's deliberative process is independent of the actions it uses and, in particular, it can concern also actions by other agents. So, for instance, consider a setting where the order lifecycle is available to the agents in a way that can be reasoned about. An agent, who is handling part of the lifecycle of an order, may conclude that, since it has to pick up three items in the warehouse, since each such item will have to be packed, since all packagings are performed by a same other agent, and since one of its goals is saving energy, it is preferable to first pick them all up and only then deliver them to the other agent. Data-awareness here is awareness that three items of a same kind are requested. Norm-awareness that items are picked because each of them is part of some order, whose lifecycle says that after being picked they will be packed. Again data-awareness allows our agent to know that the orders are different and that all parcels are to be made by a same other agent.

Notice that approaches that rely on the object force do not provide the abstractions that allow realizing the warehouse example because they do not foresee an abstraction like that of agent (not even of process). Consequently, object-orientation associates operations to data, but the paradigm did not push the study towards a normative representation. Similarly, while business artifacts provide both a rich description of their data and their lifecycle, they do not provide any link to a corresponding normative understanding, thus making impossible for the agents (could any be defined) to leverage this knowledge for reasoning about how to act. On the other hand, artifacts in the A&A model are radically different from the business artifacts because they do not come with an explicit information model for data, and they do not exhibit data lifecycles. Thus, this information cannot be exploited at design time, nor at runtime, to reason about which actions should be taken towards the achievement of the agent goals.

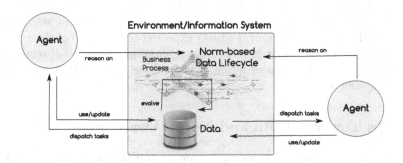

Fig. 3. Data-aware and norm-aware multiagent system.

Another reason that makes agents promising is that agents already show the capability of tackling norms. This is due to the fact that, since in the agent paradigm each agent is an independent locus of control, coordination means are deemed as essential towards regulating the overall behavior of the system. As it is well underlined in [31], the agent-based model allows to naturally tackle the issue of coordination by introducing the concepts of interaction protocol [16], and that of *norm* [26,48]. These concepts are at the heart of the design of multiagent systems. The deliberative cycle of agents is affected by the norms and by the obligations these norms generate as a consequence of the agents' actions. In principle, each agent is capable to adapt its behavior to (local or coordination) changing conditions, e.g., by re-ranking its goals based on the context or by adopting new goals, and free to do it or not. Institutions and organizations are a way to realize functional decomposition in an agent setting. Intuitively, an institution is an organizational structure for coordinating the activities of multiple interacting agents, that typically embodies some rules (norms) to govern participation and interaction. In general, an organization adds to this societal dimension a set of organizational goals, and powers to create institutional facts or to modify the norms and obligations of the normative system [7]. Agents, playing roles, must accomplish the organizational goals respecting the norms. The limit is that, despite the centrality of norms, a holistic proposal where constitutive norms are used to specify both agent actions and data operations, and where regulative norms are used to create expectations on the overall evolution of the system (agents behavior and environment evolution) is yet to be developed.

Data and Norm-aware Multiagent Systems. A data-aware and norm-aware multiagent system, see Fig. 3, should involve a group of agents and of business artifacts with the following characteristics. Agents interact with each other and with the environment by creating and modifying data which belong to an information system and that are reified by business artifacts. The conceptual model of the information system is described in terms of the norms that regulate the evolution of such data. Norms express data lifecycles, i.e. they capture how data pass from one state to another as a consequence of actions that are performed by some agent. The conceptual model is available to the interacting agents in a form that allows agents to reason on it. The agents are aware of the current state (of the lifecycle) of the data, and thus of the tasks expected of them and of their parties. At design time, norms would provide a programming interface between agents and their environment, given in terms of those state changes that are relevant in the environment.

5   Steps Towards Data and Norm Awareness

Data- and norm-awareness, in the sense introduced in this paper, are not yet realized in multiagent systems but the literature already contains independent efforts that tackle specific aspects of this direction of research, which, thus, fit in the picture we have drawn. Interestingly, many of such works focus on social commitments which emerge as currently occupying a central position in the junction between norms and data.

A first example is provided by the JaCaMo+ platform [3], which allows Jason agents [10] to engage commitment-based interactions [43], in turn reified as CArtAgO [38] artifacts (both agents and artifacts are first-class elements in the design of the multiagent system). JaCaMo+ artifacts implement the social state of the interaction, which is the social environment in which agents act, and provide the roles that are then enacted by the agents. The explicit representation of the social state enables the realization of a data-aware approach, where the data are the events occurring in the social state, while social commitments provide the information necessary to agents in their interaction. A social commitment $C(x, y, s, u)$ captures that agent x (debtor) commits to agent y (creditor) to bring about the consequent condition u when the antecedent condition s holds.

Antecedent and consequent conditions are conjunctions or disjunctions of events and commitments. The interesting point about commitments is that they have a lifecycle [47]: a commitment is *null* right before being created; *active* when it is created; active has substates *conditional* (as long as the antecedent condition did not occur), and *detached* (when the antecedent condition occurred, the debtor is engaged in the consequent condition of the commitment); an active commitment can become: *pending* if suspended; *satisfied*, if the engagement is accomplished; *expired*, if it will not be necessary to accomplish the consequent condition; *terminated* if the commitment is canceled when conditional or released when active; and finally, *violated* when its antecedent has been satisfied, but its consequent will be forever false, or it is canceled when detached (the debtor will be considered liable for the violation). JaCaMo+ explicitly represents the states of the commitments, allowing the agents to take also this information into account in their reasoning. Commitments in JaCaMo+ belong to the social state and are shared by the interacting agents as resources. So, they are information, that is created and evolves along the interaction with event occurrence, and that contributes to the specification of the environment in which the agents operate. In this light, the social state can be seen as a special kind of business artifact in the sense of [6,14,18]. JaCaMo+ allows specifying agent programs as Jason plans, whose triggering events amount to the change of the state of some commitment [2]. Suppose, to make an example, that the commitment goes to the state "detached" and that this event triggers a plan in the agent which is the debtor of that commitment: the connection between the commitment and the associated plan is not only causal (event triggers plan), but rather the plan is explicitly attached to the commitment, in the sense that its aim is to satisfy the consequent condition of the commitment (norm-awareness).

An independent proposal, i.e. [20], then shows how commitments lifecycle can be captured by a set of norms. It explains the advantages of this view which are: (1) enabling agents to take into account the evolution of commitments in their reasoning; (2) allowing the customization of the commitment lifecycle to the needs of particular application contexts. This proposal fits the understanding of norm-awareness we have explained and it provides evidence of the advantages of a norm-centered description of data evolution.

de Brito *et al.* [21] explain the limits of current approaches to artificial institutions, e.g. [25], basically residing in the fact that proposals always remain at an abstract level that does not account for the tight connection between the institution and its environment. So, for instance, the institution will say that "the winner of an auction is obliged to pay its offer, otherwise it is fined" without specifying aspects such as what an agent should do to become the winner of the auction, how payments are made, or how a fine is applied. The work overcomes the limit of the traditional approaches by allowing a specification of regulations that is based on facts occurring in the environment (an aspect that we interpret as data-awareness). The important consequence is that in this way, the institution does not depend on agents informing about norm violation, goal achievement, role adoption, etc. for the relevant information is obtained from the environment. In [21], situated artificial institutions are specified in terms of norms and constitutive rules. Norms are based on status functions, like winner, payment. Constitutive rules state the conditions for an element of the environment to carry a status function. For example, if the environment has an automatic teller machine implemented by an artifact, an operation in such artifact could count as the payment.

Other works make proposals for going beyond the propositional representation, which characterizes most studies on multiagent systems, underlining the importance of putting information in the centre. In particular, the Cupid language [17] provides a sophisticate and information-centric representation that distinguishes between a schema (what occurs in a specification) and its instances (what transpires and is represented in a database), reserving the term commitment only for schemas. This avoids the inadequacy of first-order in representing commitment instances by relying on relational database queries. The advantages, brought to the analysis of properties of a data-aware approach are proved in DACMAS [36], which incorporates commitment-based MASs but in a data-aware context. In general, in presence of data transition systems become typically infinite-state [14]. On the one hand, this is due to the fact that there is no bound on the number of tuples that can be added to database relations as the computation goes on. On the other hand, even when the number of tuples does not exceed a certain threshold, it is possible to populate them using infinitely many different data objects. Interestingly, when a DACMAS is state-bounded, i.e., the number of data that are simultaneously present at each moment in time is bounded, verification of rich temporal properties becomes decidable. Notably, this shows that, by suitably controlling how data are evolved in the system, it is possible to make agents data-aware without compromising their reasoning capabilities [5,36]. A language for representing norms that guarantees a priori the decidability of property analysis would be a great advancement being the tool that agents need to reason and decide which action to take, thus leveraging their autonomy. JaCaMo [9], simpAL [40], JaCaMo+ [2] are existing platforms for the development of MAS that have the right potential for developing the view depicted in Fig. 2. The next step would be the introduction of information-centric artifacts, whose lifecycle and data evolution are realized by way of query languages that, as for DACMAS [36], guarantee decidability when certain constraints are met. For commitment-based platforms, the Cupid [17] language would provide analogous features.

From an ontological perspective, Guarino and Guizzardi [28,29] discussed the importance of relationship reification and its connection with events/ processes. This work provides further foundation to our vision in connection to the specification of the conceptual model of an environment, seen as an information system. What this proposal currently lacks of is a methodology that will help designers to specify conceptual models. The literature on Agent-Oriented Software Engineering, on the other hand, proposes many methodologies. Briefly, SODA [35] is an agent-oriented methodology for the analysis and design of agent-based systems, adopting a layering principle and a tabular representation. It focuses on inter-agent issues, like the engineering of societies and environment for MAS, and relies on a meta-model that includes both agents and artifacts. GAIA [52] is a methodology for developing a MAS as an organization. Tropos [12] is a requirements-driven methodology for developing multiagent systems, while [4, 23] allow building declarative business process specifications in a norm-oriented fashion, see for instance. Although the last two methodologies do not consider data lifecycles in general, but rather rely on commitments and constraints, they are good candidates for extensions to a vision where norms, that capture the evolution of data, are composed into the specifications of multiagent system that are data and norm-aware. One viable direction to reach this purpose is to gather from the proposal in [44] for the realization of norm-governed socio-technical systems. Suitable methodologies should also be provided for programming the agents. In this respect, a starting point could be CoSE [2], a commitment-driven methodology for programming agents in presence of business-artifacts, that reify relationships captured as commitments.

6   Final Remarks

In this work, we have discussed the need for data-aware and norm-aware multiagent systems. In particular, we identified the importance of providing norm-based representations of the data lifecycles and of specifying the conceptual model of the underlying information system in terms of such norms. We have also commented some recent works that, independently, move along this direction facing one aspect or another.

One of the reasons of going towards data- and norm-awareness is the conviction that this will bring benefits to the design and implementation of software. The capability given to agents to take into account the data lifecycles in their reasoning process will provide the capability of reasoning about abnormal conditions in the environment, and decide how to react to them. This will enrich the already available capability agents can be equipped with of reasoning about deviations from their expected behavior. So, in principle, the robustness of the system, intended as the ability to react appropriately to abnormal conditions, would be increased. The fact that data structure and lifecycles are explicitly represented in a way that can be reasoned about makes also the agents and their environment more decoupled, reducing the need of customizing agent programs when the environment changes. This increases both the extendibility and the reusability of all the components of the MAS. Last but not the least, data-awareness joint with a norm-based representation will enable a fully fledged range of verifications, and will also help modularizing the verification of properties inside a MAS, with a positive impact on the correctness of software.

Acknowledgements. The authors would like to thank the anonymous reviewers for the helpful comments. This work was developed during the sabbatical year that Matteo Baldoni and Cristina Baroglio spent at the Free University of Bolzano-Bozen. It was partially supported by the *Accountable Trustworthy Organizations and Systems (AThOS)* project, funded by Università degli Studi di Torino and Compagnia di San Paolo (CSP 2014).

References

1. Alonso, G., Casati, F., Kuno, H., Machiraju, V.: Web Services: Concepts, Architectures and Applications. Data-Centric Systems and Applications. Springer, Heidelberg (2004)
2. Baldoni, M., Baroglio, C., Capuzzimati, F., Micalizio, R.: Empowering agent coordination with social engagement. In: Gavanelli, M., Lamma, E., Riguzzi, F. (eds.) AI*IA 2015. LNCS (LNAI), vol. 9336, pp. 89–101. Springer, Heidelberg (2015). doi:10.1007/978-3-319-24309-2_7
3. Baldoni, M., Baroglio, C., Capuzzimati, F., Micalizio, R.: Leveraging commitments and goals in agent interaction. In: Ancona, D., Maratea, M., Mascardi, V. (eds.) Proceedings of XXX Italian Conference on Computational Logic (CILC) (2015)
4. Baldoni, M., Baroglio, C., Marengo, E., Patti, V., Capuzzimati, F.: Engineering commitment-based business protocols with the 2CL methodology. JAAMAS **28**(4), 519–557 (2014)
5. Belardinelli, F., Lomuscio, A., Patrizi, F.: A computationally-grounded semantics for artifact-centric systems and abstraction results. In: Walsh, T. (ed.) Proceedings of the 22nd International Joint Conference on Artificial Intelligence (IJCAI 2011), Barcelona, Catalonia, Spain, 16–22 July, 2011, pp. 738–743. IJCAI/AAAI (2011)
6. Bhattacharya, K., Caswell, N.S., Kumaran, S., Nigam, A., Frederick, Y.W.: Artifact-centered operational modeling: lessons from customer engagements. IBM Syst. J. **46**(4), 703–721 (2007)
7. Boella, G., van der Torre, L.W.N.: Regulative, constitutive norms in normative multiagent systems. In: Dubois, D., Welty, C.A., Williams, M-A. (eds.) Proceedings of the Ninth International Conference on Principles of Knowledge Representation and Reasoning (KR 2004), Whistler, Canada, 2–5 June, pp. 255–266. AAAI Press (2004)
8. Boella, G., van der Torre, L.W. N., Verhagen, H.: Introduction to normative multiagent systems. In: Boella, G., van der Torre, L.W.N., Verhagen, H. (eds.) Normative Multi-agent Systems, 18.03. – 23.03.2007, vol. 07122 of Dagstuhl Seminar Proceedings. Internationales Begegnungs- und Forschungszentrum für Informatik (IBFI), Schloss Dagstuhl, Germany (2007)
9. Boissier, O., Bordini, R.H., Hübner, J.F., Ricci, A., Santi, A.: Multi-agent oriented programming with JaCaMo. Sci. Comput. Program. **78**(6), 747–761 (2013)
10. Bordini, R.H., Fred Hübner, J., Wooldridge, M.: Programming Multi-Agent Systems in AgentSpeak Using Jason. Wiley, Chichester (2007)
11. Bratman, M.E.: What is intention? In: Cohen, P., Morgan, J., Pollack, M. (eds.) Intensions in Communication, pp. 15–31. MIT Press, Cambridge (1990)
12. Bresciani, P., Perini, A., Giorgini, P., Giunchiglia, F., Mylopoulos, J.: Tropos: an agent-oriented software development methodology. Auton. Agent. Multi Agent Syst. **8**(3), 203–236 (2004)
13. Bridgeland, D.M., Zahavi, R.: Business Modeling: A Practical Guide to Realizing Business Value. Morgan Kaufmann Publishers Inc., San Francisco (2008)
14. Calvanese, D., De Giacomo, G., Montali, M.: Foundations of data-aware process analysis: a database theory perspective. In: Hull, R., Fan, W. (eds.) Proceedings of the 32nd ACM SIGMOD-SIGACT-SIGART Symposium on Principles of Database Systems (PODS 2013), New York, NY, USA, 22–27 June, pp. 1–12. ACM (2013)
15. Chopra, A.K., Singh, M.P.: Constitutive interoperability. In: Proceedings of the 7th International Joint Conference on Autonomous Agents and Multiagent Systems, vol. 2, pp. 797–804. International Foundation for Autonomous Agents and Multiagent Systems (2008)

16. Chopra, A.K., Singh, M.P.: Agent communication. In: Weiss, G. (ed.) Multiagent Systems, 2nd edn. MIT Press, Cambridge (2013)
17. Chopra, A.K., Singh, M.P.: Cupid: commitments in relational algebra. In: Bonet, B., Koenig, S. (eds.) Proceedings of the Twenty-Ninth AAAI Conference on Artificial Intelligence, 25–30 January, Austin, Texas, USA, pp. 2052–2059. AAAI Press (2015)
18. Cohn, D., Hull, R.: Business artifacts: a data-centric approach to modeling business operations and processes. IEEE Data Eng. Bull. **32**(3), 3–9 (2009)
19. Criado, N., Argente, E., Noriega, P., Botti, V.: Reasoning about constitutive norms in BDI agents. Logic J. IGPL **22**(1), 66–93 (2013)
20. Dastani, M., van der Torre, L., Yorke-Smith, V.: Commitments and interaction norms in organisations. In: Autonomous Agents and Multiagent Systems, pp. 1–43 (2015)
21. Brito, M., Hübner, J.F., Boissier, O.: A conceptual model for situated artificial institutions. In: Bulling, N., Torre, L., Villata, S., Jamroga, W., Vasconcelos, W. (eds.) CLIMA 2014. LNCS (LNAI), vol. 8624, pp. 35–51. Springer, Heidelberg (2014). doi:10.1007/978-3-319-09764-0_3
22. Demazeau, Y.: From interactions to collective behaviour in agent-based systems. In: Proceedings of the 1st European Conference on Cognitive Science, pp. 117–132, Saint-Malo (1995)
23. Desai, N., Chopra, A.K., Singh, M.P.: Amoeba: a methodology for modeling and evolving cross-organizational business processes. ACM Trans. Softw. Eng. Methodol. **19**(2), 6 (2009)
24. Di Leva, A., Femiano, S.: The BP-M* methodology for process analysis in the health sector. Intell. Inf. Manage. **3**(2), 56–63 (2011)
25. d'Inverno, M., Luck, M., Noriega, P., Rodríguez-Aguilar, J.A., Sierra, C.: Communicating open systems. Artif. Intell. **186**, 38–94 (2012)
26. Gibbs, J.P.: Norms: the problem of definition and classification. Am. J. Sociol. **70**(5), 586–594 (1965)
27. Governatori, G.: Law, logic and business processes. In: Third International Workshop on Requirements Engineering and Law (RELAW 2010), Sydney, NSW, Australia, 28 September, pp. 1–10. IEEE (2010)
28. Guarino, N., Guizzardi, G.: "We need to discuss the relationship": revisiting relationships as modeling constructs. In: Zdravkovic, J., Kirikova, M., Johannesson, P. (eds.) CAiSE 2015. LNCS, vol. 9097, pp. 279–294. Springer, Heidelberg (2015). doi:10.1007/978-3-319-19069-3_18
29. Guarino, N., Guizzardi, G.: Relationships, events: towards a general theory of reification and truthmaking. In: Advances in Artificial Intelligence - XVth International Conference of the Italian Association for Artificial Intelligence (AI*IA 2016), Genova, Italy, Proceedings, LNCS. Springer (2016, to appear)
30. Hewitt, C., Bishop, P., Steiger, R.: A universal modular ACTOR formalism for artificial intelligence. In: Nilsson, N.J. (ed.) Proceedings of the 3rd International Joint Conference on Artificial Intelligence, Standford, CA, pp. 235–245. William Kaufmann (1973)
31. Jennings, N.R.: On agent-based software engineering. Artif. Intell. **117**(2), 277–296 (2000)
32. Jones, A.J.I., Carmo, J.: Deontic logic and contrary-to-duties. In: Gabbay, D. (ed.) Handbook of Philosophical Logic, pp. 203–279. Kluwer (2001)
33. Meyer, B.: Object-Oriented Software Construction, 2nd edn. Prentice-Hall Inc., Upper Saddle River (1997)

34. Mitchell, J.C.: Concepts in Programming Languages. Cambridge University Press, Cambridge (2002)
35. Molesini, A., Omicini, A., Denti, E., Ricci, A.: SODA: a roadmap to artefacts. In: Dikenelli, O., Gleizes, M.-P., Ricci, A. (eds.) ESAW 2005. LNCS (LNAI), vol. 3963, pp. 49–62. Springer, Heidelberg (2006). doi:10.1007/11759683_4
36. Montali, M., Calvanese, D., De Giacomo, G.: Verification of data-aware commitment-based multiagent system. In: Bazzan, A.L.C., Huhns, M.N., Lomuscio, A., Scerri, P. (eds.) International conference on Autonomous Agents and Multi-Agent Systems (AAMAS 2014), Paris, France, 5–9 May, pp. 157–164. IFAA-MAS/ACM (2014)
37. Neykova, R., Yoshida, N.: Multiparty session actors. In: Kühn, E., Pugliese, R. (eds.) COORDINATION 2014. LNCS, vol. 8459, pp. 131–146. Springer, Heidelberg (2014). doi:10.1007/978-3-662-43376-8_9
38. Omicini, A., Ricci, A., Viroli, M.: Artifacts in the A&A meta-model for multi-agent systems. Auton. Agents Multi Agent Syst. **17**(3), 432–456 (2008). Special Issue on Foundations, Advanced Topics and Industrial Perspectives of Multi-Agent Systems
39. Ricci, A., Piunti, M., Viroli, M.: Environment programming in multi-agent systems: an artifact-based perspective. Auton. Agents Multi Agent Syst. **23**(2), 158–192 (2011)
40. Ricci, A., Santi, A.: From actors and concurrent objects to agent-oriented programming in simpAL. In: Agha, G., Igarashi, A., Kobayashi, N., Masuhara, H., Matsuoka, S., Shibayama, E., Taura, K. (eds.) Papers dedicated to Akinori Yonezawa on the Occasion of His 65th Birthday. LNCS, vol. 8665, pp. 408–445. Springer, Heidelberg (2014). doi:10.1007/978-3-662-44471-9_17
41. Russell, S.J., Norvig, P.: Artificial Intelligence: A Modern Approach, 2nd edn. Pearson Education, Upper Sadle River (2003)
42. Shoham, Y.: Agent-oriented programming. Artif. Intell. **60**(1), 51–92 (1993)
43. Singh, M.P.: An ontology for commitments in multiagent systems. Artif. Intell. Law **7**(1), 97–113 (1999)
44. Singh, M.P.: Norms as a basis for governing sociotechnical systems. ACM TIST **5**(1), 21 (2013)
45. Singh, M.P., Huhns, M.N.: Service-Oriented Computing - Semantics, Processes, Agents. Wiley, Chichester (2005)
46. Tasharofi, S., Dinges, P., Johnson, R.E.: Why do scala developers mix the actor model with other concurrency models? In: Castagna, G. (ed.) ECOOP 2013. LNCS, vol. 7920, pp. 302–326. Springer, Heidelberg (2013). doi:10.1007/978-3-642-39038-8_13
47. Telang, P.R., Singh, M.P., Yorke-Smith, N.: Relating goal and commitment semantics. In: Dennis, L., Boissier, O., Bordini, R.H. (eds.) ProMAS 2011. LNCS (LNAI), vol. 7217, pp. 22–37. Springer, Heidelberg (2012). doi:10.1007/978-3-642-31915-0_2
48. Therborn, G.: Back to norms! on the scope and dynamics of norms and normative action. Current Sociol. **50**, 863–880 (2002)
49. Weske, M.: Business Process Management: Concepts, Languages, Architectures. Springer, Heidelberg (2007)
50. Weyns, D., Omicini, A., Odell, J.: Environment as a first class abstraction in multiagent systems. JAAMAS **14**(1), 5–30 (2007)
51. Wooldridge, M.J.: Introduction to Multiagent Systems, 2nd edn. Wiley, Chichester (2009)
52. Zambonelli, F., Jennings, N.R., Wooldridge, M.: Developing multiagent systems: the Gaia methodology. ACM Trans. Softw. Eng. Methodol. **12**(3), 317–370 (2003)

Monitoring Patients with Hypoglycemia Using Self-adaptive Protocol-Driven Agents: A Case Study

Angelo Ferrando[✉], Davide Ancona, and Viviana Mascardi

DIBRIS, University of Genova, Genoa, Italy
angelo.ferrando@dibris.unige.it,
{davide.ancona,viviana.mascardi}@unige.it

Abstract. Trace expressions are a compact and expressive formalism for specifying complex patterns of actions. In this paper they have been used to model medical protocols and to generate agents able to execute them, also adapting to the context dynamics. To this aim, we extended our previous work on "self-adaptive agents driven by interaction protocols" by allowing agents to be guided by trace expressions instead of the less concise and less powerful "constrained global types". This extension required a limited effort, which is an advantage of the previous work as it is relatively straightforward to adapt it to accommodate new requirements arising in sophisticated domains.

Keywords: Medical protocol execution · Remote patient monitoring · Hypoglycemia in newborns · Protocol-driven agents · Trace expressions

1 Introduction and Motivation

The demographic changes in our societies are causing an explosion of care requests and, as a consequence, of the healthcare expenses.

Care requests for minor problems that could be managed without the direct intervention of a doctor divert the healthcare resources from more serious situations. One possible solution to this problem, addressed since the beginning of the millennium, is *Remote Patient Monitoring* (RPM [9]) which consists in the remote and distributed monitoring of a specific category of patients in order to limit the number of visits to doctors and hospitals.

Health telematics can play a major role in improving the lives of patients [16], particularly in the weaker sections of the society including disabled, elderly and chronically ill patients [34]. Mobile health-monitoring devices offer great help for such patients who may afford good healthcare without having to visit their doctor on a regular basis. These technologies bring potential benefits to both the patient and the doctor; doctors can focus on priority tasks by saving time normally spent with consulting chronically ill patients, and patients can be properly looked after whilst remaining in their environment without having to make tiring and time-consuming visits.

© Springer International Publishing AG 2016
M. Baldoni et al. (Eds.): EMAS 2016, LNAI 10093, pp. 39–58, 2016.
DOI: 10.1007/978-3-319-50983-9_3

From a technological point of view, RPM requires a low level physical infrastructure made up of sensors and a software middleware monitoring the sensors output and implementing rules for warning either the patient or the doctor, or both, if the pattern of perceived data diverges from the expected pattern for that patient. In order to achieve its goals, the middleware should:

1. manage data coming from decentralized and heterogeneous sensors;
2. support the addition and removal of sensors and other components at runtime;
3. be adaptive to changes taking place in the environment and in the care protocols that must be adopted;
4. interact with the human beings involved in the RPM process by means of a user friendly interface;
5. be fault tolerant.

A multiagent system (MAS) with one agent in charge of each patient and one of each doctor involved in the RPM process seems a very natural choice to implement a middleware satisfying all these requirements, due to the MAS intrinsic structure where each agent has incomplete information or capabilities for solving the problem, there is no global system control, data is decentralized, computation is asynchronous, the system is open and highly dynamic [24]. Consistently with a holonic approach to MAS engineering and development [22], the agent in charge of the patient (Patient's Agent, PA in the sequel) might be a MAS as well, with one agent in charge of each sensor, one agent in charge of the user interface, one agent in charge of the identification of threats based on sensory input, and so on.

The PA should monitor the behavior of the patient and the data coming from the sensors he/she wears, and should verify that they are consistent with a known "protocol". A simple protocol could be, for example, "if the blood pressure is below a given threshold, then the patient should sit down for 10 min, the saturation sensor should be switched on, and the heartbeat monitoring frequency should be increased". The PA should be able to make actions in the patient's environment in order to ensure that the protocol is followed. For example if, by checking data coming from the blood pressure sensor, the PA realizes that the value is below the expected threshold, then it should ask the patient, via its user friendly interface, to sit down for ten minutes. Since the protocol guiding the patient's treatment can change over time, the PA should be able to dynamically move from one protocol to another, upon request of some trusted entity like the doctor. This protocol switch might take place also when sensory input shows a situation not compliant with the protocol. For example if, by checking data coming from the motion sensor, the PA realizes that the patient did not remain seated as long as required, it should immediately detect a protocol violation; it might then switch to a higher priority protocol, involving for example the doctor. To summarize, the PA should be driven by the protocol and should be able to adapt to new situations by changing the followed protocol when needed.

In our recent research [3] we designed and implemented a framework for protocol-driven self-adaptive agents, where agents are characterized by one interaction protocol specified using constrained global types [2,6] and by some components that should be directly implemented in the underlying agent framework, be it JADE [10], Jason [12], or any other else.

Being protocol-driven means that the agent behaves according to a given protocol expressed in some suitable formalism. In each time instant, the protocol-driven agent can make only those internal choices which are allowed by the protocol in the current state. In case of events which depend on external choices, the agent can only verify whether the event that took place is compliant with the protocol or not ("runtime verification"). Deciding what to do after a violation has been detected is up to the MAS designers and developers and might range from switching to some special protocol for dealing with highly critical situations, to adopting some self-repair actions, to notifying a human supervisor, or even to excluding the faulty agent from the MAS.

In our work, the protocol specification is interpreted and the only framework-dependent pieces of code are the functions for generating protocol-compliant actions and for projecting one global protocol specification onto a single agent. The agent interpreter that calls these functions is framework-dependent as well. Actually, we implemented the "generate" and the "project" functions in Prolog once and for all, and we exploited the Prolog code for both the JADE and the Jason implementations of the protocol-driven interpreter. A characterizing feature of our approach is hence that we do not produce any protocol-dependent agent code into any agent-oriented programming language. This gives us the flexibility that meta-programming ensures, demonstrated for example by the easiness in implementing protocol switch: protocols can be exchanged and modified at run-time, being first class entities.

In this paper we extend the framework presented in [3] by allowing protocols to involve events of any kind and not just communicative ones. The extended framework is made more usable by allowing protocols to be expressed using "trace expressions" [7]. We show how the extended framework can be profitably adopted to specify medical protocols and to monitor them. We believe that our framework can serve as the basis for implementing a Remote Patient Monitoring software middleware. The motivating scenario that we consider is that of newborns who may suffer from hypoglycemia and the protocols we have implemented are based on medical literature [30].

The paper is organized in the following way: Sect. 2 discusses the related work, Sect. 3 introduces the background knowledge for understanding the protocol modeling and the experiments presented in Sect. 4, and Sect. 5 concludes.

2   Related Work

In the last years, the exploitation of MASs in the e-Health scenario has become more and more widespread, as discussed for example in [11]. E-Health systems pose many challenges and requirements, such as:

- context and location awareness are to be smoothly integrated, i.e., the access and the visualization of health-related information always depends on the overall contexts of the patient and of the user [14],

– fault-tolerance, reliability, security and privacy-awareness are a must in order
  to accommodate the strict requirements of all healthcare applications,
– effective mobile devices are to be used to provide access to relevant health-
  related information independently of the current physical location and physical
  condition of the user, and
– unobtrusive sensor technology is needed to gather the physiological information from the patient without hampering her daily life.

The first requirement immediately recalls "situatedness" and the others are
closely related with features of agents and MASs that, albeit not being strictly
characterizing ones, are considered relevant ones and widely studied in the agent-
oriented literature (see for example [17,25,32] for fault-tolerance, reliability, and
security in MASs, respectively; [15] for issues related with distributed coordination of mobile agents; [27] for the relationships between MASs and sensor
networks, just to cite some recent works). It comes with no surprise that many
ubiquitous and pervasive e-Health systems are designed and realized using MAS
abstractions and technologies [8,23,35].

According to [20], MASs in the e-Health context are used in the following
categories of applications: *assistive living*; *diagnosis*; *physical monitoring*; and
smart-emergency. The scenario we take under consideration in this paper falls
in the third category, where the aim is the continuous monitoring of patients at
home [29].

In [16] a system architecture consisting in a Java-based agent for each human
role (e.g. doctors, patients) is presented. Within that framework, agents reside in
three areas: the patient's mobile device (e.g. smart phone or PDA with Internet
connectivity); the healthcare personnel's mobile device (e.g. for nurses or para-
medics); and the mobile and static servers (which may be a wireless connected
notebook or an enterprise server computer). Our case study is close to that one
since we devise one protocol-driven agent for each human role as well.

A framework for representing in formal terms how clinical guidelines[1] are
realized through the actions of individuals organized into teams is presented
in [36]. The authors emphasize that the flexibility to deviate from the guideline
recommendations is indispensable if we are to build workflow systems that will be
accepted by the medical community. Even if the aim of our work is different from
that one, they share some ideas, in particular regarding the reuse of plans (which,
in our approach, are protocols), the team based definition ("global protocol
definition" in our approach), and the flexibility of changing protocol at runtime.

In [13,18] the authors describe the GPROVE framework for specifying medical guidelines[2] in a visual way and for verifying the conformance of the guideline
execution w.r.t. the specification. Except for the part regarding the visual representation of guidelines, that work is very close to ours, in particular as far as the
verification that generated events do not lead to discrepancies with the models

---

[1] Clinical guidelines are special types of plans realized by collective agents.
[2] Medical guidelines are clinical behavior recommendations used to help and support
  physicians in the definition of the most appropriate diagnosis and/or therapy within
  determinate clinical circumstances.

is concerned. The most relevant difference is when verification is performed: in [13,18] the verification is performed on a log file generated during the execution (*a posteriori*). In our work, agents are pro-actively driven by the protocol when it is up to them to decide what to do, and they verify that the protocol is respected when an event relevant for the application is intercepted. In other words, our agents accommodate runtime verification of perceived events with protocol-compliant action selection. The verification task is carried out while the agent is running, differently from [13,18].

Another work similar to ours is [31] where the SUAP project, a MAS to support and monitor prenatal care, is presented. SUAP manages electronic healthcare records of pregnant women: it models, monitors and provides advice on prenatal protocols, and models a simple referencing protocol based on pregnancy risks. In that work protocols are defined by a set of rules and there are *protocol agents* which monitor data related to appointments and exam results to identify situations in which protocols must be applied. In [31] protocols can not change during the execution: this represents the main different of that work w.r.t. ours.

3 Self-adaptive Protocol-Driven Agents

In [3] we presented a framework for implementing self-adaptive protocol-driven agents.

In this section we summarize that work and we present some extensions which make the framework more general and flexible, consistently with the extensions to the protocol formalism described in [7]. In [3], in fact, the protocol could involve communicative actions only and hence could be only used to drive the communicative behavior of the agents. In this paper we move a step forward, changing the framework implementation to cope with protocols where any kind of perceived events can be modeled. The limited effort for realizing this extension should be seen as a strength of our previous work, rather than a limitation of the current one.

Protocol-driven agents are characterized by an *interaction protocol* or, more in general, by a given "pattern of events and actions" specified in some suitable formalism, and by a *knowledge base*, a *message queue*, and an *environment representation*. As we make no other assumption on the agent architecture, our framework is as general as possible and could be implemented in any underlying environment or programming language where these three components are available (namely almost all the agents frameworks, be them BDI-oriented like Jason or not BDI-oriented like JADE).

The internal agent architecture, shown in Fig. 1, supports a combined approach to correct behavior generation (when the choice of what to do is up to the agent) and runtime verification (when the choice of what to do is made by the agent environment, and the agent must verify that it is protocol-compliant).

For supporting a protocol-driven approach to agent programming, a formalism for expressing protocols must exist together with a *generate* function for

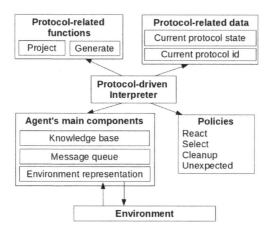

Fig. 1. Internal architecture of a protocol-driven agent.

identifying the allowed actions for moving from the current state of the protocol to the next one. What differentiates the behavior of each agent are the *select* policy to select the action to perform among the allowed ones, and the *react* policy to react to perceived events. Two more policies must be defined to state how to manage *unexpected* events and which *cleanup* actions to perform before switching from the currently executing protocol to the new one. Protocol switch is one of the major features of our approach, allowing agents to self-adapt to new situations by changing the current protocol upon reception of "switch requests". Those agents that have the power to cause a protocol switch, named *controllers*, must be explicitly stated by the agent and may change over time. Each agent can change the currently executing protocol by requesting a protocol switch to itself. Each agent *Ag* is also able to *project* a global description of a protocol involving many agents onto a local version by keeping only events that involve *Ag* itself.

The protocol-driven interpreter implements a cycle where it first checks if there is a protocol switch request and if it can be managed in the current state of the protocol. If yes, and if the protocol switch sender is a system controller, a protocol switch is performed after some cleanup operations. If no protocol switch is foreseen in that moment, the protocol-compliant actions are generated and one of them is selected for being executed. The environment representation and knowledge base are updated accordingly and the protocol moves to the next state. In case the perceived event was not foreseen by the protocol, it is managed according to the unexpected policy.

The MAS architecture is shown in Fig. 2. The protocol library may be either external, like in the figure, or hard-wired in the controller (either the doctor or the protocol-driven agent itself, in our case study) knowledge base. This makes little difference both from a logical and from a practical point of view. Protocols in the library always take a global perspective (namely, a perspective where all

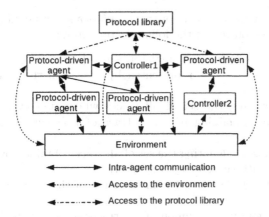

Fig. 2. Architecture of a self-adaptive MAS.

the parties involved in the protocol are managed in a homogeneous way, without taking the point of view of one of them). The local protocol for each agent can be automatically obtained from the global one by projection. This allows *the whole MAS to respect the global protocol by construction*, as the local protocol executed by each agent is obtained from the global one and is consistent with it.

Trace expressions. Trace expressions are a specification formalism expressly designed for runtime verification; they are an evolution of global types [6] and have been continuously refined and consolidated during the last 4 years [2, 4, 7, 19, 28]. Trace expressions build on top of the "event" notion. An event is something which takes place in the environment and which can be either generated or observed by the agents. It may be either a communicative event, like in [3], or any other event like the perception of some value from a sensor, the observation of some phenomenon in the environment, the expiration of a deadline.

Events. In the following we denote by $\mathcal{E}$ a fixed universe of events. An event e_1 might be, for example, "The body temperature sensor (BTS) perceived a value of $38.2°$ at time 15.32". Another similar event e_2 might be "BTS perceived a value of $39.0°$ at time 7.15" and e_3 might be "BTS perceived a value of $36.5°$ at time 22.43".

Event types. To be more general, trace expressions are built on top of event types (chosen from a set $\mathcal{ET}$), rather than of single events; an event type denotes a subset of $\mathcal{E}$. For example, an event type ϑ might be "BTS perceived a value greater than $38°$ in the afternoon". It is easy to verify that e_1 has type ϑ, whereas neither e_1 nor e_3 have. Grouping actual events into event types is convenient to specify trace expressions without dealing with all the possible values that variables in an event might assume. For example, a trace expression could model the rule "If BTS perceived a value greater than $38°$ in the afternoon, then send a message to the doctor". This rule involves the event type ϑ which, from an implementation viewpoint, can be expressed by means of the has_type predicate. An example is provided in Sect. 4.

Trace expressions. A trace expression τ represents a set of possibly infinite event traces and is defined on top of the following operators:

- ϵ (*empty trace*), denoting the singleton set $\{\epsilon\}$ containing the empty event trace ϵ (the empty trace is represented by `lambda` in the concrete language representation).
- $\vartheta{:}\tau$ (*prefix*), denoting the set of all traces whose first event e has type ϑ ($e \in \vartheta$), and the remaining part is a trace of τ (: symbol in the concrete representation).
- $\tau_1{\cdot}\tau_2$ (*concatenation*), denoting the set of all traces obtained by concatenating the traces of τ_1 with those of τ_2 (∗ symbol).
- $\tau_1{\wedge}\tau_2$ (*intersection*), denoting the intersection of the traces of τ_1 and τ_2 (/\ symbol).
- $\tau_1{\vee}\tau_2$ (*union*), denoting the union of the traces of τ_1 and τ_2 (\/ symbol).
- $\tau_1{|}\tau_2$ (*shuffle*), denoting the set obtained by shuffling the traces in τ_1 with the traces in τ_2 (| symbol).

To support recursion without introducing an explicit construct, trace expressions are regular (a.k.a. rational or cyclic) terms and can be represented by a finite set of syntactic equations, as happens, for instance, in most modern Prolog implementations where unification supports cyclic terms.

As an example, $T = \vartheta{:}T$ is equivalent to the infinite but regular term $\vartheta{:}\vartheta{:}\vartheta{:}\vartheta{:}\ldots$ Supposing that e is the only event having type ϑ ($e \in \vartheta$), the only trace represented by T is the one consisting of infinite occurrences of e, e^ω. The lack of a base case for this recursive definition is not a problem, as trace expressions are interpreted in a coinductive way in order to represent infinite traces of events.

Quoting [33], "*intuitively, a set A is defined coinductively if it is the greatest solution of an inequation of a certain form; then the coinduction proof principle just says that any set that is a solution of the same inequation is contained in A. Dually, a set A is defined inductively if it is the least solution of an inequation of a certain form, and the induction principle then says that any other set that is a solution to the same equation contains A*". Coinduction is thus the mathematical dual to structural induction; coinductively defined types are known as codata and are typically infinite data structures, such as streams. The semantics of Coinductive Logic Programming that we exploit in our implementation is discussed in [5].

To make another example of recursive definition, $T1 = (\vartheta{:}T1{\vee}\epsilon)$ represents the set of traces $\{\epsilon, e, ee, eee, \ldots, e^\omega\}$. Here, the base case is given by the possibility ($\vee$ operator) for $T1$ to rewrite into ϵ after any number of rewriting steps, which leads to the generation of e traces of any length, from 0 to ω.

The semantics of trace expressions is specified by the transition relation $\delta \subseteq \mathcal{T} \times \mathcal{E} \times \mathcal{T}$, where $\mathcal{T}$ denotes the set of trace expressions. As it is customary, we write $\tau_1 \xrightarrow{e} \tau_2$ to mean $(\tau_1, e, \tau_2) \in \delta$. If the trace expression τ_1 specifies the current valid state of the system, then an event e is considered valid iff there exists a transition $\tau_1 \xrightarrow{e} \tau_2$; in such a case, τ_2 will specify the next valid state of the system after event e. Figure 3 defines the rules for the transition function

$$\text{(prefix)} \frac{}{\vartheta{:}\tau \xrightarrow{e} \tau} \; e \in \vartheta \qquad \text{(or-l)} \frac{\tau_1 \xrightarrow{e} \tau_1'}{\tau_1 \vee \tau_2 \xrightarrow{e} \tau_1'} \qquad \text{(and)} \frac{\tau_1 \xrightarrow{e} \tau_1' \quad \tau_2 \xrightarrow{e} \tau_2'}{\tau_1 \wedge \tau_2 \xrightarrow{e} \tau_1' \wedge \tau_2'}$$

$$\text{(shuffle-l)} \frac{\tau_1 \xrightarrow{e} \tau_1'}{\tau_1|\tau_2 \xrightarrow{e} \tau_1'|\tau_2} \qquad \text{(cat-l)} \frac{\tau_1 \xrightarrow{e} \tau_1'}{\tau_1 \cdot \tau_2 \xrightarrow{e} \tau_1' \cdot \tau_2} \qquad \text{(cat-r)} \frac{\tau_2 \xrightarrow{e} \tau_2'}{\tau_1 \cdot \tau_2 \xrightarrow{e} \tau_2'} \; \epsilon(\tau_1)$$

Fig. 3. Operational semantics of trace expressions. The $\epsilon(\tau)$ side condition means that τ can move into the empty trace expression; $e \in \vartheta$ means that event e has type ϑ.

(or and shuffle rules have a symmetric or-r and shuffle-r version where τ_2 moves, instead of τ_1).

Template Trace Expressions. In order to write complex protocols in a compact and readable way, in [19] we extended global types with templates which allow parameters inside the protocol definition. In this paragraph we introduce template trace expressions which extend the notion of template global types.

Template trace expressions are a meta-formalism: they must be applied to some arguments in order to obtain normal trace expressions. Parameters are present in the template trace expression definition only.

Let us consider the following template trace expressions definition, modeling infinite loops of request reception and management each involving the same server and one different client. The loops, modeled by the SERVERT subprotocol, must be composed using the *shuffle* (|) operator. The client instances are represented, in the template trace expressions definition, by the variable var(1):

```
SERVERT = receive_request(var(1)): (serve_request(var(1)): SERVERT),
MAIN = finite_composition(|, SERVERT, [var(1)])
```

This definition says that the MAIN protocol consists of a finite composition via the shuffle operator of the SERVERT subprotocols, each of which will be characterized by having a ground client value instead of the var(1) variable. The template trace expression definition must be applied as shown in the code fragment below:

```
apply(MAIN, [t(var(1), [client1,client2,client3])], INSTANTIATED_MAIN)
```

The apply predicate takes as input the values that var(1) must assume in each instantiation of the SERVERT subprotocol, client1, client2, client3 in the example, and returns a ground value for the INSTANTIATED_MAIN variable, namely SERVER1|(SERVER2|SERVER3) where

```
SERVER1 = receive_request(client1): (serve_request(client1): SERVER1),
SERVER2 = receive_request(client2): (serve_request(client2): SERVER2),
SERVER3 = receive_request(client3): (serve_request(client3): SERVER3)
```

The value associated with INSTANTIATED_MAIN can be projected and used for protocol-driven behavior.

The advantage of using template trace expressions is that they are more compact and easy to design and understand than their "unfolding", and that the set over which the variables range can be decided at runtime, hence allowing the agents to implement a limited form of *dynamic protocol generation.*

As an example, if the clients involved in the protocol were fifty, `client1`, `client2`, ..., `client50`, the template trace expressions definition would remain the same as before. Only its application would change into

```
apply(MAIN,[t(var(1),[client1,client2,...,client50])],INSTANTIATED_MAIN)
```

allowing the protocol developers to write a very compact description instead of a 50 lines long specification (assuming to have one line for each `SERVERX = receive_request(clientX):(serve_request(clientX):SERVERX)` subprotocol).

Implementation details. With respect to the implementation described in [3], we made minor changes to the protocol-driven agent interpreter and to the project function to cope with the presence of generic events in the protocol, instead of communicative events only. The new implementation of our protocol-driven agents runs on top of both Jason and JADE. The agent interpreter is driven by the δ transition function described before and is implemented in Prolog. Since Jason can directly integrate Prolog code, the interpreter has been easily embedded into Jason agents. As far as JADE is concerned, we used a bidirectional Java-Prolog interface to make JADE agents behave according to Prolog rules.

The δ transition function is implemented by Prolog clauses defining a "`next`" predicate which are in a one-to-one correspondence with the δ transition rules, for a total of about 20 LOC (Lines Of Code). The *generate* function requires only a few lines of Prolog code, to collect all the solutions provided by `next`. The projection algorithm amounts to 60 lines of Prolog code, and the management of templates and their application required less than 200 LOC. Besides these Prolog predicates which are independent of the underlying framework, we had to develop some ad-hoc code both for JADE and for Jason, for linking the interpreter code with the agents behavior. In both cases, the required LOCs were less than 200.

4 Modeling Medical Protocols for Hypoglycemia in the Newborns

The human beings involved in our case study are doctors and newborns suffering from hypoglycemia. Each of them is associated with a protocol-driven agent. We assume that each baby can be equipped with sensors able to change the protocol-driven agent knowledge base after perception of sensory input such as *temperature, heartbeat, pressure,* O_2 saturation, *movement,* and so on. For example, if the patient has tremors, the movement sensor will update the knowledge base of the protocol-driven agent with information about the perceived tremors; this update will "fire" a move into a new protocol state where the successive foreseen events are those expected when the newborn has tremors. If the perceived event is instead an exceptional one and raises an emergency, a protocol switch might take place for allowing the agent to abandon the normal protocol it is following, and adopt an exceptional one suitable for managing the exceptional event. Finally, if the event is unknown, the agent will start following its own *unexpected events* policy. Event perception may cause the agent to perform other actions, defined by its *react* policy. Besides defining which events are expected in a given state, the protocol also asserts which actions are allowed. If the allowed actions are more than one, the agent will select one among them by using its *select* policy[3].

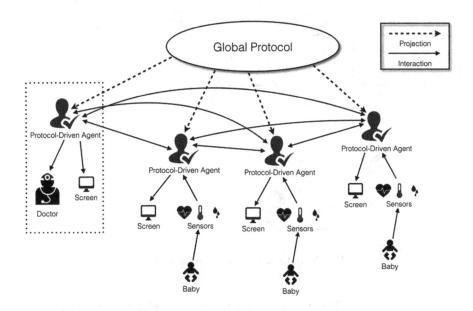

Fig. 4. Doctor-patients architecture.

The protocol-driven agent associated with newborns might need to communicate something to the patient or, to be more precise, to the patient's parents. To achieve this goal it may print some message onto a screen positioned near to the newborn. The parents can follow the monitoring process and the intervention instructions like, for example, the request to inject a dose of glucose solution. Hypoglycemia management does not require a constant presence of a doctor but needs an ongoing monitoring of some vital parameters, falling in the "patient monitoring at home" scenario discussed in Sect. 1.

---

[3] In our prototypical implementation, these policies are the default ones: unexpected events are discarded, no reaction is associated with perceived events, and selection selects the first action returned by the *generate* function.

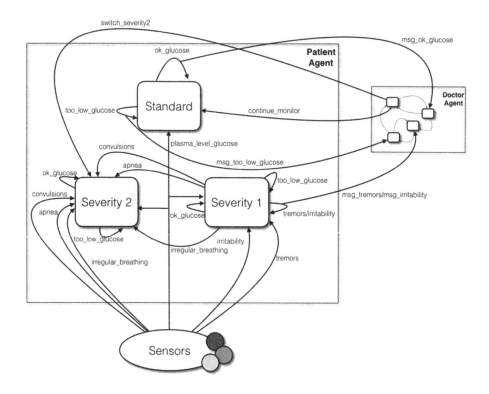

Fig. 5. Patient's protocols execution.

For sake of readability, in the sequel we will consider the situation where there are *1* doctor and *N* patients (Fig. 4), even if the protocols can be easily – and has been – generalized to *M* doctors.

The doctor's agent is driven by a single protocol while the patients' agents may be driven, in each time instant, by one of the three protocols below:

– *standard protocol*, which models the situation where the newborn has no symptoms of the disease;
– *severity 1 protocol*, associated with the lowest severity level of the disease;
– *severity 2 protocol*, associated with the highest severity level of the disease.

Figure 5 shows part of the interactions among the patients and doctors protocols. Protocol switches are fired by reception of a switch request from a trusted agent. Each agent may send a switch request to itself upon perception of an exceptional event, and this allows us to model in a neat and simple way event perception as a trigger of a protocol switch. For sake of readability, not all the messages involved in the protocols are shown Fig. 5. In particular, switch requests from a patient agent to itself are omitted.

Doctor protocol. The protocol DP of the agent associated with the doctor is conveniently represented by a template trace expression (the trace expression associated with the DoctorPatientProtocol logical variable, which will be replicated as many times as necessary during the application stage) consisting of the union (\/ operator) of three sub-protocols describing three mutually exclusive situations that the agent can experience. The event types appearing in the protocol may be communicative ones. In this case, for sake of readability, we prefix their name by msg. The first argument of communicative event types will be instantiated with the sender of the message and the second with the receiver. The agent associated with the doctor has the power to request a protocol switch to the patient's agent. A protocol switch in the patient may take place also in response to sensory input, as anticipated before and described in more details later. A switch request is modeled by the switch_request(Sender,Receiver,NewProtocolIdentifier) event type.

- Ok sub-protocol: if the doctor agent receives a message reporting that the glucose level in the blood of its patient is ok, then things are going on in the right way: the agent moves to the DoctorPatientProtocol state again (: operator, modeling sequence) and continues to monitor;
- SevereProblem sub-protocol: if the doctor agent receives a message reporting that the glucose level in the blood of its patient is too low, then it sends a protocol switch request to the patient (switch_request(var(doctor), var(patient), severity2) bringing the patient's protocol to severity2) and continues to monitor (namely, it moves to the DoctorPatientProtocol again thanks to the concatenation operator, *);
- SwitchedToSeverity1 sub-protocol: if the doctor agent receives a message reporting that the patient has switched its protocol to severity1 (communicative event type msg_switched_to_severity1(var(patient),var(doctor))), then the situation requires a more careful monitoring as it might change into a severe health status:
  • if the agent either receives a message reporting that the patient has tremors or he/she is irritable (TremorsOrIrritability sub-protocol), then it either sends a protocol switch request bringing the patient's protocol to severity2, or it asks the patient's agent to continue to monitor without switching to the severity2 protocol;
  • if, before or after the messages related to either tremors or irritability (I models the occurrence of events in any order), the doctor's agent receives a message from the patient (or from his parents) reporting an intervention request (InterventionRequest sub-protocol), then the agent communicates this request to the doctor using the screen.

In both cases, the agent can move to the "standard" monitoring state modeled by the trace expression associated with DoctorPatientProtocol.

```
trace_expr_template(doctor_protocol, DP) :-
DoctorPatientProtocol = Ok \/ SevereProblem \/ SwitchedToSeverity1,
Ok = msg_ok_glucose(var(patient),var(doctor)):DoctorPatientProtocol,
SevereProblem =
    msg_too_low_glucose(var(patient),var(doctor)):SwitchToSeverity2,
SwitchedToSeverity1 = (msg_switched_to_severity1(var(patient),var(doctor))
    :(TremorsOrIrritability|InterventionRequest))*DoctorPatientProtocol,
SwitchToSeverity2 =
    (switch_request(var(doctor),var(patient),severity2) \/
    msg_continue_monitor(var(doctor),var(patient)))*DoctorPatientProtocol,
TremorsOrIrritability =
    (msg_tremors(var(patient),var(doctor)):lambda \/
    msg_irritability(var(patient),var(doctor)):lambda)*SwitchToSeverity2,
InterventionRequest =
    msg_intervention_request(var(patient),var(doctor)):
    print_intervention_request(var(patient),var(interface)):lambda,
DP = finite_composition(|, DoctorPatientProtocol,
    [var(patient),var(doctor),var(interface)]).
```

During the application stage, var(patient) varies on the patients (for example [patient1, patient2, patient3]), var(doctor) varies on the doctors (for example, doctor1 if we want to keep the scenario as simple as possible) and var(interface) varies on the artifacts in the MAS that can act as an interface between the humans involved in the loop and the system. For example, we might decide that messages that the patients must see are printed on a screen named screen1. We could also send messages to more than one artifact, for example to [local-screen, doctor-mobile-phone, father-mobile-phone, mother-email][4]. The code for the instantiation of the template trace expression above is

```
apply(DP, [t(var(patient), [patient1, patient2, patient3]),
          t(var(doctor), [doctor1]),
          t(var(interface), [screen1])],
       INSTANTIATEDPROTOCOL)
```

Patient standard protocol. The StandardProtocol trace expression models three situations, corresponding to three sub-protocols:

- Ok sub-protocol, modeling the normal situation where the perceived glucose level is ok (event type ok_glucose(var(patient)), representing a perception event); the doctor is informed (msg_ok_glucose(var(patient),var(doctor))) and the protocol moves to the situation modeled by StandardProtocol.
- TooLowGlucose sub-protocol: the perceived event has type too_low_glucose(var(patient)); the agent in charge of the patient informs the doctor (msg_too_low_glucose(var(patient),var(doctor))) and then it receives either a message from the doctor saying to continue to monitor, or a protocol switch request.

---

[4] In the Jason implementation discussed later on, we modeled these artifacts as "dumb" agents which can receive FIPA-ACL messages. This was an easy and quick way to build a working prototype including all the relevant MAS components, without needing to actually implement Java classes for the artifacts in the system.

– `OtherSymptoms` sub-protocol: in case the patient has tremors or he/she is irritable (perception event types `irritability(var(patient))` and `tremors(var(patient))`), then a switch of the patient agent to the `severity1` protocol is required: the agent informs the doctor and then sends a switch request to itself; if the symptoms are convulsions, apnea, or irregular breathing, then the patient agents switches to the `severity2` protocol by sending the `switch_request(var(patient),var(patient),severity2)` message to itself.

```
trace_expr_template(standard_protocol, Standard) :-
StandardProtocol = Ok \/ TooLowGlucose \/ OtherSymptoms,
Ok = ok_glucose(var(patient)):
     msg_ok_glucose(var(patient),var(doctor)):StandardProtocol,
TooLowGlucose =  too_low_glucose(var(patient)):
   msg_too_low_glucose(var(patient),var(doctor)):
     (msg_continue_monitor(var(doctor),var(patient)):StandardProtocol)
        \/ switch_request(var(doctor),var(patient),severity2):lambda)),
SwitchToSeverity1 =
   msg_switched_to_severity1(var(patient),var(doctor)):
   switch_request(var(patient),var(patient),severity1):
   lambda,
LightSymptoms =
   ((irritability(var(patient)):lambda) \/ (tremors(var(patient)):lambda))
   * SwitchToSeverity1,
SevereSymptoms =
   ((convulsions(var(patient)):lambda) \/
   (apnea(var(patient)):lambda) \/
   (irregular_breathing(var(patient)):lambda)) *
   (switch_request(var(patient),var(patient),severity2):lambda),
OtherSymptoms = LightSymptoms \/ SevereSymptoms,
Standard = finite_composition(|,StandardProtocol,
                              [var(patient),var(doctor)]).
```

To make an example of how an event type can be defined, the `has_type` definition of `too_low_glucose(Patient)` is given below:

```
has_type(percept(Patient,plasma_level_glucose(PlasmaLevel)),
too_low_glucose(Patient)) :-
   hours_after_birth(Patient,HoursBirth),
   ((HoursBirth >= 1,  HoursBirth <= 2,  PlasmaLevel < 28);
   (HoursBirth >= 3,  HoursBirth <= 47, PlasmaLevel < 40);
   (HoursBirth >= 48, HoursBirth <= 72, PlasmaLevel < 48)).
```

This predicate associates the `percept(Patient, plasma_level_glucose (PlasmaLevel))` event (first argument of the `has_type` predicate), modeling the perception of the glucose level in the plasma, to the `too_low_glucose(Patient)` event type (second argument). The glucose level is too low (body of the rule defining `has_type`, namely the logical expression after the :- symbol where "," stands for "and", and ";" stands for "or") either if the perceived plasma glucose concentration level is less than 28 mg/dL and the baby is born less than 2 h ago, or if the plasma glucose concentration is less than 40 mg/dL and the baby is born between 3 and 47 h ago, or if the plasma glucose concentration is less than 48 mg/dL and the baby is born between 48 and 72 h ago. These data are based on medical literature.

For space constraints we do not show the `severity1` protocol. A fragment of the `severity2` protocol is shown below and the most relevant aspect is that, if during the execution of this protocol a low level of glucose is perceived, then a message is prompted on the screen associated with the patient, asking for an intravenous injection of glucose solution, and the intervention of the doctor is requested. Since the patient is following a `severity2` protocol, this means that he/she is in an almost critical situation. For this reason, even in case the glucose level is ok, the high-frequency and high-severity monitoring continues to go on (`NormalGlucose = ok_glucose(var(patient)):Severity2Protocol`). When the doctor will be confident enough that the most critical period has been overcome, he/she will explicitly send a protocol switch request to the patient, to roll back to the normal or lower severity protocol (not shown).

```
trace_expr_template(severity2, T) :-
    Severity2Protocol=
        TooLowGlucose \/ NormalGlucose,
    NormalGlucose =
        ok_glucose(var(patient)):Severity2Protocol,
    TooLowGlucose =
        too_low_glucose(var(patient)):
        intravenous_inj_glucose_sol(var(patient), var(interface)):
        CheckGlucoseAfterInjection,
    . . . . . . . . . .
```

Implementation in Jason

The doctors' and patients' agents driven by the protocol introduced in the previous section have been implemented on top of Jason. We run tests with up to 10 patients and 3 doctors, as shown in Fig. 6.

Figure 7 shows a portion of a run involving only one doctor and one patient, to make it easier to follow the protocol evolution. The *patient1* agent has just received a protocol switch request from the *doctor1* agent, due to a low glucose level in the patient's blood; the switch request cannot be managed immediately, so the agent saves it. When *patient1* can implement the required protocol switch, it has to project the new protocol to follow (in this case the *severity 2* protocol) onto itself. The message "Instantiated protocol" is printed after the protocol projection and switch have completed. After that, *patient1* sends a message to the *screen1* agent, which simulates a user interface in this simplified scenario, that will print the message: "An intravenous injection of a 10% glucose solution is necessary"; this message will be read by the parents who will do the injection.

We simulated different situations where different sensory input was perceived by the patients' sensors, hence changing the course of actions and reactions, in order to test both our infrastructure and the protocols we have designed and implemented.

Fig. 6. Protocol execution in Jason: the MAS configuration is shown in the background.

```
● ● ●                          MAS Console - health_protocol
[doctor1] time.resetTimes
[doctor1] React, move to new state and reset the timer!
[patient1] Percept: (tremors)
[doctor1] Send: (patient1,tell,switch(hypoglycemia_protocol_severity2,[t(var(1),patient1),t(var(2),doctor1),t(var(3),screen1)]))
[patient1] Receive: (doctor1,tell,switch(hypoglycemia_protocol_severity2,[t(var(1),patient1),t(var(2),doctor1),t(var(3),screen1)]))
[patient1] Message selected from the Message Queue: msg(doctor1,patient1,tell,switch(hypoglycemia_protocol_severity2,[t(var(
[doctor1] NewState:
fork(fork(...fork(choice([seq(msg_ok_glucose(patient1,doctor1),...choice([seq(msg_ok_glucose(patient1,doctor1),_31422779_31
[doctor1] time.resetTimes
[patient1] Save switch request because now I can't manage it
[patient1] SwitchMsg: msg(doctor1,patient1,tell,switch(hypoglycemia_protocol_severity2,[t(var(1),patient1),t(var(2),doctor1),t(va
[patient1] Instantiated protocol:
...seq(intravenous_inj_glucose_sol(patient1,screen1,10),choice([seq(ok_glucose(patient1),seq(msg_ok_glucose(patient1,doctor1
[patient1] Monitoring protocol
...seq(intravenous_inj_glucose_sol(patient1,screen1,10),choice([seq(ok_glucose(patient1),seq(msg_ok_glucose(patient1,doctor1
...seq(intravenous_inj_glucose_sol(patient1,screen1,10),choice([seq(ok_glucose(patient1),seq(msg_ok_glucose(patient1,doctor1

[patient1] time.resetTimes
[patient1] Send: (screen1,tell,intravenous_injection_glucose_solution(10))
[screen1] It's requested an Intravenous Injection of a 10% Glucose solution
[patient1] NewState: choice([seq(ok_glucose(patient1),seq(msg_ok_glucose(patient1,doctor1),...seq(intravenous_inj_glucose_sol
[patient1] time.resetTimes
```

Fig. 7. Protocol execution in Jason: protocol switch request.

5 Conclusions and Future Work

The features of an autonomous software agent make the agent metaphor extremely suitable to describe, design, and implement RPM systems made up of Patient's Agents in charge of the monitored patients.

However, there are other features not characterizing intelligent agents that must be taken into account for developing models, methodologies, and software infrastructures for RPM applications, including user friendliness, knowledge-intensity, and runtime verification ability: the RPM system should continuously verify that the pattern followed by perceived sensory data is compliant with the expected medical protocol; in order to do so, it should implement a protocol-driven behavior, with a run-time verification mechanism embedded in it.

The work presented in this paper addresses that issue in order to start building the framework for "FRIENDLY & KIND systems (Human-friendly

Knowledge-INtensive Dynamic Systems)" that we designed with an oncological doctor [1]. FRIENDLY & KIND systems (F&Ks) extend the notion of MASs by providing flexible access to dynamic, heterogeneous, and distributed sources of knowledge in a highly dynamic computational environment consisting of computational entities, devices, sensors, and services available in the physical environment, in the Internet, and in the cloud. F&Ks are driven by terminological, bridge, and pattern rules. Terminological rules ensure interoperability among the F&K components by defining a common domain vocabulary. Bridge rules connect knowledge sources together and provide devices for selection, abstraction and conflict resolution among them. Pattern rules can be verified at run-time to guarantee that the system actual dynamics conforms to the expected one. Finally, an F&K must present a human-friendly interface.

Trace expressions are a compact and expressive formalism suitable for modeling pattern rules in F&Ks and exploiting the pattern rule (a.k.a. protocol) representation for driving the agents behavior. The advantage of using trace expressions w.r.t. other pattern and business process formalisms, is that they are already integrated on top of two widespread agent frameworks, Jason and JADE, and might be integrated on top of others, with limited effort, thanks to the interpreted approach. In fact, many agent-oriented frameworks are either based on logic programming like [21,26], or can integrate Prolog code thanks to the existing interfaces between Prolog and most programming languages.

As far as the expressive power of trace expressions is concerned, in [7] we have formally compared trace expressions with Linear Temporal Logic (LTL), a formalism widely adopted in runtime verification, and we have proved that for the purpose of runtime verification, trace expressions are strictly more expressive than LTL: trace expressions are able to specify context-free and non context-free languages, while LTL is not. Although the protocols discussed in this paper are simple enough to be specified using regular languages, the ability of trace expressions to specify context-free and non context-free languages gives a great advantage over other widely used formalisms, in any application domain where a high modeling expressive power is required included the e-Health one. Also, their ability to model patterns involving general events rather than communicative events only turned out to be a key feature to cope with the hypoglycemia in the newborns scenario. We would not have been able to model this scenario using our previous work on constrained global types, as we missed the notion of "event generated by a sensor" there.

The future developments of our work will be mainly devoted to study which kind of properties of a protocol expressed using the trace expression formalism can be verified statically. Static verification would be particularly relevant for F&Ks in the e-Health domain, where reliability is a main goal to achieve.

References

1. Aielli, F., Ancona, D., Caianiello, P., Costantini, S., Gasperis, G.D., Marco, A.D., Ferrando, A., Mascardi, V.: FRIENDLY & KIND with your health: human-friendly knowledge-intensive dynamic systems for the e-health domain. In: Bajo, J., et al. (eds.) PAAMS 2016. CCIS, vol. 616, pp. 15–26. Springer, Heidelberg (2016). doi:10. 1007/978-3-319-39387-2_2

2. Ancona, D., Barbieri, M., Mascardi, V.: Constrained global types for dynamic checking of protocol conformance in multi-agent systems. In: Proceedings of SAC 2013, pp. 1377–1379 (2013)

3. Ancona, D., Briola, D., Ferrando, A., Mascardi, V.: Global protocols as first class entities for self-adaptive agents. In: Proceedings of AAMAS 2015, pp. 1019–1029 (2015)

4. Ancona, D., Briola, D., Ferrando, A., Mascardi, V.: Runtime verification of fail-uncontrolled and ambient intelligence systems: a uniform approach. Intelligenza Artificiale **9**(2), 131–148 (2015)

5. Ancona, D., Dovier, A.: A theoretical perspective of coinductive logic programming. Fundamenta Informaticae **140**(3–4), 221–246 (2015)

6. Ancona, D., Drossopoulou, S., Mascardi, V.: Automatic generation of self-monitoring MASs from multiparty global session types in Jason. In: Baldoni, M., Dennis, L., Mascardi, V., Vasconcelos, W. (eds.) DALT 2012. LNCS (LNAI), vol. 7784, pp. 76–95. Springer, Heidelberg (2013). doi:10.1007/978-3-642-37890-4_5

7. Ancona, D., Ferrando, A., Mascardi, V.: Comparing trace expressions and linear temporal logic for runtime verification. In: Ábrahám, E., Bonsangue, M., Johnsen, E.B. (eds.) Essays Dedicated to Frank de Boer on the Occasion of His 60th Birthday. LNCS, vol. 9660, pp. 47–64. Springer, Heidelberg (2016). doi:10.1007/ 978-3-319-30734-3_6

8. Annicchiarico, R., Corts, U., Urdiales, C.: Agent Technology and e-Health. Whitestein Series in Software Agent Technologies and Autonomic Computing, 1st edn. Birkhuser, Basel (2008)

9. Bayliss, E.A., Steiner, J.F., Fernald, D.H., Crane, L.A., Main, D.S.: Descriptions of barriers to self-care by persons with comorbid chronic diseases. Ann. Family Med. **1**(1), 15–21 (2003)

10. Bellifemine, F.L., Caire, G., Greenwood, D.: Developing Multi-Agent Systems with JADE. Wiley, Chichester (2007)

11. Bergenti, F., Poggi, A.: Developing smart emergency applications with multi-agent systems. Int. J. E Health Med. Comm. **1**(4), 1–13 (2010)

12. Bordini, R.H., Hübner, J.F., Wooldridge, M.: Programming Multi-Agent Systems in AgentSpeak Using Jason. Wiley, Chichester (2007)

13. Bottrighi, A., Chesani, F., Mello, P., Montali, M., Montani, S., Storari, S., Terenziani, P.: Analysis of the GLARE and GPROVE approaches to clinical guidelines. In: Riaño, D., Teije, A., Miksch, S., Peleg, M. (eds.) KR4HC 2009. LNCS (LNAI), vol. 5943, pp. 76–87. Springer, Heidelberg (2010). doi:10.1007/978-3-642-11808-1_7

14. Bricon-Souf, N., Newman, C.R.: Context awareness in health care: a review. Int. J. Med. Inf. **76**(1), 2–12 (2007)

15. Cao, Y., Yu, W., Ren, W., Chen, G.: An overview of recent progress in the study of distributed multi-agent coordination. IEEE Trans. Ind. Inf. **9**(1), 427–438 (2013)

16. Chan, V., Ray, P., Parameswaran, N.: Mobile e-health monitoring: an agent-based approach. IET Commun. **2**, 223–230 (2008)

17. Chen, S., Ho, D.W., Li, L., Liu, M.: Fault-tolerant consensus of multi-agent system with distributed adaptive protocol. IEEE Trans. Cybern. **45**(10), 2142–2155 (2015)
18. Chesani, F., Matteis, P., Mello, P., Montali, M., Storari, S.: A framework for defining and verifying clinical guidelines: a case study on cancer screening. In: Esposito, F., Raś, Z.W., Malerba, D., Semeraro, G. (eds.) ISMIS 2006. LNCS (LNAI), vol. 4203, pp. 338–343. Springer, Heidelberg (2006). doi:10.1007/11875604_39
19. Ferrando, A.: Parametric protocol-driven agents and their integration in JADE. In: Proceedings of CILC (2015)
20. Furmankiewicz, M., Sołtysik-Piorunkiewicz, A., Ziuziański, P.: Artificial intelligence and multi-agent software for e-health knowledge management system. Informatyka Ekonomiczna - Business Informatics **2**(32), 51–62 (2014)
21. Hindriks, K.V., de Boer, F.S., van der Hoek, W., Meyer, J.C.: Agent programming in 3APL. Auton. Agents Multi Agent Syst. **2**(4), 357–401 (1999)
22. Horling, B., Lesser, V.: A survey of multi-agent organizational paradigms. Knowl. Eng. Rev. **19**(4), 281–316 (2005)
23. Isern, D., Moreno, A.: A systematic literature review of agents applied in healthcare. J. Med. Syst. **40**(2), 43: 1–43: 14 (2016)
24. Jennings, N.R., Sycara, K.P., Wooldridge, M.: A roadmap of agent research and development. Auton. Agents Multi Agent Syst. **1**(1), 7–38 (1998)
25. Jung, Y., Kim, M., Masoumzadeh, A., Joshi, J.B.: A survey of security issue in multi-agent systems. Artif. Intell. Rev. **37**(3), 239–260 (2012)
26. Korstanje, R., Brom, C., Gemrot, J., Hindriks, K.V.: A comparative study of programming agents in POSH and GOAL. In: Proceedings of ICAART 2016, pp. 192–203. SciTePress (2016)
27. Lesser, V., Ortiz Jr., C.L., Tambe, M.: Distributed sensor networks: a multiagent perspective, vol. 9. Springer Science & Business Media (2012)
28. Mascardi, V., Ancona, D.: Attribute global types for dynamic checking of protocols in logic-based multiagent systems. TPLP 13(4-5-Online-Supplement) (2013)
29. Meystre, S.: The current state of telemonitoring: a comment on the literature. Telemed. J. e Health **11**(1), 63–69 (2005)
30. Wight, N., Marinelli, K.A.: ABM clinical protocol #1: guidelines for blood glucose monitoring and treatment of hypoglycemia in term and late-preterm neonates. Breastfeed. Med. **1**(3), 178–184 (2006)
31. Nunes, I., Choren, R., Nunes, C., Fábri, B., Silva, F., de Carvalho, G.R., de Lucena, C.J.P.: Supporting prenatal care in the public healthcare system in a newly industrialized country. In: Proceedings of AAMAS 2010, pp. 1723–1730 (2010)
32. Rosaci, D., Sarné, G.M., Garruzzo, S.: Integrating trust measures in multiagent systems. Int. J. Intell. Syst. **27**(1), 1–15 (2012)
33. Sangiorgi, D.: On the origins of bisimulation, coinduction. ACM Trans. Program. Lang. Syst. **31**(4), 15: 1–15: 41 (2009)
34. Schwaibold, M., Gmelin, M., von Wagner, G., Schöchlin, J., Bolz, A.: Key factors for personal health monitoring and diagnosis device. In: Mobile Computing in Medicine, vol. 15 of LNI, pp. 143–150. GI (2002)
35. Shakshuki, E.M., Reid, M.: Multi-agent system applications in healthcare: current technology and future roadmap. In: Proceedings of ANT 2015, vol. 52 of Procedia Computer Science, pp. 252–261. Elsevier (2015)
36. Smith, B., Pisanelli, D.M., Gangemi, A., Stefanelli, M.: Clinical guidelines as plans - an ontological theory. Methods Inf. Med. **45**(2), 204–210 (2006)

Using Automatic Failure Detection
for Cognitive Agents in Eclipse
(AAMAS 2016 DEMONSTRATION)

Vincent J. Koeman$^{(\boxtimes)}$, Koen V. Hindriks, and Catholijn M. Jonker

Delft University of Technology, Delft, The Netherlands
{v.j.koeman,k.v.hindriks,c.m.jonker}@tudelft.nl

Abstract. In order to reduce debugging effort and enable automated failure detection, we proposed an *automated testing framework* for detecting failures in cognitive agent programs in previous work. This approach is based on a minimal set of temporal operators that enable the specification of test conditions with sufficient expressiveness for detecting all failures in an existing failure taxonomy. We also introduced an according approach for specifying *test templates* that supports a programmer in writing tests. In this demonstration paper, the automated test framework for the GOAL agent programming language that has been created for the Eclipse platform is introduced, with a focus on its practical aspects, i.e., how to use it to detect failures in cognitive agents. As fault localization is an important follow-up to failure detection, the integration of the test framework in the existing source-level debugger for GOAL is discussed as well. In addition, an empirical evaluation of the automated testing framework implementation for GOAL is presented based on the work of almost 200 novice agent programmers.

1 Introduction

In order to reduce debugging effort and enable automated failure detection, we proposed an *automated testing framework for cognitive agent programs* that provides support for detecting frequently occurring failure types in [17]. Automated testing yields a reduction in the effort needed to detect a failure and is more effective than manual code inspection methods [20].

A *failure* is an event in which a system does not perform a required function within specified limits [13]. Failures thus are manifestations of undesired behaviour. They are caused by a *fault*, an incorrect step, process, or data definition in a program [13] or mistake in a program [22]. Upon detecting a failure, a programmer needs to locate and correct the fault that causes the failure.

In general, different techniques for detecting failures of program code are available, ranging from *inspection* of source code and logs to automated *testing*

An earlier version of this paper was demonstrated at the 2016 AAMAS conference and was published in its proceedings [18].

© Springer International Publishing AG 2016
M. Baldoni et al. (Eds.): EMAS 2016, LNAI 10093, pp. 59–80, 2016.
DOI: 10.1007/978-3-319-50983-9_4

tools [20]. The need for debugging techniques and test approaches for agent-oriented programming has been broadly recognized [2,4,5]. Techniques for agent-oriented programming need to be based on the underlying agent paradigm [19,23]. However, this is a significant challenge, as they should for example take into account that agents execute a specific decision cycle and operate in non-deterministic environments [1,3,12].

In previous work [17], we introduced a test language based on two basic temporal operators, and use this language to specify test templates for detecting failure types. These test templates refine a failure taxonomy introduced previously in [22]. A test approach has also been specified that explains how to instantiate test templates and derive test conditions for specific failure types. The main steps of this approach are (i) to define success in terms of functional requirements, (ii) to test cognitive state updating, and (iii) to classify failures that concern actions and goals. The developed testing framework thus provides a *systematic approach for detecting failures in cognitive agent programs*.

This paper is organized as follows. Section 2 introduces the automated test framework for the GOAL agent programming language [8] that has been created for the Eclipse platform, with a focus on its practical aspects, i.e., how to use it to detect failures in cognitive agents. As fault localization is an important follow-up to failure detection, the integration of the test framework in the existing source-level debugger for GOAL [15,16] is discussed in Sect. 3. In Sect. 4 some implementation details are highlighted, and in Sect. 5 this concrete implementation is evaluated. Finally, Sect. 6 concludes this paper with recommendations for future work.

2   Automated Testing of Cognitive Agents

Manual testing, using, for example, a debugger to identify differences between observed and intended behaviour, is not the most efficient failure detection method. It also heavily relies on the programmer to identify the failure and does not support performing the same test repeatedly. The **automated testing framework** [17] for GOAL [8] in Eclipse that we introduce in this section facilitates running tests repeatedly at no additional costs, reducing the total debugging effort. We also provide **test templates** for writing tests for specific aspects of an agent program such as event processing and action selection, and an according **test approach** for deriving such test templates given some initial functional requirements. We assume the reader is familiar with the basic concepts of cognitive agents, such as beliefs, goals and percepts, and refer to [8] for more details about the GOAL language itself. A classic Blocks World toy example[1] will be used to demonstrate the testing framework in this section.

---

[1] See https://github.com/eishub/blocksworld for a description of this environment, and https://github.com/goalhub/agents/tree/master/src/main/goal/BlocksWorld for the agent system that is used as an example here.

2.1   Modules as Basic Unit for Testing

As is important for any other testing framework, it is important to identify what the unit that will be tested should be. A testing framework for agent programs, for example, should not focus on the knowledge that an agent uses. That would be reinventing the wheel as developers can already use existing (unit) testing frameworks for the underlying KR technology used by an agent program. For example, when using SWI Prolog, a developer should use the available unit testing framework PlUnit [21] to test Prolog programs. Testing at the level of individual goals or rules is too fine-grained and also not that useful. Writing tests for individual rules, for example, would not only result in more test than source code, but even worse, would not focus on the failures that need to be detected. A more suitable level is the aggregate level that collects multiple rules in a single unit. We therefore focus on *modules* as units for testing.

2.2   Test Language

Tests are programs themselves that we write in a **test language**. The test language is built on top of the GOAL programming language and re-uses parts of that language. The language provides support for two main tasks: *setting up a test* and *specifying* which *test conditions* should be evaluated. The grammar of the test language is specified in Table 1.

Test Conditions. Test conditions are built on top of the cognitive state queries that are used in program rules. A condition **done**(*action*) can be used to test whether some action has just been performed. We call cognitive state queries and conditions of the form **done**(*action*) also state conditions.

Table 1. The test language grammar.

test	:= *useclause*$^+$ [*timeout*] *moduletest** *agenttest*$^+$
useclause	:= **use** *id* [*ascase*] .
ascase	:= **as** (**knowledge** | **actionspec** | **module** | **mas**)
timeout	:= **timeout** = *integer* .
moduletest	:= **test** *id* **with**
	[**pre**{ *statecond* }] [**in** { *testcond*$^+$ }] [**post**{ *statecond* }]
statecond	:= *stateliteral* | *stateliteral*, *statecond*
stateliteral	:= *stateatom* | **not**(*stateatom*)
stateatom	:= *stateop*(*qry*) | **done**(*action*)
testcond	:= (**always** | **never** | **eventually**) *statecond* . |
	statecond **leadsto** *statecond* .
agenttest	:= *id* (, *id*)* { *testaction*$^+$ }
testaction	:= **do**(*action*) [**until** *statecond*] .
stateop	:= **bel** | **goal** | **a-goal** | **goal-a** | **percept** | **sent**
id	:= *alphanumeral with underscores that starts with letter or underscore*
qry	:= *a valid KR query*
action	:= *a valid action of the programming language or environment*

A test condition is a temporal condition that expresses that something should happen always, never, eventually, or when some other condition has been true before. Test conditions are of the form:

- `always sc`, which means that the state condition `sc` should continuously (always) hold while executing a module.
- `never sc`, which means that the state condition `sc` should never hold while executing a module.
- `eventually sc`, which means that the state condition `sc` should hold at least once during the execution of a module.
- `sc1 leadsto sc2`, which means that whenever the state condition `sc1` holds, some time thereafter the state condition `sc2` should hold.

The conditions `always sc` and `never sc` can be used to specify *safety conditions*, i.e., things that always or never should occur. The conditions `eventually sc` and `sc leadsto sc` can be used to specify *liveness conditions*, i.e., things that are supposed to occur sooner or later after something else has happened. `eventually sc` is a shorthand for `true leadsto sc`.

Test Setup. A test needs to specify everything that is needed for the test. The first thing that is needed is a multi-agent system (MAS) specification. A MAS file is used by GOAL to launch an environment, and to launch and connect agents to this environment. As an example, we will test for a failure to handle 'incomplete' goals of our agent. We need to include the MAS we want to test:

```
use  BlocksWorld as  mas.
```

With our test we will show that something we want to happen eventually actually never happens. Our agent operating in the Blocks World should move a block in order to achieve its goal but does not do it. We thus want our test to fail. But to show that something will never happen takes a long time. We will instead be satisfied if our agent does not move the block within a window of 1 s. This is a reasonable time window because the agent is very fast and we will use a problem with only 8 blocks. We can use a **time out** to ensure termination of the test after a specified time. A time out is global and specifies how much time (in seconds) is allowed to pass before the entire test should be completed. If a time out happens, the test is aborted. It is useful to note that a test that is aborted does not always fail. A test that is aborted only fails if at least one test condition failed (see below). We add a time out as follows:

```
timeout  = 1.
```

Test Programs. A test is a program that specifies what should be done. First, a test should make clear which agents should take part in a test. Not all agents of a MAS have to be part of a test. The agents that take part in a test need to be referenced explicitly in a test program by naming them using their *ids*. These agents are launched when the test is started and automatically connected to an environment, if available, to receive percepts from and perform actions in that environment.

In a test we can also execute only part of an agent and even make the agent do things it would not otherwise do. The latter is useful for modifying the cognitive state of an agent and prepare it as desired for the test. Although we can execute the program code of an agent it does not need to be executed. Instead, the *testactions* that are specified in an *agenttest* clause (see Table 1) are performed when the test is run. Test actions can be preparatory actions **do** *action* for, e.g., initializing an agent's state, where *action* can be a combo action that consists of one or more actions that are available to the agent. Test actions can also be instructions **do** *id* to execute a module with name *id*. We want the `stackBuilder` agent to execute as is, which we can achieve by "doing" the `stackBuilder` module that is used as main module (the same name is used to name the agent and the module used as main module in this example):

```
stackBuilder {
  do stackBuilder.
}
```

It is important to note that modules that are used as init or event modules will also be executed like they usually would during agent cycles (see Fig. 1).

An agent test can also be shared by multiple agents by listing all agent names that should perform the test actions separated by commas. By specifying multiple agent tests it is possible to define different actions for different agents, which will then be executed in parallel.

Finally, a condition **until** *sc* can be associated with a module (or an action but that is not very useful) that terminates execution when the state condition *sc* holds. An agent test thus determines which actions and modules are executed and when they should be terminated.

Tests for Modules. The most important part of writing a test is specifying the conditions that should be evaluated while executing a module. The conditions that should be evaluated when a module is executed are specified by a **test** *id* **with** statement, where *id* is a module name. It is possible to associate a pre-condition **pre**{*sc*}, a post-condition **post**{*sc*}, and an in-condition **in** {*tc*$^+$} with the module test. The pre-condition of a module is a state condition *sc* that should hold when a module is entered (otherwise, the test fails). Similarly, a post-condition is a state condition *sc* that should hold when a module is exited. An in-condition *tc* is a temporal test condition that specifies which behaviour is expected of a module while it is executed.

We want to check whether our agent will move a block at some point in time during the execution of its main module. More precisely, we want to know whether at some point in time the agent will perform the action `move(b8,X)` where X can be any other block or the table. We can use the **eventually** operator

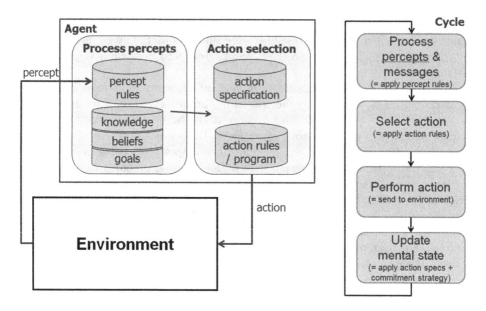

Fig. 1. The structure and decision cycle of a GOAL agent [8].

for this. As temporal conditions are specified as in-conditions, and we want to evaluate the `stackBuilder` module, we get the following module test:

```
test   stackBuilder with
 in { eventually  done(move(b8,X)). }
```

Test Evaluation. By putting everything together, we get our first test. We need to add one use clause to indicate that the module `stackBuilder` is used:

```
use  BlocksWorld as  mas.
use  stackBuilder as  module.

timeout  = 1.

test  stackBuilder with
 in { eventually  done(move(b8,X)). }

stackBuilder {
 do stackBuilder.
}
```

Because we do not want our agent to fail because there is no block 8, we moreover made sure that a block 8 that sits on top of block 1 to the MAS we developed. For completeness, the goal of the agent is:

```
on(b1,b5), on(b2,table), on(b3,table), on(b4,b3),
on(b5,b2), on(b6,b4), on(b7,table).
```

Note that this goal does not include block 8.

A run or trace of an agent program consists of a (finite or potentially infinite) sequence of cognitive states of the agent. Test conditions associated with a module are evaluated on (partial) traces generated by that module. These conditions are assigned one of three values: *undetermined, passed,* or *failed*. Initially, all test conditions of a module have the value *undetermined*. The pre-condition of a module, if specified, is evaluated on the current state when entering the module and assigned *passed* when the condition succeeds, and *failed* otherwise. Similarly, the post-condition is evaluated on the current state when a module is exited. The value of an in-condition is (re-)evaluated every time the cognitive state of the agent changes while the module is being executed.

Now it is time to run our test. We refer to the User Manual [11] for instructions on how to do this. The test's output will look like this:

```
test failed:
 test: ...\BlocksWorld2Agents\incompleteGoal.test2g
 mas: ...\BlocksWorld2Agents\BlocksWorld.mas2g
 module 'stackBuilder' did not complete successfully
 during the test of agent 'stackBuilder' because:
 In-condition(s) failed: 'eventually done(move(b8, X))'.
```

We have identified a failure in our program: the agent never moves block 8 (at least not within the 1 s window that we used).

2.3   Test Templates

Test templates facilitate writing tests. Test templates also help increase the coverage of aspects that need testing. We introduce test templates for all aspects of an agent program. The test templates are split into three main categories: templates for percepts with labels that start with **P**, templates for goals with labels that start with **G**, and templates for actions with labels that start with **A**. We briefly introduce the templates here and discuss how to use them in the next section.

P-Templates: Failures in Percept Processing. In order to support various options for percept processing, we distinguish between the four percept types[2]. and associate specific test templates with each type, based on the assumption that the percept information needs to be made persistent in the agent's belief state one-to-one. Test conditions for percepts should be associated with the module that processes the percept. This is usually a module used as either init

---

[2] See Sect. 6.10 of the GOAL Guide [10] for more details on percept types in GOAL.

or event module. This ensures the templates are evaluated while percept are processed in the module. Because the event module is executed once each cycle of the agent, in order to not violate the test conditions, percepts must have been processed and beliefs updated accordingly at the end of that module.

Template P-once: concerns percepts p that are only received *once*, typically when the agent is launched to inform about static information such as locations on maps. The test template expects that after receiving the percept, it will be made persistent such that the agent believes it. This templates should be associated with a module used as **as init module**.

```
percept(p) leadsto bel(p)
```

Template P-always: concerns percepts about facts p that are *always* received when p is true. This also implies that if such a percept is not received that p does not hold. The test template therefore consists of two test conditions. The first is the same as the condition of the ***P-once*** template. The second condition says that when p is not perceived, which indicates that p does not hold, a belief p should be removed (if present).

```
percept(p) leadsto bel(p)
not(percept(p)), bel(p) leadsto not(bel(p))
```

Template P-on-change: concerns percepts p(*t*) that are sent only when the parameters *t* of a percept p change. A percept loc(place), for example, might be sent only when an agent's location changes.

```
percept(p(t)) leadsto bel(p(t))
percept(p(s)), bel(p(t), not(s = t)) leadsto not(bel(p(t))
```

Template P-on-change-with-negation: concerns percepts p that are received once when p becomes true, and percepts not(p) that are received once when p becomes false (again). For example, in(room) is received when an agent enters a room, and not(in(room)) is received when it leaves again.

```
percept(p) leadsto bel(p)
percept(not(p)), bel(p) leadsto not(bel(p))
```

G-Templates: Failures in Goal Management. There are five failure templates that concern the management of goals. Each of these categories, with the exception of *G4*, suggests that a *reason* for (not) having a goal has *not* been adequately taken into account.

Template G-adopted (G1): concerns a goal p that the agent should adopt because of some reason sc. If the agent does not adopt the goal when the reason holds, this template will identify the failure.

```
sc  leadsto  goal(p)
```

Template G-reconsideration (G2): concerns a goal p that should be reconsidered and dropped for reason sc. If an agent does not drop the goal when sc holds, a failure to drop a goal that should be dropped is identified. The agent did not adequately reconsider the goals that it has.

```
sc  leadsto  not(goal(p))
```

An agent would normally reconsider its goals if the environment has changed outside the control of that agent. Failures of this type would therefore most likely only occur in dynamic environments or in a multi-agent context.

Template G-incorrect (G3): concerns a situation in which there is a reason sc for *not* adopting or having a goal. This template can be viewed as the counterpart of the template *G-adopted*. Instead of a liveness (leadsto) condition we use a a safety (never) condition here.

```
never  goal(p), sc
```

Template G-duplicate (G4): concerns a single-instance goal that should be instantiated at most once. Some goals should only occur once and it should never be the case that the goal is instantiated twice. For example, an agent might have a goal in('RoomA1') of visiting a room but should never have another goal of the same form, e.g., in('RoomB1'), at the same time.

```
never  goal(p(s)), goal(p(t)), not(bel(s = t))
```

Template G-maintain (G5): concerns a situation in which sc is a reason why an agent should have a goal p, and should maintain it for that reason. This template can be viewed as the counterpart of template *G-reconsideration* that requires an agent to reconsider, i.e. to not maintain a goal.

```
never  not(goal(p)), sc
```

A-Templates: Failures in Action Selection. The final two templates concern failures in the action selection strategy of an agent. An agent may have a reason to perform an action but not do so, or, vice versa, may have a reason to not perform an action but do so nevertheless.

Template A-selected (A1): concerns an action `action` that the agent is should select because of reason `sc`. Failure to meet this test condition suggests that some reason for selecting an action has not been adequately taken into account.

```
sc leadsto  done(action)
```

Template A-incorrect (A2): concerns a situation `sc` in which an action `action` should never have been selected. A failure to meet the test condition suggests that something happened that should never have happened. This template can be viewed as the counterpart of the previous template.

```
never (done(action)), sc
```

2.4   Test Approach

The test templates provide a useful starting point for writing tests. They facilitate a structured approach to testing an agent. Here we introduce a systematic test approach that consists of a number of concrete steps. The main steps of this approach are:

1. define success in terms of functional requirements,
2. test cognitive state updating, and
3. classify failures that concern actions and goals.

We also provide guidelines for instantiating the templates for a specific application. These guidelines suggest ways, for example, for finding specific reasons for instantiating the state conditions `sc` that need to be filled in the *G-* and *A*-templates. For this purpose, it is important to be able to retrieve relevant information from the sources that we have available. Table 2 lists information resources that are particularly useful for writing tests.

Table 2. Information sources for testing [17].

Source	Type of Information
Agent program (comments)	Clues for reasons & design
Agent trace (screen, logs)	Observable behaviour
Agent design & specification	Functional requirements
Environment (documentation)	Percepts, actions available

Step 1: Defining Success. The first step is to identify **functional requirements** from available agent design documentation (see Table 2). These requirements define success and provide a concrete method for checking that a program does what it is supposed to do. A program can be considered free of failures if it meets requirements. In order to automatically check this, functional requirements must also be specified in the test language. Typically, these requirements will be associated with a module `modname` that is used as main module. We can specify functional requirements as the pre-, post-, or in-conditions of this module using `test modname with` statements, or by adding a test action of the form `do modname until sc`.

Using a test action is particularly useful for checking that some overall objective `sc` is realized. If the objective is achieved, the test action will be automatically terminated. A `timeout` should be specified to guarantee termination in case `sc` would never occur. For example, the requirement or objective to pickup and deliver a sequence of packages `[p1,...,pn]` can be specified by `do modname until bel(delivered([p1,...,pn]))`.

Step 2: Testing Cognitive State Updating. What an agent decides to do depends to a large extent on the content of its cognitive state. Test conditions also depend on the evaluation of state conditions on the cognitive state of an agent. If these state conditions incorrectly succeed or fail because the updating of the state of an agent has not been implemented correctly, tests will also very likely fail for unclear reasons. For example, a condition `neverdone(putDown),not(bel(in(Room)))`, which says that a package should never be put down when not in a room, could fail just because the beliefs about `in(Room)` are not updated correctly. It is therefore important to first make sure that the updating of an agent's state works as expected.

Identify the Percepts, Actions, and Goals used in a MAS. As a preparatory step, it is useful to collect all percepts that may be received and the actions that may be performed from environment documentation (see Table 2). Similarly, all goals that an agent may have should be collected from the agent program code.

Validating Percept Processing. The first step now is to instantiate the appropriate test templates ***P-once***, etc. for each percept based on their type. Tests should be repeated sufficiently often as percepts generated will differ per run, if only because environments are more often than not non-deterministic. To gain confidence that percepts are correctly handled, it is important to check against the list of actions created above whether a sufficient variation of actions has been performed during runs, as different actions often yield other percepts.

Check Single-Instance Goals. Based on program design, and intended use of goals in comments in a program (see Table 2), for example, and using the overview of goals in the ontology, the subset of goals that are single-instance goals should be identified. For each of these goals, the test template ***G-duplicate*** should be instantiated and associated as an in-condition with the module where the goal is adopted. If these initial tests succeed, this will give a high level of confidence that cognitive states are updated correctly.

Step 3: Classifying Failures. Instantiating the remaining template types requires some understanding of the program design and the agent's behaviour in order to be able to instantiate the required state conditions sc.

Action Failures. For identifying action related failures, *A*-templates should be instantiated with actions and a state condition needs to be identified that provides a reason, i.e. a state condition sc, for (not) selecting it. For the template *A-selected* (respectively, *A-incorrect*), the question is in which situations sc an action should (never) be executed. The instantiated conditions should be associated as in-conditions with the module(s) where the action might (not) be selected. There are two basic approaches for identifying the conditions sc.

First, by inspecting the agent program, clues may be obtained for useful state conditions sc. In particular, the conditions of rules can be useful, as they typically indicate reasons for selecting an action. For example, a condition bel(in('DropZone'), holding(Block)) that triggers execution of an action putDown suggests that an agent should execute putDown when it is holding a block in the 'DropZone'. By using this condition for sc, we can instantiate template *A-selected* as follows: bel(in('DropZone'), holding(Block))leadstodone(putDown).

This approach is already able to detect failures, e.g., in case the rule order prevents the rule for putDown from ever being applied. Similarly, by negating conditions found in a program, we can find useful conditions for instantiating *A-incorrect*. It is important to note that this works only if the condition used must always hold if the action is selected. This is not always the case, but when it can be assumed, this approach provides a useful starting point. Moreover, you can consider how weakened or strengthened variants of conditions used in program rules can be used in test conditions.

Alternatively, if an action failure is suspected because, for example, a functional requirement is not satisfied, observing an agent's behaviour may provide clues for identifying a useful condition sc for instantiating a test template for that action. Suppose that a requirement bel(in(Room)) leadsto not(bel(in(Room))) formulated in step 1 fails. That is, an agent does not always leave a room after entering it. If we now observe that the goTo action is never performed, we can conclude that we have identified a failure to select this action. To confirm this by a test, we can use the template *A-selected* and instantiate sc with the reason for leaving and action with the goTo action. This would give: bel(in(Room), not(Room=OtherRoom)) leadsto done(goTo(OtherRoom)). We can repeat this line of reasoning until a root cause for the failure has been identified.

Goal Failures. The approach for instantiating *G*-templates, apart from identifying the goal that might cause the failure, is similar to that for *A*-templates. The questions that you should ask for each of the templates are:

- *G-adopted*: for which sc should a goal p be added?
- *G-reconsideration*: for which sc should a goal p be dropped?
- *G-incorrect*: for which sc should a goal p never be added?
- *G-maintain*: for which sc should a goal p never be removed?

The instantiated conditions should be associated as in-conditions with the module(s) that are related to the goal.

As an example, we create a test for a goal in(Room). We assume that this goal is adopted by a rule with the following condition: bel(room(Place)), not(bel(visited(Place))). This condition suggests that the agent should adopt (multiple) in(Room) goals for each room that it has not visited before. By using the goal and this condition for sc to instantiate the template *G-adopted*, we get: bel(room(Place)),not(bel(visited(Place))) leadsto goal(in(Place)).

This rather straightforward approach of re-using rule conditions can already provide an effective method for detecting failures, e.g., in case the rule order prevents the rule from ever being applied. Similarly, the negations of conditions found in a program can sometimes be used to instantiate the template *G-incorrect* to obtain useful test conditions. This approach for instantiating *G-incorrect* only works if the condition must hold whenever the goal is adopted, e.g., if an agent never wants to go to rooms it has visited before. A similar approach can be used for the templates *G-reconsideration* and *G-maintain*.

2.5 Debugging, Testing, and Fault Localisation

It is important to realize that the way in which agents are executed can make a difference for testing. For example, agents that are executed using the automated testing framework are never paused, whilst debugging agents with a debugger by pausing and/or stepping a program may result in agent behaviour that is different from an agent that is executed without pausing it. Moreover, each run can produce different behaviour (and thus failures) because of non-determinism in the agent (e.g., due to random rule order evaluation), the environment, or executing multiple agents. You should therefore always run the same tests multiple times in different scenarios to gain assurance that the agents work as expected.

When a failure is detected, i.e., a test fails, the fault must be located. The program location where the agent is at when the test failed is indicated by the testing framework. Although it is often the case, it is not always true that this location also is the fault location, i.e., the place of the actual error in the code. If the fault is not located immediately, additional debugging is needed using a debugger. In particular, faults related to actions that are performed but should not have been performed are usually more difficult to locate. In the next section, debugging cognitive agents specifically will be discussed.

3   Debugging a Multi-agent System

This section explains how debug a GOAL MAS. Debugging is the process of detecting, locating, and correcting faults in a program. Compared to other programming paradigms, agent-oriented programming introduces several specific challenges [9]. In this introduction, we briefly discuss the relevant background for debugging cognitive agents, based on previous work [15]. Next, in the subsections, all practical details are presented (i.e., how to use the debugger).

An agent's decision cycle provides a set of points that the execution can be suspended at, i.e. **breakpoints**. These points do not necessarily have a corresponding code location. For example, receiving a message from another agent is an important state change that is not present in an agent's source, i.e., there is no code in the agent program that makes it check for new messages. Thus, two types of breakpoints can be defined: *code-based* breakpoints and (decision) *cycle-based* breakpoints. Code-based breakpoints have a clear location in an agent program. Cycle-based breakpoints, in contrast, do not always need to have a corresponding code location. Together, these are referred to as the set of *pre-defined* breakpoints. When single-stepping through a program, these points are traversed. A user is also be able to mark specific locations in an agent's source at which execution will always be suspended, even when not explicitly stepping. To facilitate this, the debugger identifies such a marker (e.g., a line number) with the nearest code-based breakpoint. These markers are referred to as *user-defined* breakpoints. A user is also be able to suspend execution upon specific decision cycle events, especially when those do not have a corresponding location in the source. Such an indication is referred to as a *user-selectable* breakpoint.

A user is able to **control the granularity** of the debugging process. In other words, a user can navigate the code in such a way that a specific fault can be investigated conveniently. For example, skipping parts of an agent program that are (seemingly) unrelated in order to examine (seemingly) related parts in more detail. This is supported by three different step actions: *step into*, *step over*, and *step out*. At any breakpoint, a detailed **inspection of an agent's cognitive state** is facilitated. In addition, support for **evaluable cognitive state expressions** is provided, allowing a user to pose queries about specific rule parts to identify which part fails. Modifying the agent's cognitive state is supported as well.

3.1   Stepping an Agent

A paused agent can be single-stepped. This means that the agent will execute until the next pre-defined breakpoint is reached. For each such breakpoint, there is a specific result of a stepping action (i.e., the flow of stepping). In Fig. 2, this flow for the step into and step over actions on each breakpoint has been illustrated. For readability, the step out action has been left out[3]. Note that the broken edge indicates a link to the event module. After the event module has

---

[3] We refer to Koeman *et al.* [15] for more details on the step out action.

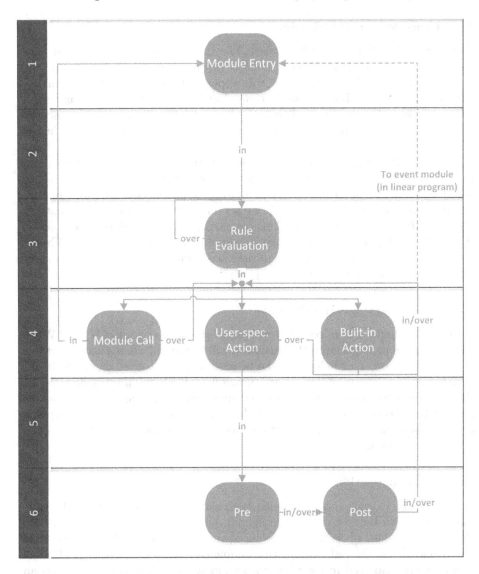

Fig. 2. The flow of step into and step over actions for a GOAL agent. A 'User-spec. Action' indicates an action that has been defined in an action specification (**act2g** file), whilst a 'Built-in Action' is something like **insert** or **adopt** [15]. (Color figure online)

been processed, depending on the rule evaluation order, either the first rule in the module or the rule after the performed action will be evaluated. In addition, a module's exit conditions might have been fulfilled at this point as well, which means that the flow may return to the action combo in which the call to the exited module was made. Note that the stepping flow is heavily influenced by the rule evaluation order and/or exit conditions in general.

3.2   User-Defined Breakpoints

User-defined breakpoints are line-based. They can be set in Eclipse at any time (i.e. also whilst running a MAS) by *double-clicking on the line number you want to break at*, on which a red marker will appear. When double-clicking on this red marker again, a yellow marker appears. Finally, when double-clicking on this yellow marker, the marker (and thus the breakpoint) will be removed entirely. These coloured markers indicate the two different types of user-defined breakpoints that are supported.

A red marker indicates a **regular breakpoint**. A user-defined breakpoint will be set on the first module entry, rule condition, or pre-condition that can be found after the indicated line. A yellow marker indicates a **conditional breakpoint**. A user-defined breakpoint will be set on the first action(combo) that can be found after the indicated line. This means that if the condition of the action (i.e., of the rule) does not hold, the breakpoint will not be reached. When a user-defined breakpoint is reached during execution, the agent will always be paused (even when not explicitly stepping).

3.3   User-Selectable Breakpoints

GOAL has a single user-selectable breakpoint: the achievement of a goal. When stepping an agent, by default, the execution will be paused when a user-selectable breakpoint occurs. This behaviour can be modified (i.e., turned on or off) in the preferences. The stepping flow after a user-selectable breakpoint is dictated by the existing (surrounding) node. For example, achieving a goal is only possible after either executing an action or applying a post-condition, so the stepping actions from the relevant node will be used when stepping away from a goal-achieved breakpoint.

3.4   State Inspection

Each time the execution is suspended (i.e., a breakpoint is reached), the code that is about to be executed is highlighted, and any relevant evaluations (i.e., the possible values of variables referenced in a rule) of this highlighted code are displayed (on the right side). An example can be seen in Fig. 3. Additional messages are displayed in the evaluation window as well, for example when an agent has been terminated.

In addition, when paused, *the cognitive state of an agent* is displayed at the top-right, split in four tabs: beliefs, goals, messages, and percepts. Searching is possible in all of these views. Note that both the displayed cognitive state and the interactive console (see the next paragraph) use the agent that is currently selected in the agent overview (at the top-left).

3.5   Interactive Console

A single 'interactive console' is provided in which both cognitive state queries (e.g. `bel` or `goal`) and actions (e.g. `delete` or `drop`) can be performed in order

Fig. 3. An example of how a rule evaluation is displayed in the GOAL debugger [15].

to respectively *inspect* or *modify* the displayed cognitive state. All solutions for a query are shown in the interactive console as a list of substitutions for variables. For actions, one needs to make sure that they are closed, i.e., have no free (unbound) variables. It is possible to execute a user-defined (environment) action as well when the environment is running.

3.6 Watch Expressions

It is also possible to continuously evaluate and thus inspect one or more cognitive state queries whilst a system is running by using so-called 'Watch Expressions'. The evaluation of each expression will be shown for all agents, and is updated every tenth of a second.

3.7 Logging

In debug mode, the bottom area contains various tabs for inspecting agents and the actions they perform. Besides the main console tab, an action history tab is present that provides an overview of actions that have been performed by all (running) agents. In addition, when an agent is launched, a dedicated console is added for that agent for inspecting various aspects of the agent program during runtime.

Main Console. The main console shows all important messages, warnings and errors that may occur. These messages include those generated by GOAL at runtime, but possibly also messages produced by environments and other components.

Action History. The action history tab shows the actions that have been performed by all running agents that are part of the multi-agent system. These actions include both user-defined actions that are sent to the environment as well built-in actions provided by GOAL.

Agent Consoles. Upon launching an agent, a dedicated tab is added for that agent. This tab typically contains more detailed information about the agent. The exact contents of the tab can be customized through the preferences. Various items that are part of the reasoning cycle of an agent can be selected for viewing. If checked, related reports will be produced in the console of an agent.

Customizing the Logging. The logging can be customized in the preferences. A timestamp with millisecond accuracy can be added to each printed log. The action history and dedicated logging tabs for agents can also be turned on or off here. It is also possible to write all logs to separate files. These files will be stored in a directory within the currently executed project. Logs for each agent, the action log, warnings, results from GOAL log actions etcetera are all written to separate files.

4   Testing GOAL Agents in the Eclipse IDE

The automated testing framework for GOAL [8] has been embedded in the GOAL agent programming plug-in[4] for Eclipse. This plug-in provides a full-fledged development environment for agent programmers, integrating all agent and agent-environment development tools in a single well-established setting [16]. The Eclipse platform is based on an open architecture that allows for building on top of well-known existing frameworks [6]. By using Eclipse and the DLTK framework [7], for example, a state-of-the-art editor for GOAL has been created, which forms a solid foundation for further tools. The GOAL language itself has been recently updated to use a more modular approach, i.e., better facilitating re-use. In addition, a source-level debugger for agents has been fully implemented in the plug-in based on previous work [15]. The test framework has been integrated into this source-level debugger, facilitating for example the inspection of an agent's state as soon as a test condition has failed, as illustrated in Fig. 4. The new modular approach of the GOAL agent programming language also better facilitates the testing of individual, separate pieces of functionality.

In the plug-in there are several examples embedded that can be used to demonstrate this test framework. Most of these are based on educational environments[5] that include an assignment for (novice) agent programmers.

---

[4] See http://goalhub.github.io/eclipse for a demonstration(video) of the testing framework implementation and instructions on how to install GOAL in Eclipse.

[5] All (educational) agent environments are available at https://github.com/eishub.

Fig. 4. An example of how test failures are displayed in the source-level debugger.

5   Evaluation

An empirical investigation was performed on a large set of solutions handed in by novice GOAL agent programmers, who were working in a total of 94 pairs. These pairs were given the same assignment[6], for which they had to develop a single agent together. At three fixed points in time, they were asked to (voluntarily) send us their work up till that point; only the third (and final) version was actually graded. This set-up specifically allowed us to investigate failures in non-final submissions through a set of evaluations (i.e., using test conditions we formulated based on the assignment), accompanied by a short questionnaire.

In Table 3, the descriptive statistics of the automated evaluations using test conditions are presented. Notice that at each deadline, more students sent in their work. In addition, when the agent programs grow larger towards the final deadline, the number of P-failures (i.e., failures in percept processing) decreases each time, whilst there is a simultaneous increase in both A- and G-failures[7]. Failures in goals seem closely related to failures in actions, most likely because failures in goal management often cause problems in action selection.

Table 3. Descriptive statistics of the evaluations on the student assignments at each of the three hand-in moments (see Sect. 2.3 for descriptions of the failure types).

Failure Type	Mean	Std. Dev.	N
P-failures (1)	1.8	1.5	29
G-failures (1)	0.5	0.6	" "
A-failures (1)	2.3	1.4	" "
P-failures (2)	0.9	1.0	64
G-failures (2)	2.7	2.1	" "
A-failures (2)	4.0	2.2	" "
P-failures (3)	0.5	0.8	94
G-failures (3)	3.7	1.4	" "
A-failures (3)	4.5	2.2	" "

---

[6] See https://github.com/eishub/BW4T and/or Jonhson *et al.* [14].

[7] Note that missing functionality was not considered a failure in these evaluations.

Table 4. Descriptive statistics of questionnaire answers at each of the three hand-ins.

Question	Mean	Std. Dev.	N
Hours spent (1)	3.6	2.3	29
Hours spent (2)	5.4	2.2	64
Hours spent (3)	14.0	4.5	94
Time spent on testing	19 %	16 %	94
Effectiv. of testing	1.1	0.8	” ”

In Table 4, the descriptive statistics of the questionnaires that student pairs filled in at each deadline are given. They were asked to report the total number of hours spent on the assignment at each hand-in, and at the final deadline the percentage of that time they spent on testing and how effective they found the agent testing framework (on a Likert scale of 0–3). Interestingly, the amount of time spent on testing is quite high (and also quite different per student pair), but the effectiveness of the testing framework is not that high. A qualitative evaluation of the feedback that students could provide at the final hand-in indicated some problems. The most frequently occurring feedback was:

- Tests can take a long time to complete.
- Failures can be hard to reproduce.
- A full integration of the testing results in Eclipse is missing (i.e., there is only console output currently).

Most of these problems are related to the environment in which the agent operated, as it could only run at a certain maximum speed, and by default randomly generates the world in which the agent operates. This indicates that agent environments also require changes specifically to facilitate reproducible and repeatable testing. Moreover, even though an integration of the testing in the source-level debugger exists, students would like to see more integration of the testing results in Eclipse itself.

Finally, a correlation analysis of the number of hours spent on the assignment (and the percentage of time spent on testing) with the amount of failures in the different categories supports the conclusion that initially most of the failures are in the P category, whilst in the end most of the failures are in the G and A categories.

6   Conclusion

In this paper, we showed how our automated testing framework for cognitive agents facilitates the detection of failures and aids in the localization of faults. In previous work [17], we have proposed an automated testing framework for cognitive agents and an associated test approach based on test templates for frequently occurring failure types. By using a concrete implementation of the testing framework for the GOAL agent programming language, an integration with the existing source-level debugger was created within the Eclipse environment, thus fully implementing the design within a state-of-the-art setting. This implementation and its source are publicly available, and used in this paper in order to illustrate concrete examples of its use and provide insight into practical implementation details that may be valuable for the adaptation into other agent programming languages.

An empirical investigation on a large set of solutions handed in by novice GOAL agent programmers lead to several interesting results, suggesting directions for future work. For instance, students spent a considerable amount of time on testing, indicating the importance of proper support for this task. However, some problems were present in the current implementation, mostly related to the fact that an external environment was used, causing problems for both reproducibility and (fast) repetition. In addition, the evaluation showed that action failures were present most, and therefore tools that can explain why actions were performed might be useful.

References

1. Bordini, R.H., Dastani, M., Winikoff, M.: Current issues in multi-agent systems development. In: O'Hare, G.M.P., Ricci, A., O'Grady, M.J., Dikenelli, O. (eds.) ESAW 2006. LNCS (LNAI), vol. 4457, pp. 38–61. Springer, Heidelberg (2007). doi:10.1007/978-3-540-75524-1_3
2. Bordini, R.H., Braubach, L., Gomez-sanz, J.J., Hare, G.O., Pokahr, A., Ricci, A.: A survey of programming languages and platforms for multi-agent systems. Informatica **30**, 33–44 (2006)
3. Caire, G., Cossentino, M., Negri, A.: Multi-agent systems implementation and testing. In: Proceedings of the 4th From Agent Theory to Agent Implementation Symposium, AT2AI-4 (2004)
4. Dastani, M.: Programming multi-agent systems. Knowl. Eng. Rev. **30**, 394–418 (2015)
5. Dix, J., Hindriks, K.V., Logan, B., Wobcke, W.: Engineering multi-agent systems (dagstuhl seminar 12342). Dagstuhl Rep. **2**(8), 74–98 (2012)
6. Geer, D.: Eclipse becomes the dominant Java IDE. Computer **38**(7), 16–18 (2005)
7. Gomanyuk, S.: An approach to creating development environments for a wide class of programming languages. Program. Comput. Softw. **34**(4), 225–236 (2008)
8. Hindriks, K.V.: Programming rational agents in GOAL. In: El Fallah Seghrouchni, A., Dix, J., Dastani, M., Bordini, R.H. (eds.) Multi-Agent Programming: Languages, Tools and Applications, pp. 119–157. Springer, US (2009)
9. Hindriks, K.V.: Debugging is explaining. In: Rahwan, I., Wobcke, W., Sen, S., Sugawara, T. (eds.) PRIMA 2012. LNCS (LNAI), vol. 7455, pp. 31–45. Springer, Heidelberg (2012). doi:10.1007/978-3-642-32729-2_3
10. Hindriks, K.V.: Programming cognitive agents in GOAL (2016). https://bintray.com/artifact/download/goalhub/GOAL/GOALProgrammingGuide.pdf
11. Hindriks, K.V., Pasman, W., Koeman, V.J.: GOAL-Eclipse user manual (2016). https://bintray.com/artifact/download/goalhub/GOAL/GOALUserManual.pdf
12. Houhamdi, Z.: Multi-agent system testing: a survey. Int. J. Adv. Comput. Sci. Appl. **2**(6), 135–141 (2011)

13. ISO: ISO/IEC/IEEE 24765: 2010 systems and software engineering - vocabulary. Technical report, Institute of Electrical and Electronics Engineers, Inc. (2010)
14. Johnson, M., Jonker, C., Riemsdijk, B., Feltovich, P.J., Bradshaw, J.M.: Joint activity testbed: blocks world for teams (BW4T). In: Aldewereld, H., Dignum, V., Picard, G. (eds.) ESAW 2009. LNCS (LNAI), vol. 5881, pp. 254–256. Springer, Heidelberg (2009). doi:10.1007/978-3-642-10203-5_26
15. Koeman, V.J., Hindriks, K.V.: Designing a source-level debugger for cognitive agent programs. In: Chen, Q., Torroni, P., Villata, S., Hsu, J., Omicini, A. (eds.) PRIMA 2015. LNCS (LNAI), vol. 9387, pp. 335–350. Springer, Heidelberg (2015). doi:10.1007/978-3-319-25524-8_21
16. Koeman, V.J., Hindriks, K.V.: A fully integrated development environment for agent-oriented programming. In: Demazeau, Y., Decker, K.S., Bajo Pérez, J., de la Prieta, F. (eds.) PAAMS 2015. LNCS (LNAI), vol. 9086, pp. 288–291. Springer, Heidelberg (2015). doi:10.1007/978-3-319-18944-4_29
17. Koeman, V.J., Hindriks, K.V., Jonker, C.M.: Automating failure detection in cognitive agent programs. In: Proceedings of the 2016 International Conference on Autonomous Agents & Multiagent Systems, AAMAS 2016, International Foundation for Autonomous Agents and Multiagent Systems, Richland, SC, pp. 1237–1246 (2016)
18. Koeman, V.J., Hindriks, K.V., Jonker, C.M.: Using automatic failure detection for cognitive agents in Eclipse: (demonstration). In: Proceedings of the 2016 International Conference on Autonomous Agents & Multiagent Systems, AAMAS 2016, International Foundation for Autonomous Agents and Multiagent Systems, Richland, SC, pp. 1507–1509 (2016)
19. Nguyen, C.D., Perini, A., Bernon, C., Pavón, J., Thangarajah, J.: Testing in multiagent systems. In: Gleizes, M.-P., Gomez-Sanz, J.J. (eds.) AOSE 2009. LNCS, vol. 6038, pp. 180–190. Springer, Heidelberg (2011). doi:10.1007/978-3-642-19208-1_13
20. Runeson, P., Andersson, C., Thelin, T., Andrews, A., Berling, T.: What do we know about defect detection methods? IEEE Softw. **23**(3), 82–90 (2006)
21. Wielemaker, J., Schrijvers, T., Triska, M., Lager, T.: SWI-Prolog. Theory Pract. Logic Program. **12**, 67–96 (2012)
22. Winikoff, M.: Novice programmers' faults & failures in GOAL programs. In: Proceedings of the 2014 International Conference on Autonomous Agents and Multiagent Systems, AAMAS 2014, International Foundation for Autonomous Agents and Multiagent Systems, Richland, SC, pp. 301–308 (2014)
23. Zhang, Z., Thangarajah, J., Padgham, L.: Model based testing for agent systems. Softw. Data Technol. **22**, 399–413 (2008)

PriGuardTool: A Web-Based Tool to Detect Privacy Violations Semantically

Nadin Kökciyan$^{(\boxtimes)}$ and Pınar Yolum

Department of Computer Engineering,
Bogazici University, 34342 Bebek, Istanbul, Turkey
nadin.kokciyan@boun.edu.tr, pinar.yolum@boun.edu.tr

Abstract. Online social networks contain plethora of information about its users. While users enjoy sharing information online, not all information is meant to be seen by the entire network. Managing the privacy of users has become an important aspect of such online networks. An important part of this is detecting privacy violations and notifying the users so that they can take appropriate actions. While various approaches for detecting privacy violations exist, most of the approaches do not have a running tool that can exhibit the principles of its underlying approach.

This paper presents PRIGUARDTOOL, a Web-based tool that can detect privacy violations in online social networks. Each user is represented by a software agent in the system that first collects user's privacy concerns, explicitly specified as what types of content are meant to be seen by which audience. The system represents these privacy constraints as commitments between the user and the online social network. The user constraints are converted into commitments automatically by the agent. The system then monitors which commitments are violated based on the content shown to users, such that a violated commitment represents a privacy violation in the system. While checking for violations, the effects of posts on the system as well as the semantic relations and rules are considered. We evaluate PRIGUARDTOOL by using various real-life scenarios and real data that have been collected over Facebook. Our initial results show that realistic privacy violations can be detected using PRIGUARDTOOL.

Keywords: Privacy · Online social networks · Commitment · Ontology

1 Introduction

Privacy is the right of an individual to express herself selectively. An individual may prefer to expose certain information about herself to a certain group of others, but may choose to hide another set of information. This right is difficult to maintain on the Web since information can propagate easily. It is even worse on online social networks since different users can share content about an individual, without expecting an explicit confirmation from the individual. This results in tremendous privacy violations to take place [5].

© Springer International Publishing AG 2016
M. Baldoni et al. (Eds.): EMAS 2016, LNAI 10093, pp. 81–98, 2016.
DOI: 10.1007/978-3-319-50983-9_5

Consider the following examples: A user herself misconfigures the system and reveal unintended content (e.g., the user shares holiday pictures with colleagues when not intending to); or a friend of a user shares a content not knowing that the user would not want the content online (e.g., a friend shares a picture where the user is drunk). These simple examples show that both a user herself or friends can take simple actions that lead to privacy violations. More importantly, sometimes the privacy violations are more subtle. In order to be discovered, they require various pieces of information to be put together. For example, a user does not reveal her location but shares a picture that has an embedded geotag. Any software that can process the geotags can help others discover the user's location [6]. Sometimes, the information needed to decipher the violations is not that straightforward. For example, looking at two friends check-ins to a remote island could signal that they are together. Inferring this information, when neither have explicitly specified it, could easily violate their privacy. In all cases, the users seek tools that will help them to preserve their privacy and catch privacy breaches if any, so that they can take an action.

Most of the existing commercial systems on the Web allow a user to specify constraints on her own posts only and enforce them. However, this does not necessarily avoid privacy violations. That is, if a user does not want her colleagues to see her holiday pictures but her group holiday picture is shared publicly by a friend, her privacy is still violated. Various approaches to deal with privacy violations exist in the literature. One set of approaches aim to prevent privacy violations in the first place [15]. The approaches that employ argumentation or negotiation techniques among users to reach agreements before sharing content fall into this category [9,17,25]. Another set of approaches aim to detect privacy violations. This set of approaches represent user's privacy constraints formally and try to find out if the network evolves into a state where these constraints are violated. An important work is that of Hu *et al.*, where privacy concerns are represented as multiparty access control rules [7]. Their work is based on a social network model, a multiparty policy specification scheme and a mechanism to enforce policies to resolve multiparty privacy conflicts. They benefit from Answer Set Programming (ASP) to represent their proposed model. Another important work is that of Carminati *et al.* that studies a semantic web based framework to manage access control in OSNs by generating semantic policies [3]. Their proposed social network operates according to agreed system-level policies. In a similar line, we have previously proposed a semantic meta-model for representing agent-based online social networks [12]. We further proposed a model PRIGUARD that represents privacy constraints as commitments between users and the online social network, which are widely-used constructs for modeling interactions between agents [26]. This paper formally describes PRIGUARD-TOOL, a Web-based tool that implements PRIGUARD model that detects privacy violations and notifies users to take an action.

PRIGUARDTOOL is a privacy management system. It enables users to enter their privacy constraints and then to check for privacy violations at desired times, similar in principle to virus checks. The privacy constraints capture a user's expectation from the network; e.g., a user may not want her colleagues to see her pictures but might be fine if friends see them. A privacy violation can happen explicitly (e.g., if the user shares a picture with colleagues by mistake) or implicitly (e.g., if the actions of the user or the others lead colleagues to have access to the picture). PRIGUARDTOOL is equipped to check for both kinds of privacy violations. Implicit violations are especially difficult to detect because they require inferences to be made. To deal with this, PRIGUARDTOOL uses ontologies to represent knowledge and semantic rules, then it can check for violations both on the ontologies and on the inferred knowledge. To demonstrate its workings, we have implemented it so that it can work on real data that are extracted from Facebook. That is, a user can login with her Facebook credentials, allow the tool to download all her data (which are converted to an ontology), and check for privacy violations there.

The rest of this paper is organized as follows: Sect. 2 explains our approach for detecting privacy violations in online social networks. Section 3 develops the principles behind our developed tool. Section 4 explains in detail the design choices made to implement the proposed tool. Section 5 evaluates the tool in the context of a real online social network. Section 6 discusses the work in relation to other approaches for managing users' privacy in online social networks, and several limitations of current work.

2 Background: PriGuard Approach

PRIGUARD is a commitment-based model for privacy-aware online social networks [12] that enables users to detect privacy violations. Each user in the social network is represented by an agent that is responsible for keeping track of the user's privacy constraints and checking for violations when needed. The online social network is defined by the set of relationships, content types and a set of semantic rules. The set of relationships pertains to the users (e.g., friend, colleague, and so on). The content types capture allowed contents (e.g., picture, check-in, text, and so on). The semantic rules capture how the social network operates (e.g., content can be reshared, contents are shown selectively, and so on). A snapshot of the online social network captures the agents, their relationships and the content in the online social network. Even for a single snapshot, one can focus on different views of it. For example, the global view of the system would contain all the content of all the agents in the system; while a smaller, local view can contain the content shared by a single agent last month. PRIGUARD uses views to check if privacy of users are violated or not. Depending on the view, the extent of privacy check can be managed.

In PRIGUARD, the social network domain is formally defined using Description Logics (DL). The domain consists of concepts (e.g., `Agent`), relations (e.g., *isFriendOf*) and individuals names (e.g., `:alice`)[1]. On the other hand, there is a

---

[1] We denote a `Concept` with text in mono-spaced format, a *relation* with italic text, and an `:individual` with a colon followed by text in mono-spaced format.

need for semantic rules so that a social network can operate accordingly. In PRI-GUARD, the semantic rules are specified as Datalog rules. These Datalog rules capture the fundamental operations of OSN, independent from specific users. For example, $sharesPost(X,P) \rightarrow canSeePost(X,P)$ is a Datalog rule, which states that an agent can see the posts that it shares. In this rule, $sharesPost$ and $canSeePost$ are predicate symbols; X and P are universally quantified variables.

While the OSN has its operation rules, the users have privacy expectations from the system. These privacy expectations are captured with conditional commitments [22, 26]. Informally, conditional commitments represent a contract between two parties, such that each party commits to realizing certain predicates. In terms of privacy, this maps to a situation where a user commits to specifying information about friends, colleagues, and so on correctly and the OSN commits to ensuring the correct set of individuals will be shown the content (based on user's specification). A commitment is denoted as a four-place relation: *C(debtor; creditor; antecedent; consequent)*. The *debtor* is committed to the *creditor* to bring about the *consequent* if the *creditor* brings about the *antecedent*. First, each user specifies her privacy concern. Second, the agent transforms such a privacy concern into a commitment so that it can later be verified. Consider the following example:

Example 1. Charlie shares a concert picture with everyone and tags Alice in it. However, Alice does not want other users to see her pictures.

Here, Alice has a privacy concern such that she does not want to be seen by others. She does not have any control on what is shared by her friends. After Alice specifies her concern, Alice's agent (:alice) generates a commitment between :alice and the social network operator. The antecedent of the commitment describes the individuals affected by the commitment (e.g., agents except Alice) and the content that the commitment is about (e.g., pictures). The consequent of the commitment says whether the specified individuals should see or not see the content. Overall, Alice only promises to share content on this online social network if the online social network promises not to reveal information about her whereabouts.

A commitment violation occurs, when the antecedent holds but not the consequent. In another words, the social network operator fails to bring about the consequent. This signals a breach of privacy. To detect such commitment violations, each agent computes under which conditions a commitment would be violated and generates a violation statement. For example, people seeing Alice's pictures would violate Alice's commitment that is in an active state (i.e., the antecedent is achieved).

Agents use the domain information, the semantic rules, the view information and the violation statements to detect privacy violations. Then, each agent reports the detection results; it depends on the creditor of the commitment (e.g., the user) to take an action accordingly.

3   PriGuardTool

PRIGUARDTOOL is a Web-based tool that implements PRIGUARD model [12]. We use ontologies to capture the domain, view, and the semantic rules of the social network.

Domain: The social network domain is represented using PRIGUARD ontology specified in OWL 2 Web Ontology Language [18]. PRIGUARD model is a DL model, which can be completely defined in an OWL 2 ontology. In this ontology, there are classes that define domain concepts, object properties that relate individuals and data properties that describe individual-specific properties. For example, `Agent` is a class, which describes a set of users in the social network. `:alice` and `:bob` might be individuals that are elements of `Agent` class. These two individuals can be connected to each other via the object property *isFriendOf*. `:alice` can have a name "Alice Kingsleigh", which is described by the data property *hasName*.

In a social network, it is important to model the users, the relationships between users and the posts being shared by the users. As mentioned before, users are represented as `Agent` individuals in the ontology. The relationships are defined as object properties between agents. *isConnectedTo* is the most general property that defines a connection between two agents. However, it is possible to describe more specific relationships such as *isColleagueOf*. `Post` class is the most general class to represent a post. In an ontology, one can define complex classes. For example, we use complex classes to model specific posts such as `LocationPost`, which can be defined as: `Post` ⊓ ∃*hasLocation*.`Location` (posts that have at least one location). Each post is initialized by an agent (*hasCreator*). Moreover, an agent can share posts (*sharesPost*) and see posts (*canSeePost*). A post can be about an agent (*isAbout*). Posts can include textual, visual or locational information represented as `Text`, `Medium` and `Location` respectively. Mediums can include geotags (*hasGeotag*). A `Post` is related to these classes via *hasText*, *hasMedium* and *hasLocation* properties. A person can be mentioned in a text (*mentionedPerson*), tagged in a medium (*taggedPerson*) or at a location (*withPerson*). Each post can be associated with contextual information (`Context`) as well. A specific `Audience` is meant to see a post. *hasAudience* relates audience individuals to post individuals. Hence, members of this audience are described by the use of *hasMember* property.

View: In PRIGUARD ontology, a view is a set of class assertions (e.g., ClassAssertion(`Agent` `:alice`)) and object property assertions (e.g., ObjectPropertyAssertion (*isFriendOf* `:alice` `:charlie`)). In Table 1, we show the system view for Example 1. We use the abbreviations CA and OPA for ClassAssertion and ObjectPropertyAssertion respectively. The view of Example 1 is specified in functional-style syntax. At this particular view, `:charlie` creates and shares a post (`:pc1`) including a medium (`:picConcert`), an `:audience` with `:alice`, `:bob`, `:diane` as members and a person tag of `:alice`. The relationships are defined as follows: `:alice`, `:bob` and `:charlie` are friends of each other; `:diane` is a friend of `:bob`. The remaining assertions include the class assertions for each instance.

Table 1. System view of Example 1 : `charlie` shares a post : `pc1`

CA(`Agent` :`alice`)	CA(`Agent` :`bob`)
CA(`Agent` :`charlie`)	CA(`Agent` :`diane`)
CA(`Post` :`pc1`)	CA(`Picture` :`picConcert`)
CA(`Audience` :`audience`)	
OPA(*isFriendOf* :`alice` :`bob`)	OPA(*isFriendOf* :`alice` :`charlie`)
OPA(*isFriendOf* :`bob` :`charlie`)	OPA(*isFriendOf* :`bob` :`diane`)
OPA(*sharesPost* :`charlie` :`pc1`)	OPA(*hasAudience* :`pc1` :`audience`)
OPA(*hasMedium* :`pc1` :`picConcert`)	OPA(*taggedPerson* :`picConcert` :`alice`)
OPA(*hasMember* :`audience` :`alice`)	OPA(*hasMember* :`audience` :`diane`)
OPA(*hasMember* :`audience` :`bob`)	OPA(*hasCreator* :`pc1` :`charlie`)

DL Rules: A social network needs a set of semantic rules to operate. Recall that, in PRIGUARD, rules are defined as Datalog rules. OWL 2 is an expressive language to represent some Datalog rules as DL rules. For example, consider the rule r_7 in Table 2. This rule states that a post that includes a geotagged picture is an instance of `LocationPost` class in the ontology. The remaining DL rules are as follows. If an agent shares a post, then the agent can see it (r_1). An agent can see a post if it is in the audience of that post (r_2). If an agent creates a post then this post is about that agent (r_3). Similarly, a post is about an agent if the agent is tagged at a specific location (r_4), in a medium (r_5) or mentioned in a text (r_6). If an agent is tagged in a picture and shares another post by declaring its location then the location information of other agents tagged in that picture is revealed as well (r_8).

Table 2. Example semantic rules as Description Logic (DL) rules

r_1:	$sharesPost \sqsubseteq canSeePost$
r_2:	$hasMember^- \circ hasAudience^- \circ R\_sharedPost \sqsubseteq canSeePost$
r_3:	$hasCreator \sqsubseteq isAbout$
r_4:	$hasLocation \circ withPerson \sqsubseteq isAbout$
r_5:	$hasMedium \circ taggedPerson \sqsubseteq isAbout$
r_6:	$hasText \circ mentionedPerson \sqsubseteq isAbout$
r_7:	$\textbf{Post} \sqcap \exists hasMedium.\exists hasGeotag.\textbf{Location} \sqsubseteq \textbf{LocationPost}$
r_8:	$R\_locPost \circ sharesPost^- \circ taggedPerson^- \circ hasMedium^- \circ sharesPost^- \sqsubseteq isAbout$

Commitments: Users input their privacy concerns via PRIGUARDTOOL interface as depicted in Fig. 1. The user can specify her privacy concerns regarding medium posts, location posts and posts that the user is tagged in. For each category, the user declares two groups of people: one group that can see that category and a group that cannot. If the user specifies conflicting privacy concerns (e.g., a user is part of both groups), the agent adopts a conservative approach to minimize privacy violations to occur; i.e., it finds conflicting users and move them to the group that cannot see the content.

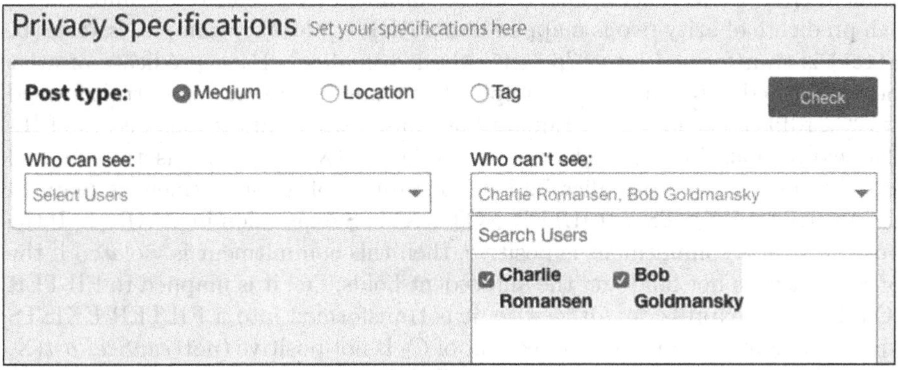

Privacy Specifications Set your specifications here

Post type: ⦿ Medium   ○ Location   ○ Tag   [Check]

Who can see:

Select Users ▼

Who can't see:

Charlie Romansen, Bob Goldmansky ▼

Search Users

☑ **Charlie Romansen**   ☑ **Bob Goldmansky**

Fig. 1. Alice declaring her friends to not see her medium posts.

PRIGUARD ontology is used to semantically describe the commitments. Table 3 shows the commitments that Alice is in involved in. Since current OSNs are centralized, our commitments are among users and the OSN operator (:osn). Recall that Alice wants to be the only one who can see her medium posts (see Example 1). Hence, two commitments are generated C_1 and C_2. In C_1, :osn promises :alice to show her medium posts to :alice. In C_2, :osn promises :alice to not reveal her medium posts to others.

Table 3. Commitments for Example 1

C_i	<Debtor;	Creditor;	Antecedent;	Consequent>
C_1:	<:osn;	:alice;	X==:alice, $isAbout$(P, :alice), MediumPost(P);	$canSeePost$(X, P)>
C_2:	<:osn;	:alice;	**Agent**(X),not(X==:alice),$isAbout$(P, :alice),MediumPost(P);	not($canSeePost$(X, P))>

Violation Statements: After all the semantic inferences are made by the use of PRIGUARD ontology and DL rules, the agent should be able to query this knowledge to detect privacy violations in the social network. A violation statement is a statement wherein a commitment would be violated. Here, agents use SPARQL queries to represent commitment violations. In another words, a violation statement is mapped to a SPARQL query.

SPARQL is a way of querying RDF-based information [21]. Note that ontological axioms can also be seen as RDF triples. In a SPARQL query, there are query variables, which start with a question mark (e.g., ?x), to retrieve the desired results. We only focus on *SELECT* queries with filter expressions *NOT EXISTS* and *EXISTS* to represent violation statements. Recall that the antecedent of a commitment includes information about agents that are the target audience of the commitment, and the set of posts being shared. The consequent of a commitment specifies whether agents could see or not the content. In the antecedent, each predicate of arity two is mapped into a RDF triple. For example, *isAbout*(P, :alice) is transformed into "?p osn:isAbout osn:alice". Each predicate of arity one is mapped into an *rdf:type* triple. For example, Agent(X) is transformed into "?x rdf:type osn:Agent". Equality or non-equality expressions become FILTER expressions in SPARQL. For example, not(X ==:alice) is transformed into "FILTER (?x != osn:alice)". The consequent of a commitment is mapped into a FILTER EXISTS or FILTER NOT EXISTS expression in SPARQL. If the consequent of a commitment is positive, then this commitment is violated if the consequent does not hold and the antecedent holds; i.e., it is mapped to FILTER NOT EXISTS expression. Otherwise, it is transformed into a FILTER EXISTS expression. For example, the consequent of C_2 is not positive (not(*canSeePost*(X, P))) hence it is transformed into "FILTER EXISTS { ?x osn:canSeePost ?p }".

A complete SPARQL query is shown in Table 4. The *PREFIX* declares a namespace prefix. *osn* prefix shows where to find PRIGUARD ontology for querying. This *SELECT* query declares two query variables (?x and ?p) to be retrieved. The core part of the query is defined in the *WHERE* block, which consists of four triples (one is used in a filter expression). This query returns the set of posts that can be seen by agents except Alice.

:charlie shares a post :pc1, which includes a picture of :alice and :charlie. The audience is set to everyone. :alice checks for possible privacy violations. PRIGUARDTOOL finds the corresponding commitments: C_1 and C_2. C_1 is not violated since Alice can see her posts. However, the violation statement of C_2 (as shown in Table 4) holds in the system with the substitutions $\{?x/\{\text{:bob, :charlie}\}\}$ and $\{?p/\text{:pc1}\}$. Here, a privacy violation occurs because

Table 4. The violation statement of C_2

```
PREFIX rdf: <http://www.w3.org/1999/02/22-rdf-syntax-ns#>
PREFIX osn: <http://mas.cmpe.boun.edu.tr/ontologies/osn#>

SELECT ?x ?p WHERE {
          ?x rdf:type osn:Agent .
          ?p osn:isAbout osn:alice .
          ?p rdf:type osn:MediumPost .
          FILTER EXISTS {
                    ?x osn:canSeePost ?p .
                    FILTER (?x != osn:alice)
          }
}
```

Alice and Charlie have conflicting privacy concerns; i.e., one wants to keep it personal while the other prefers sharing it with everyone. Thus, it is not possible to fulfill both of their concerns at the same time.

4   Implementation

We have implemented PRIGUARDTOOL as a Web application[2]. We have used PHP for the front-end development and Java for the back-end development. PRIGUARDTOOL is able to work with various social networks. For this, a gateway should be developed for user authentication and data collection. Here, we decided to work with Facebook since it is widely used around the world. We integrated *Facebook Login* to our web application to enable user authentication. We also implemented a Facebook gateway to collect data from Facebook users.

Figure 2 shows the information flow of PRIGUARDTOOL. The tasks are represented as rectangles. A human task is depicted as a task with a figure on top while the other tasks are automated tasks. The solid arrows represent the flow between tasks. The data operations are shown as dashed arrows. First, the user logs into the system by providing her Facebook credentials. The tool collects the user data and stores in a database (MongoDB). The user inputs her privacy concerns, which are stored as a JSON document. These privacy concerns are transformed into commitments between the user and the social network (Facebook) operator, and the corresponding violation statements (SPARQL queries) are generated as well. On the other branch, *Generate Ontologies* task takes care of reading user data from MongoDB, creating and storing ontologies in MongoDB. *Detect Privacy Violations* task uses SPARQL queries and the user's ontologies to monitor the social network for privacy violations. Finally, the user is shown a list of posts that violate her privacy if any. Then, the user can take an action such as modifying a post (e.g., removing a person from the audience of that post). Once the user logs out from the system, the tool removes the user data and the generated ontologies. This ensures that no information remains in the database after the detection is completed.

Data Collection: We extract information about the user from Facebook by the use of Facebook Graph API[3]. We request the following login permissions: *email*, *public_profile*, *user_friends*, *user_photos*, *user_posts*. These permissions allow us to collect information about Facebook posts together with the comments and likes of other users. We use MongoDB[4], which is an open-source document-oriented database, to keep the extracted information. Graph API supports the exchange of JSON documents, and it becomes reasonable to store the user data as a JSON document in MongoDB. Note that we only extract information of the user, which may be shared by the user itself or by a friend of the user (i.e., the user is tagged in a post shared by a friend).

---

[2] http://mas.cmpe.boun.edu.tr/priguardtool.
[3] https://developers.facebook.com/docs/graph-api.
[4] https://www.mongodb.com/.

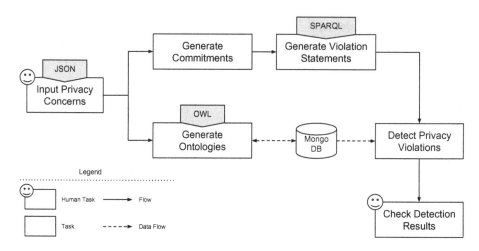

Fig. 2. PRIGUARDTOOL implementation steps

Facebook Graph API (v2.5) enables extraction of some information of a user, such as the user's posts, the comments on the posts or the likes of the posts. However, it does not allow us to extract some important information about the users, such as the list of friends of a user. Further, it is not possible to extract any information about the posts of other users. As another limitation, one cannot extract information about user-defined lists (e.g., if the user has a family list, it is not possible to get users that belong to that list). We analyze the collected information of the user so that we can come up with an approximate list of friends. For this, we analyze the interactions of other users with the user. For example, if a person makes a comment about a post shared by the user, then we consider this person as being a friend of the user. So, this list includes more users than the actual list of friends of the user. Consider the user N_3 in Table 5. The actual number of friends for this user is 671. However, by analyzing the interaction data of the user, we come up with a list of 1060 users. Since the constructed list is only a partial view of the social network, our tool may not detect all of the violations. Moreover, the approximate list of friends may contain users who are not actual friends of the user (e.g., a friend of friend of the user will be included in the approximate list as a result of liking a post of the user). In such cases, the tool can report false positive violations. For example, if the user does not want her content to be seen by her friends, the tool can report a violation where a friend of friend of the user sees her content. However, if PRIGUARDTOOL was a service of the online social network with access to more information, such false positives would not take place.

Ontology Generation: Recall that PRIGUARDTOOL makes use of ontologies to keep information about the social network domain and the user. The user data, which is a JSON document, should be transformed into class and property assertions in PRIGUARD ontology. This transformation is realized by a Java application, which parses a JSON document and generate an ontology for the user. We use Apache Jena[5], which is an open-source Java framework to work with ontologies. The user may choose to check for privacy violations for a subset of her posts. Hence, ontologies of different sizes can be generated per request.

Note that the ontology generation module can take a long time if the user has lots of friends and posts. Hence, we adopt multi-threading to generate large ontologies. It is important to keep large ontologies in a database since privacy violations can also be detected offline. The maximum size of document that can be stored in MongoDB is 16 MB. We use GridFS specification in MongoDB, which divides a document into various chunks that are stored separately as documents.

Fig. 3. Alice checks the posts that violate her privacy.

Detection Results: The users input their privacy concerns to detect privacy violations on Facebook as shown in Fig. 1. Once the user checks for violations, a list of posts that violate the privacy of the user are displayed on the Web application. For example, Alice did not want Bob and Charlie to see her medium posts. When she checks for violations, she is notified that Charlie's post violates her privacy as shown in Fig. 3. Here, Alice can get in touch with Charlie so that he modifies or removes this post since she is not the owner that post.

PRIGUARDTOOL can be used in two modes: online and offline. In both modes, agents use the user data to generate an ontology, which is loaded into memory for checking privacy violations. In online mode, PRIGUARDTOOL only considers posts that have been shared about the user in last three months. We do this to return recent privacy violations first in a short time. However, in offline mode, privacy violations are detected by the use of large ontologies. The user can also check the detection results that have been computed in offline mode. Then, the user can try to minimize the privacy violations to occur by modifying the posts if possible.

---

[5] https://jena.apache.org/.

5   Evaluation

In the context of privacy, it is difficult to evaluate approaches and tools since there are no established data sets. Moreover, privacy is subjective hence it becomes difficult to talk of a gold standard that works for all. One way to go about this is to create synthetic data. However, ensuring that the synthetic data will adhere to real life properties is also difficult. Instead of working with synthetic data, it is ideal to work with real users. For this, we show the applicability of PRIGUARD approach in a Web application that is integrated to Facebook.

5.1   Experiments with Facebook Users

To evaluate our PRIGUARDTOOL implementation, we have worked with real data of Facebook users. We have collected data from Facebook users who used our tool to protect their privacy. Here, we generate five ontologies regarding the user data. The first four ontologies include posts shared last one month, three months, six months and last year. The fifth ontology includes the latest five hundred posts shared by the user. Additionally, the users specified their privacy concerns, which were translated into commitments. Then, the user agents checked for commitment violations in generated ontologies to report privacy violations.

We perform our experiments on Intel Xeon 3050 machine with 2.13 GHz and 4 GB of memory running Ubuntu 14.04 (64-bit). In Table 5, we present the evaluation results for three Facebook users. Each user inputs a privacy concern such that she chooses five people who should not see her medium posts. Then, the user checks for privacy violations. The user agent transforms this privacy concern into a commitment. Then, the user agent searches for commitment violations and reports if any.

Table 5. Results for Facebook users

$N_x(Friend\#, TotalPost\#)$		1mo.	3mo.	6mo.	12mo.	All
$N_1(293, 123)$	Post number	2	9	27	47	123
	Violation number	1	8	25	43	100
	Detection time (s)	0.65	1.21	5.5	11.36	26.08
	Ontology gen. time (s)	1.2	2.24	4.6	6.34	11.12
$N_2(590, 1894)$	Post number	5	19	51	134	500
	Violation number	5	14	37	89	332
	Detection time (s)	3.07	5.16	18.48	70.87	696.51
	Ontology gen. time (s)	2.33	6.51	10.79	18.07	33.7
$N_3(1060, 2945)$	Post number	18	77	124	330	500
	Violation number	9	44	69	164	237
	Detection time (s)	3.28	76.74	187.53	783.06	1285.73
	Ontology gen. time (s)	3.34	9.85	16.23	41.23	67.14

The users have different numbers of friends and posts (N_1, N_2 and N_3). For each generated ontology of the user, we give information about the number of posts and the number of detected violations. Moreover, we measure the time that it takes to detect violations and to generate the corresponding ontology. For example, the user N_2 has 590 friends and 1894 posts. Her ontology includes information about posts shared in last six months. This ontology was generated in 10.79 s from the 51 posts she has made on Facebook. The tool detected 37 privacy violations regarding the user's privacy concerns. The detection took 18.48 s. Whenever the social network of a user is small in size, the time for generating an ontology and detecting violations is less. For example, it takes only 11.12 s to generate an ontology for N_1 and 26.08 s for detecting 100 violations when we consider all posts. However, it takes longer when users are part of a large network. Even if the ontology generation time is reasonable (i.e., 67.14 s to generate the largest ontology for N_3), the detection takes a long time since the axiom number in the ontology increases as the result of ontological reasoning. For example, for N_3, the detection took approximately 20 min. Hence, such a detection should be done in offline mode if the detection is not achieved in a distributed manner as we do here. In online mode, the tool can report results in less than 80 s (considering that the user N_3 is a very active user) since we only consider posts shared in last three months. The user can then check the privacy violations and try to minimize them. She can modify the post attributes if she is the owner of the violating post. Otherwise, she can contact the post's owner to modify that post or to remove it completely.

5.2 Variations on Example Scenarios

We introduce two more examples that demonstrate privacy violations in an online social network. The first example requires multiple posts to be processed together to identify a privacy violation. We show that PRIGUARDTOOL can detect this successfully. The second example contains a privacy violation that can only be detected by processing non-structured data about the post (e.g., the image or text). In its current form, PRIGUARDTOOL cannot accommodate such processing and thus cannot detect the violation.

Consider the following example that shows how a privacy violation occurs indirectly in the presence of other users' posts.

Example 2. Bob shares a picture where he tags Diane. After a while Diane shares her location in a post. Alice and Charlie, who are friends of Bob, get to know Bob's location. However, Bob did not want to reveal his location.

In Example 2, a privacy violation occurs through inference. By combining Bob's post with Diane's post, one can infer Bob's location (see the inference rule r_8). However, in order to detect such violations, we should be able to collect Diane's posts as well. In the current implementation, we focus on collecting the user's data. For this example, Diane's post would not be extracted since it does not have any explicit tag for Bob. Note that PRIGUARDTOOL is able to detect violations of different types by the use of semantic rules when data is available. Another solution would be to integrate PRIGUARDTOOL to Facebook. In another words, if PRIGUARDTOOL ran as an internal application rather than an external one, then it would have access to the data and detect the privacy violation easily.

In the following example, the user shares a post that includes textual information, which reveals the location of the user.

Example 3. Bob shares a status message: "Hello Las Vegas, nice to finally meet you!". This message is shared with his friends.

In Example 3, Bob discloses his location himself. Hence, a privacy breach occurs because of the user itself. However, such a privacy violation cannot be identified by PRIGUARDTOOL because current agents do not analyze textual information to extract meaningful information. That is, a human can easily understand that Las Vegas is a city and that Bob is currently there. However, an agent would need to use Natural Language Processing (NLP) tools to find that Las Vegas is a location name, and the post being shared is indeed a location post. Thus, his friends reading this message would be violating Bob's privacy. This task is not straightforward in the context of privacy. An agent can recognize entities in a text by the use of external tools. However, it is unknown how these entities would affect the privacy of the user. We leave this point as a future work.

6   Discussion

This paper describes PRIGUARDTOOL, which is a concrete implementation of PRIGUARD, a semantic approach for detecting privacy violations in OSNs. PRIGUARDTOOL allows a user to specify her privacy constraints using a Web-based interface. The specified constraints are then converted into commitments. The tool then checks for commitment violations in a given system, which signals a privacy breach.

6.1   Related Work

While various approaches for privacy management exist, the number of tools is scarce. CoPE is a collaborative privacy management system that is developed to run as a Facebook application [24]. The idea is that each post is co-owned by multiple users that are affected by the post; e.g., because the individual is tagged or mentioned in the post. First, each co-owner specifies her own privacy requirement on a particular post. Then, the co-owners vote on the final privacy requirement on the post. The post is shared accordingly.

FaceBlock is an application designed to preserve the privacy of users that use Google Glass [20]. Given that interactions happen more seamlessly with wearable devices, it is possible that an individual takes a picture in an environment and shares it without getting explicit consent from others in the environment. To help users manage their privacy, FaceBlock allows users define their privacy rules with Semantic Web Rule Language (SWRL) and uses a reasoner to check whether any privacy rule is triggered. If so, FaceBlock obscures the face of the user before sharing the picture.

PriNego [9,17] and PriArg [11] are systems that have been built over the same framework. Users' privacy constraints are represented with SWRL rules. PriNego is a negotiation framework that allows users to negotiate their privacy constraints before a post is shared. At each iteration of the negotiation, a given post is updated based on privacy concerns of the users. For example, after the negotiation is done, the post might have fewer members in its audience list or fewer individuals tagged. PriArg uses argumentation to facilitate agreement among users. It enables users to attack each other's privacy concerns with information they provide (i.e., arguments). At the end of the argumentation, whether a post will be shared or not is decided.

Kafali *et al.* develop PROTOSS [8], where the privacy agreements are again represented with commitments. However, in that work, the commitments are taken from the user as opposed to being generated as we have done here. Further, the system evolution is being tested for violations rather than the current state of the system. PROTOSS uses model checking hence in a given state of the social network, all the possible states are generated. In PRIGUARDTOOL, we are only concerned with a single state of the system, we can detect violations much faster and with less memory requirements then them.

Akcora, Carminati and Ferrari develop a graph-based approach and a risk model to learn risk labels of strangers; e.g., friends of friends [1]. The intuition is that these will enable them to detect individuals who are likely to violate privacy constraints. Our focus is not on identifying potential individuals that can view private data but on detecting violations through interactions on the OSN.

Liu and Terzi address the privacy problem in OSNs from the user's perspective [16]. They propose a model to compute a privacy score of a user. The privacy score increases with the *sensitivity* and *visibility* of the revealed information. *Sensitivity* is specific to a profile item while *visibility* of a profile item depends on the privacy settings of the user. It would be interesting to capture these concepts in PRIGUARD ontology and make inferences based on that.

Squicciarini *et al.* propose PriMa (Privacy Manager), which supports semi-automated generation of access rules according to the user's privacy settings and the level of exposure of the user's profile [23]. They further provide quantitative measurements for privacy violations. Quantifying violations is an interesting direction that we want to investigate further. Our use of an ontology can make it possible to infer the extents of the privacy violation, indicating its severity.

Fang and LeFevre propose a privacy wizard that automatically configures the user's privacy settings based on an active learning paradigm [4]. Their approach is based on the user's privacy preferences while we consider the privacy preferences of the user and her social graph. Moreover, we focus on detecting privacy violations that would happen because of conflicting privacy concerns of the users.

Krishnamurthy points out the need for privacy solutions to protect the user data from all entities who may access it [14]. He suggests that OSN users should know what happens to their privacy as a result of their actions. For this, a Facebook extension called Privacy IQ is developed where users can see the privacy reach of their posts and the effect of their past privacy settings. PRIGUARDTOOL is similar to this work in that we can also compare the user's privacy expectations with the actual state of the system. However, our major contribution is on detecting privacy breaches that take place because of interactions among users and inferences on information.

6.2   Limitations and Future Developments

The main obstacle we faced in adapting PRIGUARDTOOL to Facebook was that the current Facebook API does not allow a user to obtain much of the information she sees programatically. For example, a user can see her list of friends when she logs in to Facebook, but she cannot get the same list using the API. Hence, we could only construct a partial list of friends using information such as comments, tags, and so on. Although most of the time, the constructed information was sufficiently accurate, it would have been much easier if the agent could access the information to begin with.

In this work, we assume that users are able to input their privacy concerns in a fine grained way. However, users have difficulties to specify their privacy concerns even if they have the necessary tools [4]. To solve this problem, one approach would be to conduct user studies to understand the user needs better. As a result, we can design better user interfaces that guide the users in specifying their privacy expectations. Another approach would be to learn the privacy concerns of the user automatically [10,19]. This would minimize the user burden and errors by suggesting privacy configurations.

The current system supports commitments between a user and the online social network. However, in principle, if the online social network itself supports a distributed architecture (e.g., GnuSocial[6]), then individual users will be responsible for managing their content and thus the system would have to support commitments among users. This would lead to interesting scenarios and could serve as a natural domain to demonstrate operations on commitments. For example, Bob could commit to Alice not to share her pictures and then follow up with his friends to ensure that Alice's pictures are not shared. This could lead to multiple commitments being merged and manipulated to preserve privacy and give rise to composition of commitments for representing realistic scenarios [2].

Another important improvement could be to detect privacy violations in a distributed manner. The current implementation receives a state of the system and checks for possible violations in that state. A distributed implementation could help process the state considerably faster. This would enable the tool to be used online easily.

---

[6] https://gnu.io/social/.

Acknowledgments. This work is supported by TUBITAK under grant 113E543. This work extends the demonstration paper that was presented at AAMAS 2016 [13]. We thank Hamza Ozturk and Safa Orhan for helping with integrating PRIGUARDTOOL to Facebook.

References

1. Akcora, C.G., Carminati, B., Ferrari, E.: Risks of friendships on social networks. In: IEEE International Conference on Data Mining (ICDM), pp. 810–815 (2012)
2. Baldoni, M., Baroglio, C., Chopra, A.K., Singh, M.P.: Composing and verifying commitment-based multiagent protocols. In: Proceedings of the 24th International Joint Conference on Artificial Intelligence (IJCAI), pp. 10–17 (2015)
3. Carminati, B., Ferrari, E., Heatherly, R., Kantarcioglu, M., Thuraisingham, B.: Semantic web-based social network access control. Comput. Secur. **30**(2), 108–115 (2011)
4. Fang, L., LeFevre, K.: Privacy wizards for social networking sites. In: Proceedings of the 19th International Conference on World Wide Web, pp. 351–360. ACM (2010)
5. Gürses, F., Berendt, B.: The social web and privacy: practices, reciprocity and conflict detection in social networks. In: Privacy-Aware Knowledge Discovery, pp. 395–432. Chapman & Hall/CRC Press, New York (2010)
6. Heussner, K.M.: Celebrities' photos, videos may reveal location. ABC News. http://goo.gl/sJIFg4
7. Hu, H., Ahn, G.J., Jorgensen, J.: Multiparty access control for online social networks: model and mechanisms. IEEE Trans. Knowl. Data Eng. **25**(7), 1614–1627 (2013)
8. Kafalı, O., Günay, A., Yolum, P.: Detecting and predicting privacy violations in online social networks. Distrib. Parallel Databases **32**(1), 161–190 (2014)
9. Keküllüoğlu, D., Kökciyan, N., Yolum, P.: Strategies for privacy negotiation in online social networks. In: Proceedings of the 1st International Workshop on AI for Privacy and Security (PrAISe), pp. 2:1–2:8 (2016)
10. Kepez, B., Yolum, P.: Learning privacy rules cooperatively in online social networks. In: Proceedings of the 1st International Workshop on AI for Privacy and Security (PrAISe), pp. 3:1–3:4. ACM (2016)
11. Kökciyan, N., Yaglikci, N., Yolum, P.: Argumentation for resolving privacy disputes in online social networks: (extended abstract). In: Proceedings of the 15th International Conference on Autonomous Agents & Multiagent Systems, Singapore, May 9–13, pp. 1361–1362 (2016)
12. Kökciyan, N., Yolum, P.: Priguard: a semantic approach to detect privacy violations in online social networks. IEEE Trans. Knowl. Data Eng. **28**(10), 2724–2737 (2016)
13. Kökciyan, N., Yolum, P.: PriGuardTool: a tool for monitoring privacy violations in online social networks (demonstration). In: Proceedings of the 2016 International Conference on Autonomous Agents and Multiagent Systems (AAMAS), pp. 1496–1497 (2016)
14. Krishnamurthy, B.: Privacy and online social networks: can colorless green ideas sleep furiously? IEEE Secur. Priv. **11**(3), 14–20 (2013)
15. Lampinen, A., Lehtinen, V., Lehmuskallio, A., Tamminen, S.: We're in it together: interpersonal management of disclosure in social network services. In: Proceedings of the SIGCHI Conference on Human Factors in Computing Systems, pp. 3217–3226. ACM (2011)

16. Liu, K., Terzi, E.: A framework for computing the privacy scores of users in online social networks. ACM Trans. Knowl. Discov. Data (TKDD) **5**(1), 6: 1–6: 30 (2010)

17. Mester, Y., Kökciyan, N., Yolum, P.: Negotiating privacy constraints in online social networks. In: Koch, F., Guttmann, C., Busquets, D. (eds.) Advances in Social Computing and Multiagent Systems, Communications in Computer and Information Science, vol. 541, pp. 112–129. Springer, Heidelberg (2015)

18. Motik, B., Patel-Schneider, P.F., Parsia, B., Bock, C., Fokoue, A., Haase, P., Hoekstra, R., Horrocks, I., Ruttenberg, A., Sattler, U., et al.: Owl 2 web ontology language: structural specification and functional-style syntax. W3C Recommendation **27**(65), 159 (2009)

19. Mugan, J., Sharma, T., Sadeh, N.: Understandable learning of privacy preferences through default personas and suggestions. Technical report CMU-ISR-11-112, School of Computer Science, Carnegie Mellon University (2011)

20. Pappachan, P., Yus, R., Das, P.K., Finin, T., Mena, E., Joshi, A.: A semantic context-aware privacy model for faceblock. In: Proceedings of the 2nd International Conference on Society, Privacy and the Semantic Web - Policy and Technology, pp. 64–72. PrivOn (2014)

21. Pérez, J., Arenas, M., Gutierrez, C.: Semantics and complexity of SPARQL. ACM Trans. Database Syst. **34**(3), 16 (2009)

22. Singh, M.P.: An ontology for commitments in multiagent systems. Artif. Intell. Law **7**(1), 97–113 (1999)

23. Squicciarini, A.C., Paci, F., Sundareswaran, S.: PriMa: a comprehensive approach to privacy protection in social network sites. Ann. Telecommun./Annales des Télécommunications **69**(1), 21–36 (2014)

24. Squicciarini, A.C., Xu, H., Zhang, X.L.: Cope: enabling collaborative privacy management in online social networks. J. Am. Soc. Inf. Sci. Technol. **62**(3), 521–534 (2011)

25. Such, J.M., Rovatsos, M.: Privacy policy negotiation in social media. ACM Trans. Auton. Adapt. Syst. (TAAS) **11**(1), 4:1–4:29 (2016)

26. Yolum, P., Singh, M.P.: Flexible protocol specification and execution: applying event calculus planning using commitments. In: Proceedings of the First International Joint Conference on Autonomous Agents and Multiagent Systems, pp. 527–534 (2002)

Application Framework with Abstractions for Protocol and Agent Role

Bent Bruun Kristensen[✉]

Maersk Mc-Kinney Moller Institute,
University of Southern Denmark, Odense, Denmark
bbkristensen@mmmi.sdu.dk

Abstract. In multi-agent systems, agents interact by sending and receiving messages and the actual sequences of message form interaction structures between agents. The development process and the resulting description of the organization of an agent (in order to handle several ongoing interactions) are comprehensive and complex. Abstraction in the form of protocols and agent roles (for internal organization of agents) support these interaction structures: The development process becomes efficient and flexible—and the description becomes understandable. The abstractions protocol and agent roles are supported by a simple and expressive application framework.

Keywords: Multi-agent system · Protocol · Agent role · Reactive and proactive role · Application framework · Qualities at development time

1 Introduction

Agents are active, autonomous, and smart, i.e. among others capable of reactive and pro-active behavior [1]. A multi-agent system consists of a number of agents interacting with one-another—and to successfully interact, agents require the ability to cooperate, coordinate, and negotiate with each other. The description of the interaction structure between agents is complex because an agent is engaged in a number of ongoing interactions with other agents. Because typically no support is available for structuring this internal organization of an agent, the development process is less efficient and less flexible, and the resulting description becomes less understandable.

The use of abstractions to describe observations is essential for our understanding: "Without abstraction we only know that everything is different" [2]. Therefore, the intention is to contribute with abstractions to support important qualities during development time (including modelling and programming). We describe interactions by protocols that relate agent roles of agents. Protocols and agent roles are abstractions, i.e. by these concepts the developer can conceive and describe the organization structure of an agent as well as the interaction structure between agents. By introducing abstraction including exemplification, composition and specialization the description process becomes efficient and flexible as well as the resulting description becomes understandable.

Protocols and agent roles, that capture the interaction structure between agents, are supported by an object-oriented application framework [3] with agents, reactive role,

M. Baldoni et al. (Eds.): EMAS 2016, LNAI 10093, pp. 99–116, 2016.
DOI: 10.1007/978-3-319-50983-9_6

proactive role and message. The underlying agent model and the application framework are illustrated by the Contract Net [1]. The model and the application framework are evaluated and related work is presented.

2 Agent Model

Reactive and Proactive Roles. Agents communicate by sending and receiving messages representing events as illustrated in Fig. 1. An agent consists of a varying number of reactive and proactive roles. Reactive and proactive roles are abstractions for internal organization of an agent and messages are sent from and received by these roles. If a message is sent to the agent itself a default reactive role of the agent receives the message.

The roles of an agent execute one at a time and in a non preemptive way [4], i.e. they exhibit cooperative multitasking, in which case a role can self-interrupt and voluntarily give up control. Reactive and proactive roles are stereotypes but combinations can be described. Each reactive and proactive role has a list of messages to be handled on a first come first served basis. A reactive role repeats the execution of an action to take care of its list of messages whenever the handling of the previous message is completed and the awaiting message list is not empty. A proactive role consists of a single execution of an action that takes care of pausing as well as waiting and handling messages until its purpose is completed.

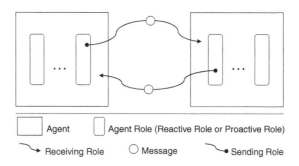

Fig. 1. Agents organized by reactive and proactive roles.

Protocols. A protocol describes a process where an initiator initializes the interaction by sending messages to a number of participants where after these participants may reply to the initiator as part of the interaction, etc. The protocol takes place between proactive roles of agents. The protocol and the proactive roles together form abstractions over an interaction structure between the involved agents.

Figure 2 illustrates a protocol P between proactive roles R_1 and R_2 in agents A_1 and A_2. Role R_1 initializes the interaction by sending a message M_1 to role R_2. Role R_2

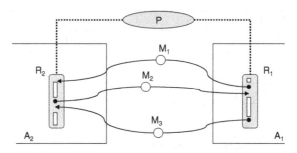

Fig. 2. Illustration of protocol and proactive roles

replies with message M_2 to R_1. In this manner a protocol between R_1 and R_2 may describe a continued interaction between R_1 (from A_1) and R_2 (from A_2). The protocol illustrated in Fig. 2 is similar to the coroutine mechanism of SIMULA [5] in the sense that a role sends a message, immediately suspends itself and the receiving role is resumed.

Example: Contract Net. Figure 3 illustrates the Contract Net with a collection of stickmen. Each stickman in the collection can, at different times or for different tasks, be involved in several simultaneous tasks as both manager and contractor. When a stickman gets a composite task (or for any reason cannot solve its present task), it breaks the task into subtasks (if possible) and announces them (acting as a manager), receives bids from potential contractors, and then possibly awards a contractor. If no bids are received after a given period of time the manager gives up the negotiation. If a bid is not awarded after a given period the contractor gives up the negotiation.

A model for the Contract Net includes: A protocol is set up with a proactive role for the manager agent (the initiator) and a proactive role for each of the contractor agents (the participants). A manager maintains a negotiation by initiating an interaction with a number of contractors. A contractor receives a task announcement and may reply with a bid to the manager. Having received bids the manager chooses among these and may reply with an award to the chosen contractor in which case a contract is established.

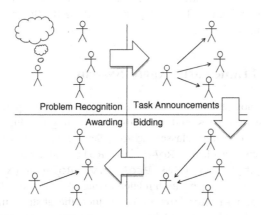

Fig. 3. Illustration of contract net

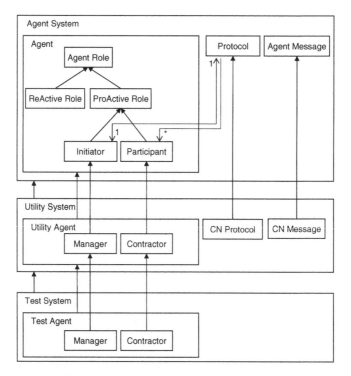

Fig. 4. Conceptual Model showing the contents of and relations between Agent System, Utility System and Test System

3 Framework Overview

Figure 4 illustrates the conceptual model of the application framework with Agent_System that is specialized to another application framework Utility_System (to support various protocols with the Contract Net as an example) that in turn is used in the application Test_System. The contents of and relations between Agent_System, Utility_System and Test_System are described in the following sections.

4 Application Framework: Agent System

Figures 5, 6 and 7 show extracts of the textual version of the application framework Agent_System with classes and methods shown in grey. Figure 5 shows class Agent_System with abstract classes Agent, Protocol and Agent_Message. Class Agent has abstract classes ReActive_Role and ProActive_Role (extending class Agent_Role). Class ProActive_Role is extended to classes Initiator and Participant both related to class Protocol. In addition classes ReActive_Role and ProActive_Role include the abstract method Act(...). The Act(...) method of class ReActive_Role returns a delay until next invocation

```
... class Agent_System {

  ... abstract class Protocol {
    ... Protocol (Agent initiator, Agent[] participant) {
      ...
      initiatorRole = initiator.newInitiatorRole(this);
      for (int i = 0; i< ...; i++) {
        participantRole[i] =
                    participant[i].newParticipantRole();
      };
    }

      ...
    ... Agent.Initiator initiatorRole;
    ... Agent.Participant[] participantRole = ... ;
  }

  ... abstract class Agent extends ... implements ... {

    ...
    ... abstract class Agent_Role extends ... {...}

    ... abstract class ReActive_Role extends Agent_Role {
      abstract ... int Act(Agent_Message am)
        ...
    };

    ... abstract class ProActive_Role extends Agent_Role {
      abstract ... void Act()
        ...
    }

    ... abstract class Initiator extends ProActive_Role {...}
    ... abstract class Participant extends ProActive_Role {...}
    ... abstract Initiator newInitiatorRole(Protocol p)
    ... abstract Participant newParticipantRole();
  }

  ... abstract class Agent_Message extends EventObject {...}
}
```

Fig. 5. Application framework: Agent_System

and is invoked repeatedly with the next message as parameter while messages are waiting. The Act() method of class ProActive_Role is invoked only once and its execution may include pausing, awaiting messages, etc. until its execution is completed. Abstract methods newInitiatorRole and newParticipantRole are used by Protocol to instruct actual specializations of Agent to instantiate actual specializations of Initiator and Participant. Class Protocol instantiates and starts the execution of InitiatorRole (with the Protocol object as parameter) for InitiatorAgent and of ParticipantRole for each of the ParticipantAgents.

```
... abstract class Agent_Role extends ... {
  ... void rolePause(int sleepTime) {...}
  ... Agent_Message roleAwait() {...}
  ... void replyMessage(Agent_Message rm, Agent_Message am) {...}
  ... Agent_Message handleMessage() {...}
    ...
}
```

Fig. 6. Interaction methods of class Agent_Role

Figure 6 shows extracts of selected interaction methods of class `Agent_Role` (inherited by `ReActive_Role` and `ProActive_Role`):

- `rolePause(...)`, the role pauses for a period of time
- `roleAwait()`, the role waits until a message is received and then returns the message
- `replyMessage(...)`, a message is sent to a role of another agent as a reply to a message received from that role
- `handleMessage()`, the next waiting message is returned (if any and else `null`)

```
… abstract class Agent_Role extends … {
  … void initiateProtocol(Agent_Message am, Participant p) {…}
  … void replyProtocol(Agent_Message ram, Agent_Message am) {…}
  …
}
```

Fig. 7. Methods `initiateProtocol` and `replyProtocol`

Class `Protocol` sets up the protocol between agent roles—the `Initiator` and the `Participants` agents. Figure 7 shows extracts of the interaction methods related to the protocol:

- `initiateProtocol(...)`, the `Initiator` sends a message am to a `Participant` to initialize the protocol.
- `replyProtocol(...)`, either the `Initiator` or a `Participant` send a message ram in reply to message am received within the protocol.

5   Application Framework: Utility System

Class `Agent_System` can be used directly to construct a multi-agent system with reactive and proactive agent roles and protocols. We choose to extend `Agent_System` to another abstract class `Utility_System` to illustrate an example of an abstract protocol—the Contract Net. Classes `Utility_System` is then specialized in class `Test_System` as an actual use.

Overview and class CN_Protocol. Figure 8 shows the ingredients of the specialization of `Agent_System` to `Utility_System`: `Protocol` is specialized to `CN_Protocol` and the proactive roles `Initiator` and `Participant` to `Manager` and `Contractor`, respectively. Classes `Manager` and `Contractor` specify their own `Act()` method according to the Contract Net. And each of these `Act()` methods makes use of additional methods (shown as dotted) to be implemented in the actual use of the `Utility_System`.

Figure 9 illustrates how `Utility_System` and `Utility_Agent` extend `Agent_System` and `Agent`, respectively. Class `Protocol` is extended to `CN_Protocol` that initializes a `Manager` role for the `Initiator` agent and a `Contractor` role for each of the `Participant` agents.

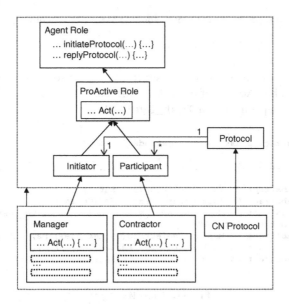

Fig. 8. Specialization of Agent_System to Utility_System

```
... abstract class Utility_System extends Agent_System {

  ... class CN_Protocol extends Protocol {
    ... CN_Protocol (Agent initiator, Agent[] participant) {
    super(initiator, participant);
      ...
    }

    ... Utility_Agent.Manager managerRole;
    ... Utility_Agent.Contractor[] contractorRole = ... ;
    ...
  }

  ... abstract class Utility_Agent extends Agent  {

    ... abstract class Manager extends Initiator {
      ... Manager (Protocol protocol)  {...}
      ... void Act() {...}
    };

    ... abstract class Contractor extends Participant {
      ... void Act() {...}
    }
  }
}
```

Fig. 9. Utility_System with CN_Protocol

When a Protocol is instantiated as shown in Fig. 10 its constructor initializes
ManagerRole through the executing agent and ContractorRoles through
otherAgents.

```
new CN_Protocol(Test_Agent.this, otherAgents);
```

Fig. 10. Creation of a CN_Protocol

Class Manager. Figure 11 shows abstract class Manager as an extension of Initiator. Method Act() of class Manager uses the abstract methods (*hot spots* cf. [6]) in italics (implemented in Test_System).

```
... abstract class Manager extends Initiator {
  ...
  ... void Act() {...}

  ... abstract CN_Task createCN_Task(int t)
  ... abstract CN_Task.Offer createOffer(CN_Task t)
  ... abstract CN_Message newOfferMessage(Agent a, CN_Task t)
  ... abstract int bidDelayTime()
  ... abstract CN_Message selectBid(CN_Message[] ms, int l)
  ... abstract CN_Task.Award createAward(CN_Task t)
  ... abstract CN_Message newAwardMessage(Agent a, CN_Task t)
}
```

Fig. 11. Class Manager

Figure 12 shows the actual sequencing in the Act() method of class Manager—illustrated by the comments: Prepare and send offers, Wait a while until bids have arrived, Collect received bids, Select a bid and prepare and send an award.

```
... void Act() {
  CN_Protocol cnd = (CN_Protocol) protocol;
  CN_Message m;
// ... ... ... ... ... Prepare and send offers ...
  int taskNo = allTasks++;
  for (int i = 0; i<cnd.contractorAgent.length; i++) {
    CN_Task t = createCN_Task(taskNo);
    if (t.addOffer(createOffer(t))) {
      m = newOfferMessage(cnd.contractorAgent[i], t);
      initiateProtocol(m, cnd.contractorRole[i]);
    };
  };
// ... ... ... ... ... Wait a while until bids have arrived ...
  rolePause(bidDelayTime());
// ... ... ... ... ... Collect received bids ...
  CN_Message[] ms = new CN_Message[...];
  int i = 0;
  while ((m = (CN_Message) handleMessage())!=null) {
    if (m.typeMessage(CN_Kind.BID)) {
      ms[i++] = m;
    };
  };
// ... ... ... ... ... Select a bid, prepare and send an award ...
  if ((m = selectBid(ms, i))!=null) {
    CN_Task t = m.cnTask;
    t.addAward(createAward(t));
    CN_Message mm = newAwardMessage(m.fromAgent, t);
    replyProtocol(mm, m);
  };
}
```

Fig. 12. Method Act() of Manager

Class Contractor. Figure 13 shows abstract class Contractor as an extension of Participant. Method Act() of class Contractor uses the abstract methods in italics (implemented in Test_System).

```
... abstract class Contractor extends Participant {

  ... void Act() {...}

  ... abstract CN_Task.Bid createBid(CN_Task t)
  ... abstract CN_Message newBidMessage(Agent a, CN_Task t)
  ... abstract int awardDelayTime()
  ... abstract void handleAward(CN_Message m)
}
```

Fig. 13. Class Contractor

Figure 14 shows the actual sequencing in the Act() method of class Contractor—illustrated by the comments: Wait to receive an offer, Possibly prepare and send a bid, Wait to receive an award, Possibly receive and handle the award.

```
... void Act() {
// ... ... ... ... ... Wait to receive an offer ...
  CN_Message m = (CN_Message) roleAwait();
  if (m.typeMessage(CN_Kind.OFFER)) {
// ... ... ... ... ... Possibly prepare and send a bid ...
    CN_Task t = m.cnTask;
    if (t.addBid(createBid(t))) {
      CN_Message mm = newBidMessage(m.fromAgent, t);
      replyProtocol(mm, m);
// ... ... ... ... ... Wait to receive an award ...
      rolePause(awardDelayTime());
// ... ... ... ... ... Possibly receive and handle the award ...
      if ((m = (CN_Message) handleMessage())!=null) {
        if (m.typeMessage(CN_Kind.AWARD)) {
          handleAward(m);
        };
      };
    } else return;
  };
}
```

Fig. 14. Method Act() of Contractor

Class CN_Message. Figure 15 shows CN_Message as an extension of Agent_Message where CN_Task represents the actual task to be undertaken (with respect to Offer, Bid and Award) and CN_Kind enumerates the actual message types in Contract Net.

```
... class CN_Message extends Agent_Message {
    ... CN_Message(... , CN_Task cnt, CN_Type cnk, ...) {
      ...
    }
    ...
    ... CN_Kind cnk;
    ... CN_Task cnt;
}

... class CN_Task {...}

enum CN_Kind {OFFER, BID, AWARD}
```

Fig. 15. Classes CN_Message, CN_Task and CN_Kind

6 Test System

Figure 16 shows Test_System, as an extension of Utility_System where class Test_Agent extends Utility_Agent. The abstract methods newInitiatorRole and newparticipantRole are implemented to return objects of the actual Manager and Contractor classes specialized from Manager and Contractor of Utility_Agent. Classes Manager and Contractor implement the abstract methods from Figs. 11 and 13, respectively.

```
... class Test_System extends Utility_System {

    ... class Test_Agent extends Utility_Agent {
      ... Initiator newInitiatorRole(Protocol protocol) {
        return (new Manager((CN_Protocol) protocol));
      }
      ... Participant newParticipantRole() {
        return (new Contractor());
      }
      ...
      ... class Manager extends Utility_Agent.Manager {...}
      ... class Contractor extends Utility_Agent.Contractor {...}
    }
}
```

Fig. 16. Test_System with Test_Agent

The protocol using the OFFER, BID and AWARD messages is simple and therefore the structures of the roles illustrated in Figs. 12 and 14 are simple too. But these roles would remain simple if they involved additional interaction, i.e. such as re-announcing subtasks, continued negotiations about details, etc. A Test_Agent involved in several simultaneous contract negotiations would not complicate the description but only require additional instantiations of the existing protocol.

Figure 17 is a snapshot of the dynamic flow of messages between agents. This feature is a part of the application framework, i.e. it is general although it is parameterized with the actual extension of the framework—in this case Contract Net. For each agent, i.e. for Test_Agent 2 there is a column of messages sent Messages Out: 6 and received Messages In: 6 showing total number of messages and a list of actual

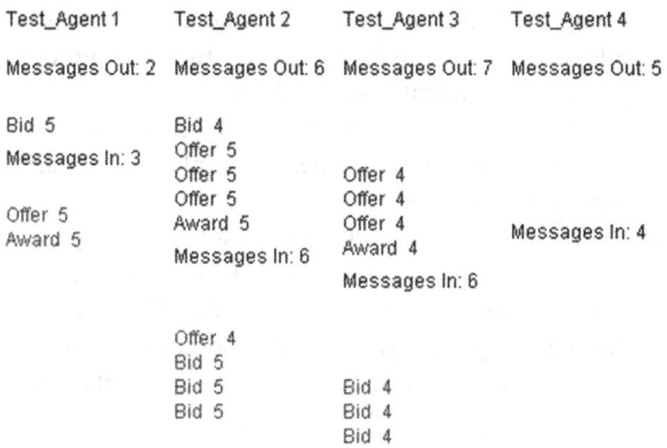

Test_Agent 1   Test_Agent 2   Test_Agent 3   Test_Agent 4

Messages Out: 2   Messages Out: 6   Messages Out: 7   Messages Out: 5

Bid 5
Messages In: 3

Offer 5
Award 5

Bid 4
Offer 5
Offer 5
Offer 5
Award 5
Messages In: 6

Offer 4
Offer 4
Offer 4
Award 4
Messages In: 6

Messages In: 4

Offer 4
Bid 5
Bid 5
Bid 5

Bid 4
Bid 4
Bid 4

Fig. 17. Flow of messages between agents (Color figure online)

messages. The actual messages are colored to indicate the status of a message, i.e. *sent*, *received*, *forwarded*, *handled* and *to be removed*. It can be seen from Fig. 17 that TEST_Agent 2 sends offer 5 that is received by TEST_Agent 1; TEST_Agent 1 replies with bid 5 that is received by TEST_Agent 2; TEST_Agent 2 replies with award 5 that is received by TEST_Agent 1. This protocol is similar to the M_1, M_2, M_3 protocol illustrated in Fig. 2.

7   Evaluation

We evaluate the proposed application framework with respect to the complexity of the resulting description of the interaction structure between agents—in terms of the Protocol and Agent_Role abstractions.

Each of the *n* agents in the Contract Net example may send an offer to the *n-1* other agents that may reply back etc.:

- Without some kind of protocol abstraction we assume each agent has one (typically reactive) role, i.e. *n* roles in total. However such a role has to manage up to *n* ongoing interactions (one of which is between up to *n* agents) each with their own state of the interaction. Without the protocol abstraction each role takes care of *n* interactions.
- With the CN_protocol abstraction each agent has a Manager role and sends an offer to *n-1* other agents each with a Contractor role, i.e. in total *n* roles. When *n* agents send an offer this becomes n^2 roles in total. However each role is simple as illustrated in Figs. 12 and 14 because each role is involved in exactly one CN_protocol, i.e. the state of the interaction is captured by the role. With the CN_protocol abstraction each role takes care of 1 interaction.

In summary the agent model and framework are simple and understandable but still expressive. By the abstractions Protocol and Agent_Role we substitute the usual complexity of describing the handling (including state and progress) of several simultaneously ongoing interactions by simple, statically structured protocols and roles.

By identifying protocol and agent roles in the Contract Net we classify the interaction and the contributions of the agents by means of CN_protocol, Manager and Contractor. However, abstraction includes not only classification but also specialization and composition: We may see CN_protocol, Manager and Contractor as a general description of the Contract Net, so that specialized versions of Contract Net can be described by specializations of each of these abstractions, e.g. CN_protocol_X, Manager_X and Contractor_X. Similarly, another more extensive protocol can be composed by using the Contract Net as a part protocol by using CN_protocol, Manager and Contractor in the description of this protocol.

Classes Protocol, Initiator and Participant together form abstractions over an interaction structure. Initiator and Participant are local to an Agent in order to have access to the local state of the Agent. Alternative solutions may be inspired from Kristensen [7] where *Association* is a central abstraction over interaction sequences and integrate activities and roles of concurrent autonomous entities.

8   Discussion

Historically, the proposed framework is motivated by and discussed during the research projects FLIP and DECIDE—however, the intention was not to construct resulting MAS software during these projects. The FLIP project [8] investigates a transportation system including moving boxes from a conveyor belt onto pallets and transporting these pallets in the high bay area of the LEGO® factory with AGVs, no human intervention and only centralized control. A toy prototype includes agents in the form of LEGOBots based on a LEGO® MindstormsTM RCX brick extended with a PDA and wireless LAN. The DECIDE project [9] includes a number of real applications: Control of a baggage handling system in a larger airport in Asia; Intelligent control of handling material with recipes in productions processes; Coordination and planning of large vehicle transports at a shipyard; Design and implementation of a very flexible packing machine. These applications illustrates that the complexity of the interaction structure between agents needs to be supported by structurally simple and expressive abstractions.

The proposed application framework has been used and subsequently revised in courses about agent oriented programming. The course includes the construction of a multi-agent system based on the application framework. The task is to design and implement the management of the evolution of a collection of animal parks. A solution is to use reactive roles to react to incoming messages concerning actual changes—and proactive roles to support buying and selling animals by negotiating with other agents. The experience includes that the complexity of the interaction structure of simple toy-like multi-agent systems is overwhelming, because the basic interaction sequence is simple but the management of several simultaneously ongoing interaction sequences is complicated.

Abstraction. The application framework is available in Java [10] and applications may be described and executed by the application framework [11]. For an agent we describe `Protocols` and `Agent_Roles` (supported by abstract classes in the application framework)—a `Protocol` describes which `Agent_Roles` of agents participate in the interaction—an `Agent_Role` describes the actual contribution of an agent to the interaction structure of the `Protocol`. `Protocols` and `Agent_Roles` are described at development time. At runtime actual instances of `Protocols` and `Agent_Roles` are created and deleted when appropriate.

`Protocol` and `Agent_Role` are abstractions, i.e. exemplification, composition and specialization are supported [12, 13]:

- *exemplification*, i.e. protocols and agent roles may be instantiated
- *composition*, i.e. whole protocols and agent roles may be described by means of part protocols and agent roles
- *specialization*, i.e. more special protocols and agent roles may be described from descriptions of more general protocols and agent roles

Qualities. Qualities for modeling time, programming time and runtime are well-known in programming languages—either for specific languages and languages in general e.g. [14–16]. However, no general framework exists for characterizing qualities of language constructs. The qualities discussed in the literature are often interlinked or overlapping—and an inherent property of qualities is, that some of these are conflicting.

Among the qualities mentioned in the literature, *abstraction* is a quality itself. The abstractions `Protocol` and `Agent_Role` do not necessarily support runtime efficiency—rather the intention of these abstractions is the support understandability by being simple and expressive. Instead of *qualities* at *runtime* we focus on the *development process*, i.e. we are concerned about qualities at *development time* (i.e. modeling and programming time). Also we do not include for example the qualities maintainability and reusability that are closely related to abstraction quality. For reasons of simplicity we focus on the following qualities:

- *Understandability:* The clarity and the sAt development time implicity of the designed models and described programs. We see simplicity and readability as aspects of understandability.
- *Efficiency:* The effort needed to develop software by using abstractions. In general, efficiency may be in conflict with understandability.
- *Flexibility:* The ability to easily change various aspects within the model or program. In general, flexibility supports both efficiency and understandability.

Exemplification. At development time *exemplification* of protocols and agent roles especially supports

- Understandability: By classifying agent interactions by protocols and agent roles we achieve some understanding and the protocols or agent roles express our understanding. As illustrated the agent interactions in the Contract Net are classified by

CN_Protocol, Manager and Contractor described as abstract classes in Utility_System and as classes in Test_System.

- Efficiency: By exemplification we save time because no redesign and programming task is necessary—the classifications by protocols and agent roles are prepared only once. As illustrated objects of CN_Protocol, Manager and Contractor are instantiated in Test_System.

Composition. At development time *composition* of protocols and agent roles especially supports

- Understandability: By having the whole protocol or the whole agent role described by the various part protocols or part agent roles the form and content of the whole protocol or whole agent role are more conceivable. As an illustration the method createBid(...) of class Contractor of Test_System may itself include several cases of the Contract Net because this Contractor itself has to initiate a number of offers in the form of subtasks to a number of subcontractors needed to complete the actual task—thus this Contractor becomes a whole Contractor agent role with a number of part Manager agent roles.
- Efficiency: The composition of a whole protocol or whole agent role from part protocols and agent roles makes the description process simple and straightforward —i.e. the simplicity from the divide-and-conquer principle. As an illustration the description process of method createBid(...) of class Contractor of Test_System as a whole Contractor agent role with a number of part Manager agent roles becomes simple and straightforward because the abstractions CN_Protocol, Manager and Contractor are available in Utility_System and are used as part protocols and agent roles.

Specialization. At development time *specialization* of protocols and agent roles especially supports

- Flexibility: Specialization of protocol and agent role is seen as structural parameterization (i.e. not parameterization by means of variables and values), i.e. at development time specialization enables flexible description of additional protocols and agent roles by parameterizing existing protocols and agent roles. As illustrated classes Protocol, Initiator and Participant in Agent_System are specialized to CN_Protocol, Manager and Contractor in Utility_System.
- Understandability: When protocols and agent roles are related by specialization, the program becomes easier to comprehend due to the underlying conceptual model. Simultaneously the model or program typically becomes smaller but more complex and thus less understandable. As illustrated the conceptual model of the Contract Net formed by CN_Protocol, Manager and Contractor in Utility_System as specializations of Protocol, Initiator and Participant in Agent_System makes the model more comprehensible, but the actual program becomes slightly more complex and less understandable.

9 Related Work

The proposed application framework is for *implementing* protocols and agent roles, i.e. for *describing* abstractions and *using* these in concrete applications. The purpose of Odell et al. [17] is *modelling* of agent interaction protocols in AUML as a set of UML idioms and extensions. In Mazouzi et al. [18] the purpose is to *specify*, *validate* and *evaluate* interaction protocols expressed as recursive colored petri nets. The purpose of Baldoni et al. [19] is to *experiment* with the enhancement of object orientation with agent-like interaction including protocol and role introduced in the powerJava extension of Java to allow session-aware interactions. In Wang et al. [20] the purpose is to load interaction protocols dynamically through role, action and message ontologies, process description with decision-making rules and a three-layer agent architecture. Dialogue games are the basis for agent interaction protocols for convincing through arguments—in Atkinson et al. [21] by formal definition of the PARMA protocol—in McBurney et al. [22] by a categorization of types of dialogue games with examples of protocols.

The use of object-oriented languages for creating frameworks with concepts from multi-agents is well known, as well as the notion of protocol, agent role, reactive and proactive agents. But the actual form of protocol, reactive and proactive roles of agents and their inclusion in the application framework is original. A protocol is between one initiator and several participants, i.e. the initiator sends a message to the participants that may send a message back to the initiator, i.e. the initiator communicate with each of the participants but the participants do not communicate together. Protocols may be organized with part-protocols to support that a participant (as part of an ongoing protocol) may be initiator of a part-protocol.

Reactive and proactive roles are related to *behaviours* in JADE [23] and *plans* in JACK [24]: In JADE the agent life-cycle is described by behaviors by extending the Behaviour class. An agent can execute several behaviors in parallel. However, behavior scheduling is not preemptive, but cooperative—and everything occurs within a single Java thread. In JACK an agent will look for the appropriate plans to handle goals and events. The plan (an abstraction above object-oriented constructs) inherits from a Plan class that implements the plan's base methods and the underlying functionality. Neither behaviors nor plans support the notion of reactive and proactive role explicitly but may be utilized to expose similar behavior. In JADE createReply() creates a new message properly setting the receivers and various fields used to control the conversation. In JACK reply(received, sendBack) sends a message back to an agent from which a previous message has been received without triggering a new plan.

JaCaMo [25, 26] includes a conceptual model for the interaction component, a programming language to specify the interaction, and how this is integrated with the organization and the environment of the multi agent system platform. The interaction is a first class abstraction and part of the platform. Protocols allow the specification, development, and execution of the interaction not considering only agents, but also the environment and the organization. The result is that the interaction is a separated component, avoiding specifying the interaction inside the code of agents or other components. 2COMM [27] (as well as 2COMM4JASON [28] and 2COMM4-JADE [29]) support the development of commitment-based interaction protocols. 2COMM is a step towards realizing a programmable communication channel by means of artifacts and its implementation relies on the JADE and CArtAgO frameworks. Commitment protocols are embodied into artifacts which are used by the interacting agents—the artifacts form the social layer of the multi-agent system and implement interaction protocols. Agents do not exchange messages directly but use the operations provided by the artifacts. The artifact explicitly provides a role that is decoupled from the interacting agent, instead of attaching it into an agent behavior or of forming agent types by atomic roles. JaCaMo and 2COMM focus on specific aspects and forms of interaction in general multi agent systems, are integrated on existing platforms, and support among others maintainability, modularity and reusability. In comparison our application framework extends the object-oriented paradigm with facilities for modeling and programming message interaction in simple multi agent systems, supports only interaction between agents, and models the interaction by experimental abstractions for protocol and agent role.

10 Summary

Typically, the description of the interaction structure between agents is complex because an agent has to organize (in order to receive messages and reply to these messages accordingly) a number of ongoing interactions with other agents. Because of the lack of support for structuring this organization, the development process is neither efficient nor flexible, and the description becomes less understandable. By introducing abstraction including exemplification, composition and specialization the description process becomes efficient and flexible as well as the resulting description becomes understandable. The development time (including modelling and programming) is supported explicitly by abstractions natural to the interaction structure and the resulting description becomes organized accordingly. Therefore, the proposed application framework with abstractions supporting protocols based on agent roles offer simple and expressive description of multi-agent interaction structures.

Acknowledgments. We thank Palle Nowack and Daniel May for inspiration and support.

References

1. Wooldridge, M.: An Introduction to Multiagent Systems, 2nd edn. Wiley (2009)
2. Booch, G.: Private communication (2007)
3. Fayad, M.E., Johnson, R.E., Schmidt D.C.: Building Application Frameworks: Object-Oriented Foundations of Framework Design. Wiley (1990)
4. Lea, D.: Concurrent Programming in Java: Design Principles and Patterns. Addison Wesley (2007)
5. Dahl, O.-J., Myhrhaug, B., Nygaard, K.: SIMULA 67 Common Base Language (Editions 1968, 1970, 1972, 1984). Norwegian Computing Center, Oslo (1968)

6. Pree, W.: Meta patterns — a means for capturing the essentials of reusable object-oriented design. In: Tokoro, M., Pareschi, R. (eds.) ECOOP 1994. LNCS, vol. 821, pp. 150–162. Springer Berlin Heidelberg, Berlin, Heidelberg (1994). doi:10.1007/BFb0052181

7. Kristensen, B.B.: Rendezvous-based collaboration between autonomous entities: centric versus associative. In: Concurrency and Computation: Practice and Experience, vol. 25, no. 3, pp. 289–308. Wiley Press (2013)

8. Jensen, L.K., Kristensen, B.B., Demazeau, Y.: FLIP: prototyping multi-robot systems. J. Robot. Auton. Syst. **53**(3, 4), 230–243 (2005)

9. Hallenborg, H.: Intelligent control of material handling systems. In: Kutz, M. (ed.) Environmentally Conscious Materials Handling. Wiley, New York (2009)

10. Arnold, K., Gosling, J.: The JAVA Programming Language. Addison Wesley, New York (1999)

11. https://www.dropbox.com/sh/pq6mj8vz17kbkhp/AABE33JRC53F4weqyN0D1Jqta?dl=0

12. Kristensen, B.B., Østerbye, K.: Conceptual Modeling and Programming Languages. SIGPLAN Notices, vol. 29, No.9 (1994)

13. Kristensen, B.B., Madsen, O.L., Møller-Pedersen, B.: The when, why and why not of the BETA programming language. In: Proceedings of the Third ACM SIGPLAN Conference on History of Programming Languages, San Diego, California (2007)

14. MacLennan, B.J.: Principles of Programming Languages Design, Evaluation, and Implementation, 3rd edn. Oxford University Press, New York (1999)

15. Liskov, B., Guttag, J.: Program Development in Java: Abstraction, Specification and Object-Oriented Design. Addison-Wesley, Boston (2000)

16. Watt, D.A.: Programming Language Design Concepts. Wiley, Chichester (2004)

17. Odell, J.J., Parunak, H., Bauer, B.: Representing agent interaction protocols in UML. In: Ciancarini, P., Wooldridge, M.J. (eds.) AOSE 2000. LNCS, vol. 1957, pp. 121–140. Springer, Heidelberg (2001). doi:10.1007/3-540-44564-1_8

18. Mazouzi, H., El Fallah Seghrouchni, A., Haddad, S.: Open protocol design for complex interactions in multi-agent systems. In: Autonomous Agents and Multi-Agent Systems, pp. 517–526 (2002)

19. Baldoni, M., Boella, G., Van der Torre, L.: Importing agent-like interaction in object orientation. In: Proceedings of the 7th WOA Workshop, From Objects to Agents, pp. 158–165 (2006)

20. Wang, M., Shi, Z., Jiao, W.: Dynamic interaction protocol load in multi-agent system collaboration. In: Lukose, D., Shi, Z. (eds.) PRIMA 2005. LNCS (LNAI), vol. 4078, pp. 103–113. Springer, Heidelberg (2009). doi:10.1007/978-3-642-03339-1_9

21. Atkinson, K., Bench-Capon, T., McBurney, P.: A dialogue game protocol for multi-agent argument over proposals for action. Auton. Agent. Multi-Agent Syst. **11**(2), 153–171 (2005)

22. McBurney, P., Parsons, S.: Dialogue games in multi-agent systems. Informal Logic **22**(3), 257–274 (2002)

23. Bellifemine, F., Caire, G., Greenwood, D.: Developing Multi-Agent Systems with JADE. Wiley, Chichester (2008)

24. JACK Intelligent Agents—Agent Manual. JACK Intelligent Agents—Agent Practicals. http://www.agent-software.com/products/jack/documentation_and_instructi/jack_documentation.html

25. Zatelli, M.R., Hübner, J.F.: The interaction as an integration component for the JaCaMo platform. In: Dalpiaz, F., Dix, J., Riemsdijk, M.B. (eds.) EMAS 2014. LNCS (LNAI), vol. 8758, pp. 431–450. Springer, Heidelberg (2014). doi:10.1007/978-3-319-14484-9_22

26. Boissier, O., Bordini, R.H., Hübner, J.F., Ricci, A., Santi, A.: Multi-agent oriented programming with JaCaMo. Sci. of Comp. Prog. **78**(6), 747–761 (2013)

27. Baldoni, M., Baroglio, C., Capuzzimati 2COMM: a commitment-based MAS architecture. In: 2nd International Workshop on Engineering Multi-agent Systems (EMAS@AAMAS), pp. 38–57 (2013)
28. Baldoni, M., Baroglio, C., Capuzzimati, F.: A commitment-based infrastructure for programming socio-technical systems. ACM Trans. Internet Techn. 14(4), 23:1–23:23 (2014)
29. Baldoni, M., Baroglio, C., Capuzzimati, F.: Social relationships for designing agent interaction in JADE. In: Santoro, C., Bergenti, F. (eds.) Proceedings of 15th Workshop from Objects to Agents, WOA 2014, vol. 1260, Italy (2014)

A Namespace Approach for Modularity in BDI Programming Languages

Gustavo Ortiz-Hernández[1,2]([✉]), Jomi Fred Hübner[3], Rafael H. Bordini[4],
Alejandro Guerra-Hernández[2], Guillermo J. Hoyos-Rivera[2],
and Nicandro Cruz-Ramírez[2]

[1] Centro de Investigaciones en Inteligencia Artificial - UV, Xalapa, Mexico
gusorh@gmail.com
[2] Institute Henri Fayol - MINES, Saint-Étienne, France
[3] Federal University of Santa Catarina, Florianópolis, SC, Brazil
[4] FACIN-PUCRS, Porto Alegre, RS, Brazil

Abstract. In this paper we propose a model for designing Belief-Desire-Intention (BDI) agents under the principles of modularity. We aim to encapsulate agent functionalities expressed as BDI abstractions into independent, reusable and easier to maintain units of code, which agents can dynamically load. The general idea of our approach is to exploit the notion of *namespace* to organize components such as beliefs, plans and goals. This approach allowed us to address the name-collision problem, providing interface and information hiding features for modules. Although the proposal is suitable for agent-oriented programming languages in general, we present concrete examples in Jason.

Keywords: Agent-oriented programming · Modularity · Namespace

1 Introduction

In the last decades, several programming paradigms have arisen, often presented as an evolution of their predecessors, and with the main purpose of abstracting more complex and larger systems in a more natural and simpler way. Particularly, the Agent-Oriented-Programming (AOP) paradigm has been promoted as a suitable option to deal with the challenges arising when developing modern systems. This paradigm offers high-level abstractions which facilitate the design of large-scale and complex software systems, and also allows software engineers to employ a suite of well-known strategies for dealing with complexity, i.e., decomposition, abstraction and hierarchy.

These strategies are usually applied at the Multi-Agent-System (MAS) level [8,15,19]. However, even a single agent is intrinsically a complex system, hence its design and development should consider the above mentioned strategies. Regarding this, the principle of *modularity* applied to individual agent development can significantly improve and facilitate the construction of agents.

© Springer International Publishing AG 2016
M. Baldoni et al. (Eds.): EMAS 2016, LNAI 10093, pp. 117–135, 2016.
DOI: 10.1007/978-3-319-50983-9_7

In this paper, we present an approach for programming agents following the principle of modularity, i.e., to develop agent programs into separate, independent, reusable and easier to maintain units of code. In order to support modularity, we identify three major issues to be addressed: (i) a mechanism to avoid name-collision, (ii) fulfilling the information hiding principle, and (iii) providing module interfaces.

Our contribution is to address these issues by simply introducing the notion of *namespace* in the AOP paradigm. In the context of BDI languages, which is the focus of this paper, the novelty of our approach is that it offers a syntactic level solution, independent of the operational semantics of some language in particular, which simplifies its implementation.

The rest of this paper is organized as follows: related and previous work are presented in Sect. 2; our proposal is described in Sect. 3; we explain details of implementation in Sect. 4 and offer an example in Sect. 5; an evaluation is presented in Sect. 6; finally, we discuss and conclude in Sects. 7 and 8 respectively.

2   Related Work

There exist much work supporting and implementing the idea of modularity in BDI languages. An approach presented by Busetta et al. [6] consists in encapsulating beliefs, plans and goals that functionally belong together in a common scope called capability. The programmer can specify a set of scoping rules to say which elements are accessible to other capabilities. An implementation is developed for JACK [17]. Further, Braubach et al. [3] extend the capability concept to fullfill the information hiding principle by ensuring that all elements in a capability are part of exactly one capability and remain hidden from outside, guaranteeing that the information hiding principle is not violated. An implementation for JADEX [4] is provided. Both approaches propose an explicit import/export mechanism for defining the interface.

The modules proposed by Dastani and Steunebrink [12] are conceived as separate mental states. This modules are instantiated, updated, executed and tested using a set of predefined operations. Executing a module means that the agent starts reasoning in a particular mental state until a predefined condition holds. This approach is extended by Cap et al. [7], by introducing the notion of sharing scopes to mainly enhance the interface. Shared scopes allow modules posting events, so that these are visible to other modules sharing the same scope. These ideas are conceived in the context of 2APL [10] and an implementation is described in [11].

Also following the notion of capability, Madden and Logan [21] propose a modularity approach based on XML's strategy of namespaces [5], such that each module is considered as a separate and unique namespace identified by an URI. They propose to handle a local belief-base, local goal-base and local events-queue for each module, and then to specify, by means of an export/import statement, which beliefs, goals and events are visible to other modules. In this system, there is only one instance of each module, i.e., references to the exported part of the module are shared between all other modules that import it. These ideas are supported by the Jason+ language, implemented by Logan and Kiss [9].

Another work tackling the name-collision issue is presented by Ortiz et al. [23]. They use annotations to label beliefs, plans and events with a source according to the module to which they belong. In this approach, modules are composed by a set of beliefs, plans and a list of exported and imported elements. Both imported and exported elements are added to a unique common scope. An implementation of this approach is developed as a library that extends Jason.

In Hindriks [16], a notion of module inspired by what they call policy-based intentions is proposed for GOAL. A module is designated with a mental state condition, and when that condition is satisfied, the module becomes the agent focus of execution, temporarily dismissing any other goal. They focus on isolating goals/events to avoid the pursuit of contradictory goals.

In Riemsdijk et al. [26], modules are associated with a specific goal and they are executed only to achieve the goal for which they are intended to be used. In this approach, every goal is dispatched to a specific module. Then all plans in the module are executed one-by-one in the pursuit of such goal until it has been achieved, or every plan has been tried. This proposal is presented in the context of 3APL [13].

A comparative overview of these approaches is given in Table 1. All solutions tackle the name-collision problem, providing a mechanism to scope the visibility of goal/events to a particular set of elements, e.g., plans. They also offer different approaches for providing the interface of modules. However, not all of them fulfill the information hiding principle.

It is also worth mentioning that all those approaches propose some particular operational semantics tied to the AOP language in which they have been conceived and implemented. The proposal that we present in this paper provides a mechanism to address those issues independently of the operational semantics.

3   Modules and Namespaces

A *module* is as a set of beliefs, goals and plans, as a usual agent program, and every agent has one initial module (its initial program) into which other modules can possibly be loaded. We refer to the beliefs, plans and goals within a module as the *module components* (cf. Fig. 1).

Modularity is supported through the simple concept of *namespace*, defined as an abstract container created to hold a logical grouping of components. All components can be prefixed with an explicit namespace reference. We write `zoo::color(seal,blue)` to indicate that the belief `color(seal,blue)` is associated with the namespace identified by `zoo`. Furthermore, note that the belief `zoo::color(seal,blue)` is not the same belief as `office::color(seal,blue)` since they are in different namespaces.

Namespaces are either *global* or *local*. A global namespace can be used by any module; more precisely, the components associated with a global namespace

Table 1. The columns represent existing features in the surveyed approaches, in respect to the issues mentioned in Sect. 1. The abbreviations stand for: (IL) implementing language; (IS) the approach is independent of the language's operational semantics; (IH) fulfills the information hiding principle; (NC) provides a mechanism to deal with the name-collision issue. The last column refers to the general notion used to provide an interface.

Approach	IL	IS	IH	NC	Interface's mechanism
Busetta et al. [6]	JACK	✗	✓	✓	Explicit import/export
Braubach et al. [3]	JADEX	✗	✓	✓	Explicit import/export
Dastani and Steunebrink [12]	2APL	✗	✗	✓	Set of predefined operations
Cap et al. [7]	2APL	✗	✗	✓	Sharing scopes
Madden and Logan [21]	Jason+	✗	✓	✓	Explicit import/export
Hindriks [16]	GOAL	✗	✗	✓	Mental-state condition
Riemsdijk et al. [26]	3APL	✗	✗	✓	Goal dispatching
Ortiz et al. [23]	Jason	✗	✗	✓	Unique-common scope
Our proposal	Jason	✓	✓	✓	Global namespaces

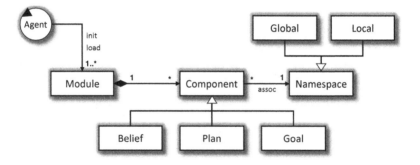

Fig. 1. Proposed model for modularity.

can be consulted and changed by any module. A local namespace can be used only by the module that has defined the namespace.

We introduce the notion of *abstract namespace* of a module to denote a namespace whose name is undefined at design-time, and will be defined at run-time when the module is loaded. To indicate that a component is in a module's abstract namespace, the prefix is simply omitted, e.g., a belief written as taste(candy,good) is in an abstract namespace and its actual namespace will be defined when the module is loaded.

The module loading process involves associating every component in the abstract namespace of the module with a concrete namespace, and then simply incorporating the module components into the agent that loaded the module. Therefore, a concrete namespace must be specified at loading time to replace the module's abstract namespace.

When a module (the loader) loads another module (the loaded), they interact in two directions: the loader *imports* the loaded module components associated with global namespaces and the loader *extends* the functionality of the module by placing components in those namespaces. Figure 2 illustrates the interaction when a module A loads some module B.

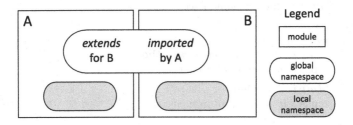

Fig. 2. The interaction between modules.

A module is formally defined as a tuple:

$$mod = \langle bs, ps, gs \rangle$$

where $bs = \{b_1, \ldots, b_n\}$ is a set of beliefs, $ps = \{p_1, \ldots, p_n\}$ is a set of plans, and $gs = \{g_1, \ldots, g_n\}$ a set of goals. As shown in Fig. 1, each of these components is associated with a namespace. We use subscripts to denote the elements of a module, e.g., mod_{bs} stands for the beliefs included in module mod.

3.1 Syntax

As in many programming languages, we use identifiers to refer to the module components, i.e., its beliefs, plans and goals. Since the syntactic identifiers depend on the programming language and our proposal is intended to be language independent, we propose to extend the syntax of identifiers allowing a namespace prefix:

$$\langle id \rangle ::= [\ \langle nid \rangle ::] \langle natid \rangle$$

where *nid* is a namespace identifier and *natid* is used to denote the native identifiers of some AOP language. For example, a belief formula like count(0), whose identifier is count, can be written ns2::count(0) to associate the belief with namespace ns2.

We use a syntactical name-mangling technique[1] to associate every component in the abstract namespace of a particular module to a concrete namespace and to bring support for local namespaces. Restriction access to local namespaces is

---

[1] A technique used in programming languages, which consists in attaching additional information to an identifier, typically used to solve name conflicts.

Algorithm 1. The *mangling(src, nid)* function associates each component in the abstract namespace of a module program *src* with a concrete namespace *nid* and renames local namespaces with an internally generated identifier.

---

1 **begin**
    Input: *src* : a module program
    Input: *nid* : a concrete namespace
2   *mod* = parse(src)
3   **foreach** *id* ∈ *ids(mod)* **do**
4   **if** *ns(id) is an abstract namespace* **then**
5   replace *id* by *nid::id* in *mod*
6   **if** *ns(id) is local* **then**
7   replace *id* by *#nid::id* in *mod*
8   **return** *mod*

---

implemented by replacing every local namespace identifier in the components of a particular module by an internally created identifier. This is generated in such a way that it is not a valid identifier according to the grammar of the native language. For instance, if `ns2` is the identifier of a local namespace, the mangling function renames `ns2::color(box,blue)` to `#ns2::color(box,blue)`, where `#ns2` is an invalid identifier and thus no developer can write a program that accesses this belief. We use *#nid* to denote a mapping from *nid* to an internally generated identifier, unique in the module program where it is being used. The mangling function is described in Algorithm 1. To avoid cluttering the notation, we define an auxiliary function $ids(mod) = \{id_1, \ldots id_n\}$ that gets all identifiers *id* that are in the components *bs*, *ps*, and *gs* of module *mod* and function *ns(id)* gives the namespace of identifier *id*.

3.2 Loading Modules

We represent an agent state as a tuple $ag = \langle B, P, G, \ldots \rangle$, where $B = \{b_1, \ldots, b_n\}$ stands for the agent's belief base, $P = \{p_1, \ldots, p_n\}$ a plan library and $G = \{g_1, \ldots, g_n\}$ the goals of the agent.[2] All identifiers used in the beliefs, plans and goals are prefixed with a proper namespace. The dots symbol (...) is used in the agent tuple to denote the existence of other components proper of the agent's mental state (such as intentions, mail box, etc.) that are not relevant for the purpose of presenting our proposal.

---

[2] Sometimes when referring to intentional agents, a distinction between desires and intentions is highlighted to focus on the commitment of the agent towards some goal. In the agent state we do not take commitment into consideration; a goal $g \in G$ can be either a desire or an intention. However, a goal $g \in gs$ in some module is considered as an initial goal.

When an agent loads a module, it incorporates the module components, i.e., beliefs, plans and goals, into its own belief base, plan library and goals, respectively. A namespace must be specified at loading time to replace the module's abstract namespace with a concrete namespace. A transition rule (**Load**) presents the dynamics of loading a module in a particular namespace. The condition (upper part) stands for the action $load(src, nid)$ that takes a module program src and a namespace nid as parameters. This rule executes the mangling function on the module and incorporates the module components into the agent's current state, already associated with a proper namespace identifier.

$$(\textbf{Load}) \frac{load(src, nid)}{\langle B, P, G, \ldots \rangle \rightarrow \langle B', P', G', \ldots \rangle}$$

$$\text{where:} \quad \begin{aligned} mod &= mangling(src, nid) \\ B' &= B \cup mod_{bs} \\ P' &= P \cup mod_{ps} \\ G' &= G \cup mod_{gs} \end{aligned}$$

The agent's *initial module* is loaded in what we call the *default namespace*. This is a predefined global namespace whose identifier is `default`. The initial module program determines the initial belief base, plan library and goals of the agent. We use src_0 to denote the initial module program. The next transition rule (**Init**) describes the agent's initialization.

$$(\textbf{Init}) \frac{src_0}{\langle B, P, G, \ldots \rangle \rightarrow \langle B', P', G', \ldots \rangle}$$

$$\text{where:} \quad \begin{aligned} mod &= mangling(src_0, \texttt{default}) \\ B' &= mod_{bs} \\ P' &= mod_{ps} \\ G' &= mod_{gs} \end{aligned}$$

4   Implementation

We present the implementation of our proposal in Jason [2], a Java-based interpreter for an extended version of AgentSpeak(L) [24]. An agent program in Jason is defined as a set of initial beliefs bs, a set of initial goals gs and a set of plans ps, where each $b \in bs$ is an atomic grounded formula (initial beliefs may also be represented as Prolog style rules). Every plan $p \in ps$ has the form $te : ctx \leftarrow body$, where te stands for a triggering event defining the event that the plan is useful for handling. A plan is considered relevant for execution when an event which matches its trigger element occurs, and applicable when the condition ctx holds. The element $body$ is a finite sequence of actions, goals and belief updates. Actions in Jason can be external or internal. An external action changes the environment, unlike an internal action which is executed internally to the agent. Jason allows the developer to extend the parsing of source code by implementing user-customized directives.

The basic syntactical construct of a Jason program is the atomic formula, which as in logic programming has the form $p(t_1, \ldots, t_n)$, where p is the functor, and each t_i denotes a term that can be either a number, list, string, variable, or a structure that has the same format of a positive literal. We say then that each p in a Jason program is a Jason identifier. For instance, a plan such as:

```
+!go(home) : forecast(sunny) ← walk_to(0,0).
```

contains the following identifiers: `go`, `home`, `forecast`, `sunny` and `walk_to`.

We have extended the syntax of Jason identifiers to allow a namespace prefix.[3] Since Jason identifiers are used for beliefs and goals, by prefixing them with a namespace these components are *scoped* within a particular namespace.[4] So, a plan written as:

```
+!ns1::go(home) : ns2::forecast(sunny) ← +b.
```

will consider only an achievement-goal addition event `+!go(home)` in namespace `ns1`, and a belief `forecast(sunny)` in namespace `ns2`; beliefs and goals in other namespaces are thus not relevant for this plan. Terms within a literal are not changed when a module is loaded. However, terms can be explicitly prefixed with a namespace. A term prefixed with `::` is in the abstract namespace (e.g. in `forecast(::sunny)` the term sunny is associated with the abstract namespace).

Jason keywords (e.g., `source`, `atomic`, `self`, `tell`, ...), strings and numbers are handled as constants and are not associated with namespaces.

The Jason internal action `.include` and parsing directive `include` were extended with a second parameter to implement the dynamics of loading a module as presented in Sect. 3.2. The first argument is the file with the module's source code and the second argument the global namespace used to replace the abstract namespace. A parsing directive `namespace/2` is provided to define the type of the namespace (local or global) and as a syntactic sugar to facilitate the namespace association of components, so that the identifiers enclosed by this directive will be associated with the specified namespace.

The beliefs related to perception are placed in the default namespace, and thus also the corresponding events (external events generated from perception). This solution keeps backward compatibility with previous source code, since the initial module is loaded in the default namespace and the previous version of Jason does not have modules other than the initial one.

5   Example

This section illustrates our proposal for modules in more detail showing an implementation of the Contract Net Protocol (CNP) [25]. The modules `initiator`

---

[3] For the unification algorithm used by Jason, we can simply consider the namespace prefix as being part of the predicate symbol of the literal.

[4] Plans are also scoped within a namespace given that their triggering events are based on beliefs or goals.

and **participant** (Codes 5 and 6) encapsulate the functionality to start and participate in a CNP, respectively. The multi-agent system is composed of the initiator agents **bob** and **alice**, whose initial module code is presented in codes 1 and 2 respectively; and the participant **company A** and **company B** (Codes 3 and 4). In this implementation, every CNP instance takes place in a different namespace to isolate the beliefs and events of each negotiation.

Agent **bob** statically loads the module initiator twice (lines 1–2) using the directive **include/2**. This agent starts two CNP's for tasks **build(park)** and **build(bridge)** (initial goals in lines 4–5) in namespaces **hall** and **comm**. Each goal is handled by the module instance loaded in the same namespace where the goal is posted.

```
1  {include("initiator.asl",hall)}
2  {include("initiator.asl",comm)}
3
4  !hall::startCNP(build(park)).
5  !comm::startCNP(build(bridge)).
6
7
8
9
10
11
12
```

Code 1. bob.asl

```
1   !start([fix(tv),fix(pc),fix(oven)]).
2
3   +!start([]).
4   +!start([fix(T)|R])
5     <- .include("initiator.asl",T);
6        .add_plan(
7          {+T::winner(W)<-
8            .print("Winner to fix",T,"is",W)
9          });
10       // sub-goal with new focus
11       !!T::startCNP(fix(T));
12       !start(R).
```

Code 2. alice.asl

Agent **alice** starts multiple CNP's. It uses the internal action **.include/2** for dynamically loading the module **initiator**. It starts one CNP for each task in a given list of tasks (line 5). Agent alice *extends* the functionality provided by the module initiator to print in the console the winner as soon as it is known. Namely, it adds one plan to the same namespace where the module is loaded (lines 6–9).

Agent **company A** participates in all CNPs. It loads the module **participant** in every namespace where it listen that a CNP has started (note that the namespace in line 2 of code 3 is a variable). The agent customizes the module by adding beliefs in the same namespace where the module is loaded (lines 3–4). The module uses these beliefs to decide what tasks can be accepted and how much to bid (cf. lines 6–7 of Code 6).

Agent **company B** plays participant only for CNPs started by agent **bob**, and taking place in namespaces **hall** or **comm**. When a CNP starts under these conditions, it loads the module **participant** in the corresponding namespace. The beliefs in lines 8–9 and the plan added in lines 14–19 extend the functionality of the module by setting the strategy for bidding and accepting tasks. This company only accepts tasks for building and its bid depends on the namespace in which the CNP is being carried on. Directive **namespace/2** in line 1 defines the local namespace **supp**. This namespace encapsulates the beliefs used to estimate the final price of tasks (lines 2–5), so that they are inaccessible to other modules.

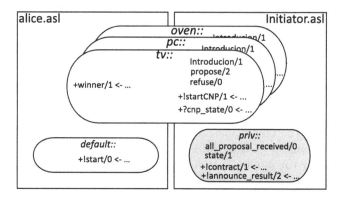

Fig. 3. The namespaces of agent alice during its execution.

The `initiator` module provides functionality to start a CNP. It starts with a forward declaration of the local namespace `priv` in line 1. The namespace of `startCNP` (line 11) is abstract and a concrete namespace is given when the module is loaded (cf. lines 1–2 and 5 of Codes 1 and 2, respectively). Because the namespace given to `startCNP` is global (as defined by the loader), this module is *exporting* the plan @p1. The identifiers without an explicit namespace between lines 30 and 55 will be placed in the local namespace `priv`. This is used to encapsulate the module's internal functionality, so that the plans to carry out contracts and announcements are only accessible from within this module (as illustrated in the line 23). Similarly, the beliefs added to memorize the current state of the CNP and the rule in lines 4–8 are private and will not interfere or clash with any other belief of the agent. However, a loader module can retrieve the current state of the CNP by means of plans @p2 and @p3. Figure 3 illustrates

```
1 +N::cnpStarted[source(A)]
2  <- .include("participant.asl", N);
3     +N::price(_,(3*math.random)+10);
4     +N::acceptable(fix(_));
5     !N::joinCNP[source(A)].
6
7
8
9
10
11
12
13
14
15
16
17
18
19
20
```

Code 3. company A.asl

```
1 {begin namespace(supp,local)}
2     price(bridge,300).
3     price(park,150).
4     gain(hall,1.5).
5     gain(comm,0.8).
6 {end}
7
8 hall::acceptable(build(_)).
9 comm::acceptable(build(_)).
10
11 +N::cnpStarted[source(bob)]
12 : .member(N,[hall,comm])
13 <- .include("participant.asl",N);
14    .add_plan({
15       +?N::price(build(T),P)
16        : supp::gain(N,G)
17        <- ?supp::price(T,M);
18           P=M*(1+G)
19    });
20    !N::joinCNP[source(bob)].
```

Code 4. company B.asl

the relation (imports and extends) between the modules `alice` and `initiator` using the same notation of Fig. 2.

```
1  {namespace(priv,local)} //Forward definition
2
3  // character :: forces a term to be considered in the abstract namespace
4  priv::all_proposals_received
5    :- .count(::introduction(participant)[source(_)],NP) &
6       .count(::propose(_)[source(_)], NO) &
7       .count(::refuse[source(_)], NR) &
8       NP = NO + NR. // participants = proposals + refusals
9
10 // starts a CNP
11 @p1 +!startCNP(Task)
12   <- .broadcast(tell, ::cnpStarted); // tell everyone a CNP has started
13      // this_ns is a reference to the namespace where this module is loaded
14      // in this example is the namespace where the CNP is being performed
15      .print("Waiting participants for task ",Task," in ",this_ns,"...");
16      .wait(3000); // wait participants introduction
17      +priv::state(propose); // remember the state of the CNP
18      .findall(A, ::introduction(participant)[source(A)], LP);
19      .print("Sending CFP for ",Task," to ",LP);
20      .send(LP,tell, ::cfp(Task)); //send call for proposals to participants
21      // wait until all proposals are received for a maximum 15secs
22      .wait( priv::all_proposals_received, 15000,_);
23      !priv::contract(this_ns).
24
25 // to let the agent to query the current state of the CNP
26 @p2 +?cnp_state(S) <- ?priv::state(S). @p3
27 +?cnp_state(none).
28
29 {begin namespace(priv)}
30    //.intend(g) is true if the agent is currently intending !g
31    +!contract(Ns) : state(propose) & not .intend(::contract(_))
32      <- -+state(contract); // updates the state of CNP
33         .findall(offer(Price,A), Ns::propose(Price)[source(A)], L);
34         .print("Offers in CNP taking place in ",Ns," are ",L);
35         L \== []; // constraint the plan execution to at least one offer
36         .min(L,offer(WOf,WAg)); // sort offers, the first is the best
37         +Ns::winner(WAg);
38         !announce_result(Ns,L);
39         -+state(finished).
40
41    // nothing todo, the current phase is not propose
42    +!contract(_).
43    -!contract(Ns)
44      <- .print("CNP taking place in ",Ns," has failed! None proposals");
45         -+state(finished).
46
47    +!announce_result(_,[]).
48    // announce to the winner
49    +!announce_result(Ns,[offer(_,Ag)|T]) : Ns::winner(Ag)
50      <- .send(Ag,tell, Ns::accept_proposal); // notify the winner
51         !announce_result(Ns,T).
52    // announce to others
53    +!announce_result(Ns,[offer(_,Ag)|T])
54      <- .send(Ag,tell, Ns::reject_proposal);
55         !announce_result(Ns,T).
56 {end}
```

Code 5. initiator.asl

The **participant** module has a plan to join a CNP by sending an introduction message to the agent playing initiator in the corresponding namespace. When a call for proposals is received, an offer is sent back only if the task is supposed to be accepted, otherwise the agent replies with a refuse message (lines

6–13). The accepted tasks and the amount to bid are not provided in the module (lines 6, 7 and 13). They are meant to be defined by a loader module that can extend every instance of this module to specify both tasks to be accepted and the strategy for bidding (e.g. as in modules company A and company B).

```
1  // participating in CNP
2  +!joinCNP[source(A)]
3    <- .send(A,tell, ::introduction(participant)).
4
5  // Answer to Call For Proposal
6  +cfp(Task)[source(A)] : acceptable(Task)
7    <- ?price(Task,Price);
8       .send(A,tell, ::propose(Price));
9       +participating(Task).
10
11 +cfp(Task)[source(A)] : not acceptable(Task)
12   <- .send(A,tell, ::refuse);
13      .println("Refusing proposal for task ", Task, " from Agent ", A).
14
15 // Answer to My Proposal
16 +accept_proposal : participating(Task)
17   <- .print("My proposal in ",this_ns," for task ", Task," won!").
18      // do the task and report to initiator
19 +reject_proposal : participating(Task)
20   <- .print("I lost CNP in ",this_ns," for task ",Task,".").
```

Code 6. participant.asl

6   Evaluation

We developed a non-modular version of the CNP to compare with the version presented in Sect. 5. Then, we performed five extensions to both versions. The first consists in modifying the vocabulary used by agents for communication. The second modifies the protocol so that every agent specifies the limit of CNP's in which it is able to participate simultaneously. In the third, initiator agents set a deadline for the call for proposals. The fourth adds one more agent playing initiator and four participants with their own acceptable tasks and strategy to bid. Finally, in the fifth only acceptable proposals are announced.

The comparison among the versions is shown in Table 2. The abbreviations stand for: (num) extension number; (ags) number of agents; (I) number of agents playing initiator; (P) number of agents playing participant; (eds) the number of files edited; (m) modular version, i.e., developed using our approach; (n) non-modular version; (adds) blocks of code added; (dels) blocks of code deleted; (chgs) changes in a line of code. The size of the implementation was calculated after compressing the source files with a zip utility. The initial size is given in bytes, then a percentage representing the increment is given. The extensions are progressive and each is compared against the previous.

For instance, to accomplish extension 2 of the modular version (starting from extension 1), we added six blocks of code and changed two lines across a total of four files, which increased the size of the system programs in 8.2% (i.e., 190 and 195 more bytes than initial implementation and extension 1, respectively) when compared with its previous extension. To extend the corresponding non-modular version, three files were edited to add twelve blocks of code and perform six changes in different lines, increasing the program size in 7% (i.e., 224 and 199 more bytes than initial implementation and extension 1, respectively). The number of agents remained the same in both versions. Total row summarizes the updates and the increase along all extensions of the system. If the same file had to be edited during two different editions it is counted twice.

Table 2. Comparison of the CNP across a series of extensions.

num	Extension	ags		eds		Size		Updates					
								adds		dels		chgs	
		I	P	m	n	m	n	m	n	m	n	m	n
	Initial implementation	2	3	-	-	2359	2864	-	-	-	-	-	-
1	Update communication vocabulary	2	3	2	5	−0.5%	0.8%	0	0	0	0	15	37
2	Participants set a limit of CNP's	2	3	4	3	8.2%	7.0%	6	12	0	0	2	6
3	Initiators set a deadline	2	3	3	2	2.1%	1.5%	3	4	0	0	1	2
4	Add more participants	3	7	5	5	50.6%	85.9%	48	126	0	0	0	0
5	Participants are not notified if lose	3	7	2	10	−1.3%	−6.6%	0	0	2	10	0	0
	Total	-	-	16	25	59.1%	88.6%	57	142	2	10	18	45

The results show that the modular version required a total of 77 updates (57 additions, 2 deletions and 18 changes) against the non-modular for which 197 updates were necessary. In this particular case study we are reducing the maintainability effort by 60% (120 updates less). We can conclude that a project developed using our approach is easier to maintain.

This results can be analyzed in terms of the Don't repeat yourself (DRY) principle.[5] Our proposal enforces this principle since it represents a mechanism to avoid the repetition of code in several parts of the system. In contrast to the non-modular version, where every component implementing the functionality of the protocol is repeated in the program of each agent, the higher the number of participant agents (interested in different tasks and having distinct bidding strategies) the greater the count of repetition occurrences. For instance, if some change is performed in the protocol, even as simple as the way in which participants introduce themselves, the change have to be propagated to the source code of every agent participating in the CNP's.

We made some initial effort in comparing our proposal with the usual `include` directive in previous releases of Jason. Due to the chosen metrics and example, the difference appeared negligible. In future work we will consider other metrics and examples where the difference to a version with the old include directive might be more significant. In any case, it should be emphasized that clearly the old directive does not solve the problem of name collision nor supports information hiding. For instance, if an agent `tom` already uses `price/2` (e.g., to record

---

[5] A principle of software development with the purpose of reducing the repetition of information [18], so that a modification of any single element of a system does not require a change in other logically unrelated elements.

the prices for supplies), when it includes the source file implementing the CNP (using an include without support for namespaces), since the belief `price/2` is also used by the CNP implementation to determine the bids, a name-collision arises and the resulting behavior is unexpected.[6] For solving this, it is necessary either to change the name of the belief used by `tom` to record the prices of supplies, or that one used in the CNP implementation. Note that the latter alternative implies updating every agent using the source file implementing the CNP.

The following section overviews how this proposal for modules addresses the issues mentioned in Sect. 1; and highlight some of its properties, as well as the major differences of our approach over related work mentioned in Sect. 2.

7   Discussion

The notion of namespaces adapted to the context of BDI-AOP languages is suitable to address the main issues related to modularity. For instance, the name-clashing problem is tackled by associating each component to a unique namespace, enabling the programmer to write qualified names for disambiguating references to components.

The interface is provided through the concept of global namespace, which supports both importing components and extending the functionality of modules. The notion of abstract namespace allows dynamic association of module components to namespaces, thus the same module can be loaded several times in different namespaces and also multiple modules can be loaded into the same namespace to compose a more complex solution. The local namespaces permit programmers to encapsulate components which facilitates independent development of modules. Moreover, loading modules at runtime can be seen as dynamic updating, i.e., the acquisition of new capabilities without stopping its execution.

The main difference of our approach resides in the strategy adopted to achieve modularity. On the one hand, the strategy adopted in this paper consists in logically organizing component names in the agent's mental state, by attaching additional information to their identifiers. On the other hand, approaches mentioned in Sect. 2, in general, are based in mechanisms for dealing with multiple mental states inside the agent, in which modules are active components of the operational semantics of the language, i.e., new transition rules are needed for handling multiple belief bases, plan libraries and/or event queues in the same reasoning cycle. The latter strategy leads to solutions that are more difficult to implement, in contrast to ours, which brings a syntactic level solution, so that it can be implemented in several BDI languages by simply extending their parsers.

---

[6] This is also reported by Madden and Logan [21] from the experience of using the usual `include` directive available in previous releases of Jason for the development of a large-scale multi-agent system [20].

7.1   Module Relationships

Next, we discuss how our approach is suited to construct association, composition and generalization relationships between modules as defined and analyzed for capabilities by I. Nunes in [22], as well as some principles from Object-Oriented programming.[7]

Association. There exists an association between a *loader* module and a *loaded* module when the execution of at least one plan of the loader requires a goal, whose plan to achieve it, is part of the loaded module. According to [22], association promotes high cohesion by allowing to modularize functionality that addresses different concerns into separate modules.

An example of association is illustrated by Codes 7 and 8. The module **one** loads module **A** and executes one of its plans. The module is loaded using a local namespace to avoid breaking the information hiding principle. In this relationship **A** is not aware of **one**.

```
1 {namespace(ia,local)}
2
3 +!do <- .include("A.asl",ia);
4       !ia::inc(2).
```
Code 7. one.asl

```
1 count(0).
2
3 +!inc(S) : count(X)
4    <- -+count(X+S).
```
Code 8. A.asl

Composition. It is a stronger relationship than association. As stated in [22] there exist situations in which the *loaded* module uses components of the *loader* module. This increases the coupling between modules, but allows to model the notion of containment ensuring the information hiding. We missed this type of relationship in our implementation, because we stand for passing information as arguments, when sharing information from *loader* to *loaded* is necessary. In this way, the information hiding principle is not broken and the coupling is reduced.

However, it is possible to model the composition relationship described by I. Nunes using namespaces, by simply adding a symbol to reference the abstract namespace of the loader module.

We provide an example in Codes 9 and 10. The module **B** access to belief **rate/1** in module **two**. The resulting output of executing plan **do/0** in module **two** will be **counter 1**. The symbol ° is used to refer the *loader*'s abstract namespace.[8]

---

[7] The concept of capability and modules are quite similar, since both are composed of a set of beliefs, plans and goals [3,6], the relationships identified for capabilities can be applied to our notion of modules as well.

[8] This can be supported by extending the mangling function (c.f. algorithm 1) in order to replace the ° symbol by the corresponding namespace at loading time.

```
1 {namespace(ib,local)}
2
3 rate(0.50).
4
5 +!do <- .include("B.asl",ib);
6       !ib::inc(2);
7       ?ib::count(X);
8       .print("counter ",X).
```

Code 9. two.asl

```
1 count(0).
2
3 +!inc(S) : count(X)
4    <- ?°::rate(R);
5       -+count(X+S*R).
6
```

Code 10. B.asl

Cardinality. Since the same module can be loaded in multiple namespaces while each instance conserves its individual beliefs, it is also possible to represent the cardinality in modules associations. For example, at Codes 2 and 5 in Sect. 5, module **bob** loads one instance of **initiator** for each contract net protocol it starts, so that each negotiation maintains its own state.

Visibility. Local namespaces can be used to keep components private within a module, and global namespaces to share components between all modules. However, sometimes it results useful to share components only among the instances of the same module, e.g., in order to avoid replicating the same information several times. It is possible to model this, by introducing a new level of visibility for namespaces (besides *global* and *local*). For instance, a *module* namespace will be accessible only from within all instances of the same module. Comparably to the class visibility level from the Object-Oriented programming as implemented by the modifier **static** in Java.

Multi-inheritance. This can be modeled as the union of modules. Typically this union is meant to form a new module which encapsulates a more complex and specialized behavior, while reusing beliefs, plans and goals from other modules.

In the following example (Codes 11 and 12), the module **C** inherits **B** by including all its components in the same namespace (line 9). The *parent*'s local namespaces of each module (if exist) still hidden from the *child* module, and vice-versa. The inclusion of the parent module is performed at the end of the source code, in order to *override* the already existing plan **inc/1** in **A**. This latter works in the particular case of Jason because, by default, the first plan listed in the code is selected for execution, in the case that multiple applicable plans to achieve the same goal exist. A more sophisticated solution for AgentSpeak(L)-style languages is presented by A. Dhaon and R. Collier in [14]. Their method consists in customizing the selection function used for the interpreter to select the next plan for execution, and thus disambiguate which plan must be executed when the same plan is implemented in different levels of the module's hierarchy.

Dynamic extension of modules can be performed too by using the notion of namespaces, in Code 2 at lines 6–9, the functionality of module **initiator** (c.f. code 5) is extended. This is useful in the case that the programmer desires to extend the functionality for only one instance without creating a new module. A similar mechanism is used in Java through the concept of anonymous classes.

A related approach for constructing inheritance relationships between modules in the realm of logic programming, that can be adapted as a more general solution for modeling multi-inheritance in Agent-Oriented programming, is presented by Baldoni et al. in [1]. They use a modal operator instead of namespaces to group rules, then a set of logic implications establishes the inheritance relationship between modules. However, it should be carefully analyzed in order to evaluate its feasibility before adopting it in the context of Agent-Oriented programming.

```
1 {namespace(ic,local)}
2
3 +!init
4    <- .include("C.asl",ic);
5       !ic::inc(2);
6       !ic::mult(2);
7       ?ic::count(X);
8       .print("counter "X).
9
```

Code 11. three.asl

```
1 //belief count/1 is inherited from A
2 +!mult(T) : count(X)
3    <- -+count(X*T).
4
5 //overrides plan inc/1 in A
6 +!inc(S) : count(X)
7    <- -+count(X+1).
8
9 {include("A.asl")}
```

Code 12. C.asl

8   Conclusion

In this paper we have presented a solution for programming BDI Agents under the principles of modularity, and we explored the assumption that the notion of namespace is enough to address the main issues related to modularity, such as avoiding name-collisions, following the information hiding principle and providing an interface. We have exemplified the properties and feasibility of the approach using the Jason language.

It is future work to provide an unload mechanism that removes components from modules that are no longer used by the agent. We also aim to implement the approach in other languages to further evaluate the generality of the approach.

References

1. Baldoni, M., Giordano, L., Martelli, A.: A modal extension of logic programming: modularity, beliefs and hypothetical reasoning (1995)
2. Bordini, R.H., Hübner, J.F., Wooldridge, M.J.: Programming Multi-Agent Systems in AgentSpeak Using Jason. John Wiley & Sons Ltd., Chichester (2007)
3. Braubach, L., Pokahr, A., Lamersdorf, W.: Extending the capability concept for flexible BDI agent modularization. In: Bordini, R.H., Dastani, M.M., Dix, J., Fallah Seghrouchni, A. (eds.) ProMAS 2005. LNCS (LNAI), vol. 3862, pp. 139–155. Springer Berlin Heidelberg, Berlin, Heidelberg (2006). doi:10.1007/11678823_9
4. Braubach, L., Pokahr, E., Lamersdorf, W.: Jadex: a BDI agent system combining middleware and reasoning. In: Software Agent-Based Applications, Platforms and Development Kits, pp. 143–168. Birkhaeuser (2005)

5. Bray, T., Hollander, D., Layman, A., Tobin, R.: Namespaces in XML 1.0. W3C recommendation, W3C, August 2006. http://www.w3.org/TR/2006/REC-xml-names-20060816. Accessed 16 Aug 2006

6. Busetta, P., Howden, N., Rönnquist, R., Hodgson, A.: Structuring BDI agents in functional clusters. In: Jennings, N.R., Lespérance, Y. (eds.) ATAL 1999. LNCS (LNAI), vol. 1757, pp. 277–289. Springer, Heidelberg (2000). doi:10.1007/10719619_21

7. Cap, M., Dastani, M., Harbers, M.: Belief/goal sharing BDI modules. In: The 10th International Conference on Autonomous Agents and Multiagent Systems (AAMAS 2011), Richland, SC, vol. 3, pp. 1201–1202. International Foundation for Autonomous Agents and Multiagent Systems (2011)

8. Cuesta, P., Gomez, A., Gonzalez, J.: Agent oriented software engineering. In: Moreno, A., Pavon, J. (eds.) Issues in Multi-Agent Systems, Whitestein Series in Software Agent Technologies and Autonomic Computing, pp. 1–31. Birkhäuser Basel (2008)

9. Logan, B., Kiss, D.N.: Jason+ - extension of the jason agent programming language. Technical report, School of Computer Science and Information Technology, University of Nottingham (2010)

10. Dastani, M.: 2APL: a practical agent programming language. Auton. Agents Multi Agent Syst. 16(3), 214–248 (2008)

11. Dastani, M., Mol, C.P., Steunebrink, B.R.: Modularity in agent programming languages. In: Bui, T.D., Ho, T.V., Ha, Q.T. (eds.) PRIMA 2008. LNCS (LNAI), vol. 5357, pp. 139–152. Springer Berlin Heidelberg, Berlin, Heidelberg (2008). doi:10.1007/978-3-540-89674-6_17

12. Dastani, M., Steunebrink, B.: Modularity in BDI-based multi-agent programming languages. In: Proceedings of the 2009 IEEE/WIC/ACM International Joint Conference on Web Intelligence and Intelligent Agent Technology (WI-IAT 2009), Washington, US, vol. 02, pp. 581–584. IEEE Computer Society (2009)

13. Dastani, M., Riemsdijk, M.B., Dignum, F., Meyer, J.-J.C.: A programming language for cognitive agents goal directed 3APL. In: Dastani, M.M., Dix, J., El Fallah-Seghrouchni, A. (eds.) ProMAS 2003. LNCS (LNAI), vol. 3067, pp. 111–130. Springer Berlin Heidelberg, Berlin, Heidelberg (2004). doi:10.1007/978-3-540-25936-7_6

14. Dhaon, A., Collier, R.W.: Multiple inheritance in agentspeak(l)-style programming languages. In: Proceedings of the 4th International Workshop on Programming Based on Actors Agents & #38; Decentralized Control (AGERE! 2014), pp. 109–120, New York, NY, USA. ACM (2014)

15. Bergenti, F., Gleizes, M.-P., Zambonelli, F.: Methodologies and Software Engineering for Agent Systems: The Agent-Oriented Software Engineering Handbook. Multiagent Systems, Artificial Societies, and Simulated Organizations, vol. 11. Springer, Heidelberg (2004)

16. Hindriks, K.: Modules as policy-based intentions: modular agent programming in GOAL. In: Dastani, M., El Fallah Seghrouchni, A., Ricci, A., Winikoff, M. (eds.) ProMAS 2007. LNCS (LNAI), vol. 4908, pp. 156–171. Springer Berlin Heidelberg, Berlin, Heidelberg (2008). doi:10.1007/978-3-540-79043-3_10

17. Howden, N., Ronnquist, R., Hodgson, A., Lucas, A.: JACK intelligent agents - summary of an agent infrastructure. In: Proceedings of the 5th ACM International Conference on Autonomous Agents (2001)

18. Hunt, A., Thomas, D.: The Pragmatic Programmer: From Journeyman to Master. Addison-Wesley Longman Publishing Co. Inc., Boston (1999)

19. Jennings, N.R.: Agent-oriented software engineering. In: Imam, I., Kodratoff, Y., El-Dessouki, A., Ali, M. (eds.) IEA/AIE 1999. LNCS (LNAI), vol. 1611, pp. 4–10. Springer, Heidelberg (1999). doi:10.1007/978-3-540-48765-4_2

20. Madden, N., Logan, B.: Collaborative narrative generation in persistent virtual environments. In: Intelligent Narrative Technologies: Papers from the 2007 AAAI Fall Symposium, Menlo Park, CA. AAAI Press, November 2007

21. Madden, N., Logan, B.: Modularity and compositionality in jason. In: Braubach, L., Briot, J.-P., Thangarajah, J. (eds.) ProMAS 2009. LNCS (LNAI), vol. 5919, pp. 237–253. Springer, Heidelberg (2010). doi:10.1007/978-3-642-14843-9_15

22. Nunes, I.: Improving the design and modularity of BDI agents with capability relationships. In: Dalpiaz, F., Dix, J., Riemsdijk, M.B. (eds.) EMAS 2014. LNCS (LNAI), vol. 8758, pp. 58–80. Springer International Publishing, Cham (2014). doi:10.1007/978-3-319-14484-9_4

23. Ortiz-Hernandez, G., Guerra-Hernandez, A., Hoyos-Rivera, G.J.: JasMo - a modularization framework for Jason. In: 12th Mexican International Conference on Artificial Inteligence (MICAI), Mexico. IEEE, November 2013

24. Rao, A.S.: AgentSpeak(L): BDI agents speak out in a logical computable language. In: Velde, W., Perram, J.W. (eds.) MAAMAW 1996. LNCS, vol. 1038, pp. 42–55. Springer, Heidelberg (1996). doi:10.1007/BFb0031845

25. Smith, R.G.: The contract net protocol: high-level communication and control in a distributed problem solver. IEEE Trans. Comput. **29**(12), 1104–1113 (1980)

26. van Riemsdijk, M.B., Dastani, M., Meyer, J.-J.Ch., de Boer, F.S.: Goal-oriented modularity in agent programming. In: Proceedings of the Fifth International Joint Conference on Autonomous Agents and Multiagent Systems (AAMAS 2006), pp. 1271–1278, New York, NY, USA. ACM (2006)

ARGO: An Extended Jason Architecture that Facilitates Embedded Robotic Agents Programming

Carlos Eduardo Pantoja[1,4]($\boxtimes$), Márcio Fernando Stabile Jr.[2],
Nilson Mori Lazarin[1], and Jaime Simão Sichman[3]

[1] Centro Federal de Educação Tecnológica (CEFET/RJ), Rio de Janeiro, Brazil
{pantoja,nilson.lazarin}@cefet-rj.br
[2] Instituto de Matemática e Estatística, Universidade de São Paulo, São Paulo, Brazil
mstabile@ime.usp.br
[3] Escola Politécnica, Universidade de São Paulo, São Paulo, Brazil
jaime.sichman@poli.usp.br
[4] Universidade Federal Fluminense, Niterói, Brazil

Abstract. This paper presents ARGO, a customized Jason architecture for programming embedded robotic agents using the Javino middleware and perception filters. Jason is a well known agent-oriented programming language that relies on the Belief-Desire-Intention model and implements an AgentSpeak interpreter in Java. Javino is a middleware that enables automated design of embedded agents using Jason and it is aimed to be used in the robotics domain. However, when the number of perceptions increases, it may occur a bottleneck in the agent's reasoning cycle since an event is generated for each single perception processed. A possible solution to this problem is to apply perception filters, that reduce the processing cost. Consequently, it is expected that the agent may deliberate within a specific time limit. In order to evaluate ARGO's performance, we present some experiments using a ground vehicle platform in a real-time collision scenario. We show that in certain cases the use of perception filters is able to prevent collisions effectively.

1 Introduction

Agents are autonomous and pro-active entities situated in an environment and are able to reason about what goal to achieve, based on its perceptions about the world [22]. In robotics, an agent is a physical entity composed of hardware, containing sensors and actuators, and software that is responsible for its reasoning. The Belief-Desire-Intention model (BDI) [3] is a cognitive approach for reasoning based on how information from the environment and the goals an agent has can activate predefined plans in order to try to achieve these goals. Jason [2] is an Agent-Oriented Programming Language (AOPL) that implements an AgentSpeak interpreter in Java, adopting the BDI cognitive architecture. However, programming robotic agents using Jason is a difficult task because a bottleneck can

© Springer International Publishing AG 2016
M. Baldoni et al. (Eds.): EMAS 2016, LNAI 10093, pp. 136–155, 2016.
DOI: 10.1007/978-3-319-50983-9_8

occur in the agent's reasoning cycle when the robot updates its belief base with perceptual information.

Javino [14] is a middleware that enables automated design of embedded agents using Jason. It allows agents to communicate with microcontrollers in hardware devices, e.g. Arduino. Both Javino and Jason can run embedded in a single-board computer such as Raspberry Pi (connected with n devices). However, when using several sensors, the agent's belief base generates events for each perception, which may compromise the robot execution time. In [20], perception filters were used to minimize the cost effects of processing all perceptions in simulation systems using Jason. The results showed that filters are able to improve agent's performance significantly.

Thus, in this paper, we present a customized Jason architecture for programming embedded robotic agents named ARGO[1], which uses a layered robot architecture separating the hardware from the reasoning agency. In ARGO, Javino enables processing data coming from sensors as perceptions in ARGO's agent reasoning cycle. Then, one can restrict the list of perceptions delivered by Javino based on filters designed by the agent's programmer. The main contribution of ARGO is to enable the use of perception filters for programming robotic agents, which reduces the cost of processing perceptions in BDI. Moreover, ARGO allows an agent to decide when to start or to stop perceiving, to fix the interval between each perception and to control the perceptual behavior by using Jason internal actions to filter perceptions at runtime.

In order to evaluate ARGO's performance, we also present some experiments using a ground vehicle platform in a real-time collision scenario constructed. We applied the experimental design methodology described by [12] to test and to statistically verify that in certain cases the use of perception filters reduces BDI processing time, thus preventing collisions effectively.

The rest of the paper is structured as follows. We briefly present in Sect. 2 the Jason framework and the Javino middleware, and then explain how we can construct embedded robotic agents with these frameworks. In the sequence, perception filters are discussed in Sect. 3. We then present ARGO architecture and its implementation in Sect. 4. Our experiments, including the case study, the experimental design and our results, are presented in Sect. 5. In Sect. 6, we discuss related work. Finally, in Sect. 7 we present our conclusions and further research.

2   Programming BDI Agents

2.1   Jason

Jason [2] is an interpreter for an extended version of AgentSpeak [17], which is an abstract AOPL based on a restricted first-order language with events and actions. Created to allow the specification of BDI agents, Jason implements the

---

[1] Download available at http://argo-for-jason.sourceforge.net.

operational semantics of AgentSpeak and provides a platform for the development of multi-agent systems.

A Jason agent operates by means of a reasoning cycle that is analogous to the BDI decision loop [2]. First, the agent receives a list of literals representing the current state of the environment. Then, the belief base is updated based on the perceptions received. Each change in the belief base generates an event that is added to a list to be used in a posterior step. The interpreter checks for messages that might have been delivered to the agent's mailbox. These messages go through a selection process to determine whether they can be accepted by the agent or not. After that, one of the generated events is chosen to be dealt with and when it is selected, all the plans related to that event are selected. From these plans, a new selection is made to separate which of them can be executed given the current state of the environment. If more than one plan can be executed, a function selects which one will be executed. If the agent has many different foci of attention, a function chooses one intention among those for execution. The final step is to execute the first non-executed action from the selected intention.

2.2   Javino

Javino is a library for both hardware and software that implements a protocol for exchanging messages between the low-level hardware (microcontrollers) and the high-level software (programming language) with error detection over serial communication [14]. There are some communicating libraries in the literature, such as RxTx Library and JavaComm, based on serial ports. However, these libraries do not provide error detection and they use byte-to-byte communication. In both cases, the programmer needs to implement a message controller on the hardware layer in order to avoid losses.

The format of a message used in a communication by Javino is composed of 3 fields: preamble, size and message content. The preamble (2 bytes) identifies the beginning of a message that arrived through a serial port. The size field (1 byte) is calculated before any transmission informing the size of the message. The field message content (up to 255 bytes) carries the message to be sent.

Both the preamble and size fields identify errors in case of loss or collision of information during the message transmission. When a message arrives on the serial port, the receiver (either software-side or hardware-side) verifies the preamble. If it is correct, the receiver then counts the size of the message content field and compares it with the value of size field: if they don't match, the message is discarded. In the case of incomplete messages, the receiver also discards the message. Javino provides three different operation modes:

– the **Send** Mode assumes a simplex message transmission by software to hardware. It uses the *sendCommand(port, msg)* method to send a message to the hardware-side. This method returns a boolean value which gives a feedback about the successful transmission to the microcontroller. This feedback is necessary because the port serial can be locked by other concurrent transmissions. The software-side do not wait for answers from the hardware;

- the **Request** Mode assumes a half-duplex transmission between software to hardware, where the hardware sends an answer message. It uses the *request-Data(port, msg)* method, that sends a message to the hardware-side through a serial port and returns a boolean value which checks if there is any answer sent by the hardware-side. The user is supposed to implement an answer message in the hardware-side using the *availableMsg()* method, that verifies if it exists a valid message from software-side, the *getMsg()* method, that gets the message sent by software-side and the *sendMsg(msg)* method, that sends a message to software-side;
- the **Listen** Mode assumes a simplex transmission by hardware to software. It uses the *listenHardware(port)* method to check if there is any message sent by the hardware-side. The Request and Listen modes get messages from hardware using the *getData()* method.

The Javino's protocol aims to be multi-platform and can be implemented using any programming language. The hardware-side library may be used in microcontrollers such as ATMEGA, PIC or Intel families. The software-side library may be coded in Java or in another programming language. In [14], it was developed a Java library for the software-side and an Arduino library for hardware-side. In this case, Javino requires both Python and pySerial installed to manage the serial port of an operational system.

2.3   Embedding Robotic Agents

Some previous research have tried to integrate robotic reasoning into hardware by using BDI agents. In [9], a framework was presented to provide a way of programming agents using AgentSpeak in Unmanned Aerial Vehicle in a simulator. The authors in [4] proposed an aquatic robot which uses Arduino together with BeagleBoard who could move from point-to-point deviating from obstacles. However, the reasoning was centralized on a computer using a Wi-Fi communication with the robot. All the decisions were sent to BeagleBoard and retransmitted, by serial communication, to Arduino, which held sensors and actuators. Another work published in [1] presented a grounded vehicle, which used Arduino and Jason to control sensors and actuators using a Java library for communication between the hardware and the Jason's environment. However, the agent's reasoning was still running on the computer. The messages to the hardware-side were sent from an Arduino connected to a USB port computer to another Arduino embedded on the robot using radio transmitters.

The work in [19] showed that it was possible to use BDI agents on embedded systems employing single-board computers. However, it was not presented an infrastructure to integrate BDI agents in a robot. Therefore, they simulated the environment on a computer to execute the decisions taken by the BDI agent.

Finally, a robotic agent platform using both Javino and Jason framework was presented in [14], which was an improvement of the platform presented in [1]. The authors used Raspberry Pi and Arduino together to provide a fully embedded BDI agent reasoning on a robot. In this case, Javino was integrated into the agent's simulated environment and the agent used a Jason external action to request the perceptions and a Jason internal action to control the actuators. In this architecture, the agent is responsible for controlling both sensors and actuators that are connected to the Arduino board and it is embedded in Raspberry Pi. The Arduino boards are connected to the USB ports of Raspberry Pi, thus, the agents use Javino to get perceptions from sensors and act with the actuators plugged in Arduino. The architecture worked in embedded robotic agents. However, according to the authors, when using too many sensors or plans in Jason code the agent's reasoning suffered a delay due to the cost of processing perceptions in Jason. We believe that using filters to overcome this issue could reduce the time employed in perceptions processing in BDI.

3 Perception Filters

3.1 Filtering Perceptions

Filtering perceptions is a widely discussed topic in MAS and Robotics. Some works try to provide an agent vision mechanism, which limits the agent range of vision simulating the human eye behavior such as [13]. In classical robotics, Kalman filters are often used to provide robot vision, playing an important role in the development of robotic platforms [5].

In [13], the authors present a technique for perceiving objects using Multi-agent Based Simulation (MABS), when agents are situated in open environments. The agents do not have access to all perceptions available in the simulated system. Adversely, they only have access to partial information about the environment determined by their vision sensor range area (modeled as a cone like the human eyes range of view). So, an agent can perceive only what is within the cone area in front of it and its decisions are based on what it can percept in the simulated system. The agent vision algorithm eliminates unseen items that are not in the sensor area and detects visually obstructed objects (objects that are completely behind another object). The algorithm verifies if an object is too far from the agent position: if this distance is less than a pre-defined range, the object is perceived, otherwise, it is not processed as a perception. The algorithm then verifies if part of an object is within the vision cone. In this case, the object is perceived. Finally, the algorithm verifies if the object is witinh the agent's vision cone and it is not obstructed to be perceived. If it is obstructed, the object is not perceived. The algorithm has as an input the environment's objects, and it returns the ones perceived by the agent. The work is specific for MABS where all the objects are pre-defined in the simulated system. So, if it is desirable to extend the solution to a real robotic domain, one needs to identify objects in the real world using a camera. The camera image can be considered as the agent's vision sensor. However, in order to use thise mechanism coupled with a BDI agent, like Jason, it would be necessary to transform the objects perceptions in Jason's beliefs.

Kalman filters variants are used for many problems in the robotic domain such as robot controlling, object tracking, data estimation and prediction, simultaneous localization and mapping (SLAM), visual navigation, among others. In robot vision for object detection and tracking, a Kalman Filter can be used to identify an object and track it based on a series of images, for instance captured from a camera. Path following can be obtained in a static road segment detecting the distance and the angle between the robot and a line using Kalman filters [5]. Since Kalman filters are based on mathematical approaches, they could also be used along with Jason in internal actions or in Jason's environment. In the same way, the objects perceived in the environment have to be transformed into Jason's beliefs.

3.2 Perception Filters in Jason

In order to identify the critical points for performance in the Jason reasoning cycle, the work in [20] used a profiling tool to analyze a piece of Jason code. By measuring memory and CPU usage, the authors verified that two sections of the code were more time-consuming: the Belief Update Function (BUF) and the method responsible for the *unification* of variables in the plans and rules. These two methods generated a bottleneck, and depending on the specification of the agent, those methods could take up to 99% of reasoning time.

Given that Jason's default implementation assumes that everything that an agent can perceive in the environment will be part of its perception list, they proposed the inclusion of a perception filter between the perceive function and the update of beliefs before starting the reasoning cycle. This filter is responsible for analyzing the perception list received and for removing from the list those literals that are not interesting for the agent. This is done through filters defined by the agent designer which are described in XML format files and define restrictions on the predicate, variables and annotations of the beliefs.

Let us suppose a robotic agent that represents his beliefs about the environment by predicates like $p(d, v)$, where predicate p identifies the sensor, d the side of the robot where the sensor is located and v the value acquired by perception. An example of such a perception is shown in Fig. 1.

```
1  temperature(right ,36)
2  temperature(back ,38)
3  light(left ,143)
4  distance(front ,227)
5  distance(right ,30)
```

Fig. 1. Example of perception list represented as beliefs.

An example of filter that is used in the experiments Sect. 5.1 is shown in Fig. 2. This filter would remove all the perceptions originated from the temperature and light sensors and would also remove the perceptions from the distance sensors that are not in the front of the robot.

```
1   <?xml version="1.0"?>
2   <PerceptionFilter>
3     <filter>
4         <predicate>temperature</predicate>
5     </filter>
6     <filter>
7         <predicate>light</predicate>
8     </filter>
9     <filter>
10        <predicate>distance</predicate>
11        <parameter operator="NE" id="0">front
12        </parameter>
13    </filter>
14  </PerceptionFilter>
```

Fig. 2. Example of perception filter.

Since the agent's intentions may change, the perceptions that are relevant for the agent may also change. To reflect these changes, a new Jason internal action called *change_filter* was also proposed in [20]. This action receives as a parameter the name of an XML file with the specific rules for the perceptions, and sets it as the current filter so that in the next reasoning cycle, the agent receives perceptions according to its new interests.

4   ARGO

4.1   Overview of a Robot's Architecture Using Javino

A robotic agent is an embedded system where software and hardware components are integrated to provide sensing and operating abilities in real-time environments. For this, it is necessary to employ an architecture capable of facilitating the robot construction and programming. Hence, we propose an architecture for programming robotic agents where it is possible to design the robot platform independently from the reasoning agency, and then to integrate them using a protocol for serial communication.

The robot platform must be composed of sensors and actuators coupled to microcontrollers, where all the desired actions that the robot can perform in the environment and the percepts it can capture from sensors are programmed. In this case, our architecture translates raw data into a format for high-level programming language in the firmware, resulting in a performance gain for the agent's reasoning. Javino's protocol is responsible for sending these percepts using the serial port of the microcontroller. In this architecture, it is possible to use any kind of microcontrollers whereas it employs a library compliant with Javino's protocol. Afterwards, a MAS programming language is employed to allow the cognitive control of the robot platform. The chosen program language should be able to host the existing versions of Javino's protocol or to implement a new one. An overview of the architecture is shown in Fig. 3.

The architecture is composed of three layers: hardware, firmware and reasoning. The hardware layer is responsible for mounting the robot platform, sensors, actuators and connecting them with respective microcontrollers employed. A single-board computer is used to connect all microcontrollers using USB and will be responsible for hosting the MAS. The firmware layer provides all actions that a robot can execute including procedures for both sensors and actuators and they are programmed directly in the microcontroller. Basically, these procedures send prepared raw data as percepts for the reasoning layer and receive agent's messages to perform some action, both using serial communication and the hardware-side of Javino's protocol.

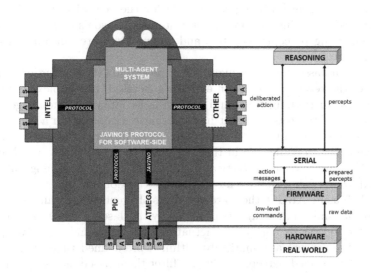

Fig. 3. Overview of a robot's architecture using Javino.

The reasoning layer represents the MAS's programming using a high-level language. The middleware in software-side transmits received percepts from serial port to the agent and sends action messages to the firmware layer. Depending on the AOPL chosen, it is possible to integrate received percepts directly into the agent's reasoning cycle or to use some structure to control the perception flow. As the architecture allows many microcontrollers in a robot platform, a strategy for capturing those percepts should be implemented. For example, it is possible to read all available serial ports one by one and after that to update the agent's percepts or to allow the agent decide which serial port it desires to use at a particular moment. Note that an agent cannot access more than one serial port at a time and more than one agent cannot access the same serial port at the same time.

In most of the commercial platforms, programmers do not have access to implementation details or they have to use an interface as a middleware for controlling the robot; on the other hand, these platforms also present a suite of functions to help in robot motion and planning. Our approach aims to be an architecture for open robot design to be used in cases where the programmer needs freedom to build his own prototype, using open platforms such as Arduino. The architecture is not bound neither to the MAS programming language, which can be interchanged, nor to the hardware adopted. However, it is necessary to adjust the raw data translation to percepts in the firmware layer, if the AOPL is changed.

4.2   ARGO Architecture

In the reasoning layer of our proposed robot architecture, it is necessary to adopt an AOPL which will be responsible for the cognitive reasoning of the robot platform. For this, we propose a customized Jason's architecture named ARGO employing perceptions filters and Javino integrated into Jason agent's reasoning cycle.

The BDI in Jason implies a high cost of processing the perceptions since for each one of the received literals an event is generated. In complex codes, plans may be added in running time, and a quite large intention stack is generated. In these cases, if the robotic agent has to achieve a goal within a time limit, it may not succeed. Our idea is to apply perception filters in these cases, so as to enable the agent to deliberate in time, in order to act in such critical applications. ARGO aims to be a practical architecture for programming automated embedded agents using BDI agents in the robotics domain.

In a MAS using ARGO, there are two types of agents which can be employed: ARGO agents and common agents provided by the Jason framework. An ARGO agent is able to directly control the actuators at runtime and it receives perceptions from the sensors automatically within a pre-defined time interval. Once the agent has received perceptions, it can filter them based on its actual configuration. It is also able to change its filters at runtime based on its needs (the same can occur when accessing its devices).

An ARGO agent is able to communicate with others common Jason agents, but only ARGO agents can control devices and receive perceptions from the real world. Because of this characteristic of the architecture, ARGO agents can send their received perceptions to other agents: they can either delegate for Jason agents the reasoning about these perceptions if i desirable or process all incoming percepts by themselves. In the first case, the ARGO agents are dedicated only to activate/deactivate devices, to get perceptions and to distribute perceptions to other agents instead of overcharging their reasoning by processing all received and filtered perceptions. In the latter case, a delay in some action response can occur if the processing cost of reasoning with the received perceptions is higher than the expected response time for example. An overview of ARGO can be seen in Fig. 4.

An agent can assume to be an ARGO agent by defining the Argo architecture in the MAS design; otherwise, the standard agent architecture of Jason is automatically defined. An ARGO agent is supposed to connect to one or more devices at runtime by choosing which serial port it wants to access (until the limit of

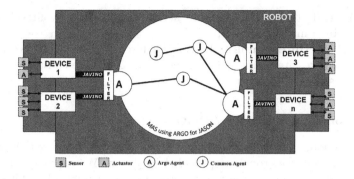

Fig. 4. ARGO overview.

127 serial ports); however it can only use one port at a time, for both sensing and acting. Besides that, different ARGO agents must not use the same serial port at the same time, because when exists a competition for communicating at the same port, there may be a data loss [8].

4.3   Internal Actions

As mentioned before, an ARGO agent has the ability to control devices at runtime. It means that it can evolve in the real world using the robot's actuators and sensors. In practice, the agent controls devices using serial communication by choosing a serial port where the desired component is connected. Once defined the serial port, the agent can start receiving perceptions or can send a command to an actuator.

However, if the serial port is fixed for an agent, it will not be able to change it or to connect to other devices. Another issue is the perceiving ability: a Jason agent receives perceptions from sensors in every BDI cycle, even when it does not need them. Since an agent is an autonomous entity, we believe that an ARGO agent has to be able to decide when to perceive the real world at runtime. This means that the agent can start and stop perceiving from sensors when needed or it can define an interval for receiving these perceptions. Similarly, it can also directly control the actuators by defining at runtime which serial port to use. Moreover, bu using the ARGO architecture perception filtering technique, an agent can change at runtime its filters based on its needs, hence customizing its perception policy.

Therefore, we propose five internal actions for programming agents in Jason along with ARGO architecture. A Jason's internal action is a kind of action that is used to extend the agent capabilities. The proposed internal actions are:

1. **limit(x):** defines the sensing interval, where x is a value in milliseconds;
2. **port(y):** defines which serial port should be used by the agent, where y is a literal representing the port identification, e.g. COM8;
3. **percepts(open—block):** decides whether or not to perceive the real world;

4. **act(w):** sends to the hardware an action, represented by literal w, to be executed by a microcontroller;
5. **change_filter(filterName):** defines the filter to constrain perceptions in runtime, where filterName is the name of the XML file containing the filter constraints.

4.4   Customizing Jason for ARGO

In Jason's reasoning cycle, as mentioned in Sect. 2.1, the agent gets its percepts from the simulated environment provided by Jason. We extended the reasoning cycle of Jason, shown in Fig. 5, to providing a customized architecture for ARGO agents. First, Javino middleware is now responsible for getting percepts coming from low-level layers and sends them to the perceive step. Before being incorporated in the belief base, percepts can be filtered based on the agent's active filter. Then, filtered perceptions are processed and the reasoning cycle flows up to the act step, where the agent can perform basic Jason's actions or an action to control the actuators of the robot, which once more involves Javino middleware.

In order to create ARGO architecture, it was necessary to customize Jason framework, in particular by extending the *AgArch* class. This class is responsible for the Jason's native architecture and provides a list of perceptions sent by the Jason's environment in Java and the communication with other agents [2]. In the extended architecture, Javino middleware was inserted as a communication bridge to the hardware sensors and actuators. Besides that, the serial port identification had to be added to the native *AgArch* class in order to define to which serial port the Javino has to communicate.

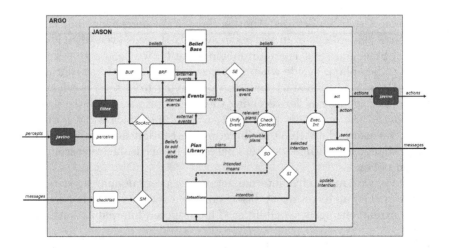

Fig. 5. ARGO reasoning cycle.

In the *TransitionSystem* class, two new attributes *blocked* and *limit* were created, as well as a new function *realWorldPerceptions*. The blocked attribute is responsible for blocking or unblocking the perceptions and the limit attribute specifies a time interval for perceiving the real world (data from sensors). The *realWorldPerceptions* verifies in each cycle *(i)* if the percepts are blocked; or *(ii)* if the time limit for the next perception has been reached. If the percepts are not blocked and the time limit was reached, Javino requests the percepts from sensors and sends them to the perceive method in Agent class.

Before the agent processes the percepts coming from Javino, they can be filtered using the method *filter* also implemented in the Agent class. In this case, all agents have the ability to filter percepts, because this method was implemented in the native Agent class. The modifications executed do not change Jason's original functionality, except for the simulated environment which is not used since Javino gets the percepts from the real world. We opted for creating a customized architecture instead of an infrastructure because the later one obliges all agents to be ARGO agents.

5 Experiments

5.1 Case Study

In order to evaluate the overall architecture and to assure the impact of the perception filter, we assembled a robot composed of four distance sensors, four light sensors, four temperature sensors, an Arduino board and an Arduino 4wd chassis. A sensor of each type was placed in each of the four sides of the robot (front, back, right and left). The robot was placed on a flat surface two meters away from a wall. When started, the robot would perceive the environment and move forward at a constant speed[2] until the distance to the wall was less than a specified value. As soon as it perceived that the distance was smaller, the robot should stop. The robot can be seen in Fig. 6.

Fig. 6. The robot used in the experiments.

---

[2] The speed is about 10 cm/s and it is not used in the experiments since it is constant.

5.2   Experiment Design

The experiment presented was designed based on the experimental design guidelines presented in [12]. According to the author, the goal of a proper experimental design is to obtain the maximum information with the minimum number of experiments. The procedure separates the effects of various factors that might affect the performance and allows to determine if a factor has a significant effect or if the observed difference is simply due to random variations caused by measurement errors and/or parameters that were not controlled. It is important to define the meaning of four terms:

1. *Response Variable* is the outcome of an experiment. In the experiments executed, the response variables are the processing time taken by the agent to stop after perceiving the wall and the distance it stopped from the wall;
2. *Factors* are the variables that affect the action response variable. Factors can be Primary or Secondary. Primary factors are those whose effects need to be quantified while secondary factors are those that impact the performance but whose impact we are not interested in quantifying. The primary factors chosen for this experiments were the distance the agent should stop from the wall, the time interval for receiving the perceptions and the filter used;
3. *Levels* are the values that a factor can assume. The factors and levels used are presented in Table 1;
4. *Replication* is the repetition of all or some experiments. If all experiments in a study are repeated three times, the study is said to have three replications.

Table 1. Factors and levels used for the experiment

Factor	Levels		
Distance	40 cm	80 cm	120 cm
Perception interval	20 ms	35 ms	50 ms
Filter	No filter	Front Side	Front Distance

The three filter levels represent the filter configurations that were used. "No filter" represents that the ARGO architecture did not make use of the perception filters, "Front Side" represents that the filter removed all the perceptions, except the ones from the sensors present on the front side of the robot. "Front Distance" represents that the filter removed all the perceptions, except the ones from the distance sensor present on the front side of the robot. Three executions were conducted for every combination of levels in Table 1.

5.3   Implementation

The agent has an initial belief that represents the distance limit from the wall that the robot should stop. It has also an initial intention that leads to a configuration plan, where it is defined both the serial port to which the Arduino board is connected and the perception interval limit. We ran experiments varying this value using 20 ms, 35 ms and 50 ms. Perceptions are then unblocked, since initially perception is blocked by default. The next action activates the filter that is responsible for filtering every perception except those from the front sensor of the robot. We ran experiments using a filter for all sensors except for the distance sensor in the front of the robot, and another round of experiments using no filters at all. The last action of the plan is an achievement action for a plan responsible for starting moving the robot.

The first action of the start plan is a message for the microcontroller to activate the motors and to move ahead. A belief with a status indicating that the robot is moving ahead is then added to the belief base of the agent. An achievement action for the moving plan is performed by the agent. The moving plan is responsible for verifying if the received filtered perception of the front distance sensor of the robot is greater than the initial belief of the distance limit. If so, the agent sends a message to the microcontroller to keep moving ahead. Otherwise, the robot crossed the distance limit and should stop. For this end, the agent sends a message to the microcontroller to stop the motors of the robot.

Some plans for using the temperature sensors and the light sensors were also provided. In this cases, when the perceptions of these both sensors are received, the agent sends a message to the microcontroller to turn on/off a specific led light positioned on each side of the robot, which informs when the received values crossed the limit specified in the agent code (in this case 100 for the light and 25°C for temperature). The agent code is shown in Fig. 7.

In our case, we used a single agent for controlling the robot, because we employed only one microcontroller where all the sensors and the robot's motors were connected to. If more than one agent tries to connect to the same serial port, conflicts arise. However, the architecture is sufficiently flexible to alow to develop a MAS for controlling the robot; in such a case, each employed ARGO agent could be responsible for controlling a kind of sensor (light, distance, and temperature), and the robot would be equipped with three microcontrollers.

5.4   Results

The first response variable analyzed was the distance the agent stopped from the wall. Figure 8 shows the results of all possible value combinations of the different factors presented in Table 1. Bars that do not appear in the Figure mean that the agent collided with the wall.

One should notice initially that in all cases, the agent that didn't filter its perceptions collided with the wall (there is no any blue bar in the Figure). In some cases, for instance the distance limit 120 cm, the agent with front side filter arrived eventually to stop before the wall; however, in these cases it stopped always closer to the wall when compared to the agent that used front distance filtering.

The agent using front distance filtering outperformed the others in quite all the experiments, and it was able to successfully stop before hitting the wall in all the experiments when the distance limit was 80 cm or 120 cm. Since this

```
1   value(40).
2   !config.
3
4   +!config: true <-
5            .port(COM5);
6            .limit(20);
7            .filter(byValue);
8            .percepts(open);
9            !start.
10
11  +!start : true <-
12           .act(front);
13           +status(front);
14           !moving.
15
16  +!moving: dist(f, X) &
17                   value(J) & X>J &
18                   status(front) <-
19           .act(front);
20           !moving.
21
22  +!moving: dist(f, X) &
23                   value(J) &
24                   X<=J & status(front) <-
25           .act(stop).
26
27  -!moving <-
28           !!moving.
29
30  +light(X,Y) : Y>100 <-
31           .act(ledLightOn).
32
33  +light(X,Y) : Y<=100 <-
34           .act(ledLightOn).
35
36  +temp(X,Y) : Y>25 <-
37           .act(ledTempOff).
38
39  +temp(X,Y) : Y<=25 <-
40           .act(ledTempOn).
```

Fig. 7. Agent code.

agent focuses only in perceptions coming from the front sensor, Jason's internal mechanism generates less events, and the agent can thus reason faster than an agent without any filter. However, in some experiments (for example, distance limit 40 cm and perception interval 50), neither agent could avoid the collision.

The second response variable analyzed was the elapsed time taken by the agent to stop after perceiving the wall. For this experiment, we calculated the variation assigned to each factor, as detailed in [12]. This statistical analysis is useful to check which factors are responsible for the differences in the response variable. The calculated values are presented in Table 2.

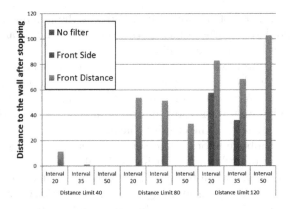

Fig. 8. Distance to the wall after stopping.

Table 2. Variation assigned to each factor in the analysis of the response time.

Factor	Variation attributed
Distance Limit (L)	1,415%
Perception Interval (I)	0,165%
Filter (F)	88,965%
Interaction between L and I	0,525%
Interaction between L and F	3,715%
Interaction between I and F	0,265%
Interaction between L and I and F	1,725%
Error	3,285%

The results confirm the importance of the perception filter in reducing the processing time, since almost all variation was attributed to this factor. This result suggests that ARGO architecture, by integrating Javino and the perception filters, can be used for developing embedded robotic agents in a way that the agent can benefit from the BDI architecture with a smaller influence of one of its major drawbacks that would be the high processing time.

6   Related Work

Robot architectures usually deal with platforms, sensors, actuators, programming language and reasoning mechanisms. One challenge is how to integrate these components in a way that a robot can deliberate to perform a task without failing to accomplish its goal. In [21] the authors propose a cognitive control architecture integrating knowledge representation of sensory and cognitive reasoning of a robotic agent using GOAL. The architecture consists of four decoupled layers: robot platform, robot behavioral control, environment interface and cognitive control. The robot platform employed was the humanoid NAO and it used URBI as middleware for interfacing with the robot's hardware via TCP/IP protocol. The robot behavioral control layer is responsible for processing sensory data and monitoring and executing behaviors. Besides, this layer communicates (using TCP/IP) with the reasoning and the robot platform layer, transmitting sensory data and actions execution respectively. The interface layer uses a translation mechanism between the sensory information acquired from the behavioral layer and the percepts sent to the cognitive layer. This layer is necessary because symbolic and sub-symbolic information can use different languages. The mechanism is based on a standard template using XML files mapping, which indicates how to map data but also when to do it. The cognitive control layer uses GOAL [10], which is a logic-based programming language for cognitive agents.

Similarly, ARGO's architecture also divides the robot programming into layers, separating sensory data from the agent's reasoning. We exploit the advantages of Jason extending it for programming robotic agents. ARGO provides three layers to be programmed: hardware, firmware and agent reasoning. Our proposed architecture provides a support for exchanging the hardware and the firmware without concerning with the reasoning layer; furthermore, it is possible to change the agent programming language without changing either the hardware or the firmware. This is possible because Javino is responsible for exchanging serial messages between these layers, and it does not link them to each other. We do not provide a translation mechanism in high-level layers because of the processing cost, which can affect the robot efficiency. However, the translation from raw data into percepts is done in the firmware layer. Since ARGO aims to be used in open platforms, the programmer must code the firmware layer. For commercial platforms such as NAO and Lego Mindstorms, a percepts mapping process must be provided.

Some other works also use Jason for this end, such as [15,16]. In [16], CArtAgO [18] is used as the functional layer for providing artifacts that represent sensors and actuators of a robot, and Jason is used as the reasoning layer. Despite using artifacts, which is an interesting abstraction for the devices employed, the authors use a simulator named Webots and do not embed the MAS. In [15], the authors provide a Jason extension for ROS named Rason.

Javino's protocol provides a mechanism for avoiding noisy data in communication between the firmware and the reasoning layer. However, we do not treat noisy data coming directly from sensors, when they provide well-formed but wrong values. In [7], the authors present a programming language for cognitive robots and software agents using the 3APL [11] language, which implements a deliberation cycle for selecting and executing practical reasoning rule statements and goal statements. They also provide an architecture consisting of beliefs, goals, actions and practical reasoning rules as a mental state. The beliefs represent the robot's percepts of an environment. The authors focused only on the programming constructs, they do not provide information about how a robot platform should interact with the high-level language.

In [6], a Teleo-Reactive (TR) extension for programming robots is presented, supported by a double tower architecture which provides a percepts handler that atomically updates the BeliefStore (a repository of beliefs). After that, the architecture reconsiders all rules affected by this change. The authors assert that actions and percepts can be dispatched through ROS interface to the robot platform. TR extension uses low-level procedures written in procedural programming languages for sensorial data and actuators actions. Concerning implementation, they used Qu-Prolog, simulators and Lego Mindstorms robots.

ARGO has the same intention of facilitating the programming of robotic agents providing a mechanism for automatically updating the agent's belief base. The TR extension provides an inhibition process of some behaviors in response to percepts while ARGO provides a runtime process for filtering percepts that are not needed at a specific moment. Filtering perceptions in ARGO prevents unnecessary event triggering in the deliberative cycle of Jason, therefore, the agent deliberation should be more efficient.

7   Conclusions and Further Work

According to our studies, we concluded that using perception filters in applications where the response time is critical is an essential feature for agents developed in Jason. For this end, we have proposed the ARGO architecture. Perception filters enhance ARGO performance and make it practical feasible since it reduces significantly the perception processing and the events generated for each perception. Hence, it is a major feature in the ARGO architecture. However, in some applications, we believe that a delay in responses for perceptions processing can be tolerated and do not interfere with the goal of the MAS (i.e. applications where the response is not time-bounded).

In the ARGO architecture, an agent in a MAS can control different microcontrollers since the programming layer is independent of the microcontroller choice. This is an important issue because it is not bonded to a specific microcontroller technology allowing mixing other microcontrollers to a single prototype. Moreover, it is not bonded even to the MAS implementation, since it is possible to change the MAS code without changing the microcontroller code. This is possible because the microcontrollers run separately and they communicate with the MAS using serial communication. Basically, every ARGO agent requests perceptions or send actions acquiring a serial port connected to a microcontroller using Javino. This creates an uncoupled development environment for prototypes and robotic platforms using Jason framework, thus offering different ways of controlling low-cost boards with agents for several purposes.

In a MAS using ARGO it is possible to merge common agents (default agents from Jason framework) and ARGO agents (customized architecture) into a single project, but separating some responsibilities. Since just ARGO agents can get perceptions from the real world, a design issue may be raised: is it a better solution that uses only ARGO agents, possibly overcharging some ARGO agents or to delegate to common agents some processing information and deliberation responsibilities, thus isolating ARGO agents only to sensing and acting functions. We leave these questions as future work.

In order to achieve the customized architecture, some modifications were performed in the Jason framework. However, they do not change the original Jason functionalities, because they are just used for ARGO agents. Hence, there is no difference between the Jason framework and the ARGO architecture when a MAS uses using only common agents. The ARGO customized architecture benefits from the Jason framework extensibility ability to provide custom made architectures.

In our experiments, we show that applying the perception filter together with Javino reduces significantly the time of processing perceptions in Jason. In a real-time collision scenario, where the agent had to reason and stop before colliding with an obstacle placed at 120 cm, 80 cm, and 40 cm, the experiments showed the agent was able to stop before colliding only by using perception filters. The ARGO architecture aims to provide programming structures that allow coding robotic agents using Jason. It means that an agent can decide when to act and to perceive at runtime. Furthermore, it is able to change perceptions filters based on its needs, and to decide what device it will be connected to at a certain time during its execution.

For future work, we intend to extend the ARGO architecture for programming multi-robot systems through a communication protocol between robotic agents. Moreover, it is necessary to test ARGO in different domains and apply robotics technics such as SLAM. We will also intend to provide other hardware-side libraries, for instance for PIC and Intel families.

Acknowledgments. Márcio F. Stabile Jr. is financed by CNPq. Carlos Pantoja is financed by CAPES. Jaime Simão Sichman is partially financed by CNPq, proc.303950/2013-7.

References

1. Barros, R.S., Heringer, V.H., Lazarin, N.M., Pantoja, C.E., Moraes, L.M.: An agent-oriented ground vehicle's automation using Jason framework. In: 6th International Conference on Agents and Artificial Intelligence, pp. 261–266 (2014)
2. Bordini, R.H., Hübner, J.F., Wooldridge, M.: Programming Multi-Agent Systems in AgentSpeak using Jason. John Wiley & Sons Ltd., Chichester (2007)
3. Bratman, M.E.: Intention, Plans and Practical Reasoning. Cambridge Press, Cambridge (1987)
4. Calce, A., Forooshani, P.M., Speers, A., Watters, K., Young, T., Jenkin, M.R.: Autonomous aquatic agents. In: ICAART (1), pp. 372–375 (2013)
5. Chen, S.Y.: Kalman filter for robot vision: a survey. IEEE Trans. Industr. Electron. **59**(11), 4409–4420 (2012)
6. Clark, K., Robinson, P.: Robotic agent programming in TeleoR. In: 2015 IEEE International Conference on Robotics and Automation, pp. 5040–5047 (2015)
7. Dastani, M., de Boer, F., Dignum, F., Van Der Hoek, W., Kroese, M., Meyer, J.J., et al.: Programming the deliberation cycle of cognitive robots. In: Proceedings of the 3rd International Cognitive Robotics Workshop (2002)

8. Guinelli, J.V., Junger, D., Pantoja, C.E.: An analysis of Javino middleware for robotic platforms using Jason and JADE frameworks. In: 10th Software Agents, Environments and Applications School (2016)
9. Hama, M.T.: Uma plataforma orientada a agentes para o desenvolvimento de software em veículos aéreos não-tripulados. Master's thesis, Universidade Federal do Rio Grande do Sul, Porto Alegre, Brazil (2012)
10. Hindriks, K.V.: Programming rational agents in GOAL. In: Seghrouchni, A., Dix, J., Dastani, M., Bordini, H.R. (eds.) Multi-Agent Programming: Languages, Tools and Applications, pp. 119–157. Springer, Boston (2009)
11. Hindriks, K.V., De Boer, F.S., Van der Hoek, W., Meyer, J.J.C.: Agent programming in 3APL. Auton. Agent. Multi-Agent Syst. **2**(4), 357–401 (1999)
12. Jain, R.: Art of Computer Systems Performance Analysis: Techniques For Experimental Design Measurements Simulation and Modeling. Wiley (2015)
13. Kuiper, D.M., Wenkstern, R.Z.: Agent vision in multi-agent based simulation systems. Auton. Agent. Multi-Agent Syst. **29**(2), 161–191 (2015)
14. Lazarin, N.M., Pantoja, C.E.: A robotic-agent platform for embedding software agents using raspberry pi and arduino boards. In: 9th Software Agents, Environments and Applications School (2015)
15. Morais, M., Meneguzzi, F., Bordini, R., Amory, A.: Distributed fault diagnosis for multiple mobile robots using an agent programming language. In: 2015 International Conference on Advanced Robotics (ICAR), pp. 395–400 (2015)
16. Mordenti, A., Ricci, A., Santi, D.I.A.: Programming robots with an agent-oriented bdi-based control architecture: Explorations using the jaca and webots platforms. Bologna, Italy, Technical report (2012)
17. Rao, A.S.: AgentSpeak(L): BDI agents speak out in a logical computable language. In: Velde, W., Perram, J.W. (eds.) MAAMAW 1996. LNCS, vol. 1038, pp. 42–55. Springer, Heidelberg (1996). doi:10.1007/BFb0031845
18. Ricci, A., Piunti, M., Viroli, M., Omicini, A.: Environment programming in CArtAgO. In: Seghrouchni, A., Dix, J., Dastani, M., Bordini, H.R. (eds.) Multi-Agent Programming: Languages, Tools and Applications, pp. 259–288. Springer, Boston (2009)
19. Santos, F.R., Hübner, J.F., Becker, L.B.: Concepção e análise de um modelo de agente BDI voltado para o planejamento de rota em um VANT. In: 9th Software Agents, Environments and Applications School (2015)
20. Stabile Jr., M.F., Sichman, J.S.: Evaluating perception filters in BDI Jason agents. In: 4th Brazilian Conference on Intelligent Systems (BRACIS) (2015)
21. Wei, C., Hindriks, K.V.: An agent-based cognitive robot architecture. In: Dastani, M., Hübner, J.F., Logan, B. (eds.) ProMAS 2012. LNCS (LNAI), vol. 7837, pp. 54–71. Springer, Heidelberg (2013). doi:10.1007/978-3-642-38700-5_4
22. Wooldridge, M.J.: Reasoning About Rational Agents. MIT Press, Cambridge (2000)

A Multi-agent Solution for the Deployment of Distributed Applications in Ambient Systems

Ferdinand Piette[1,2]([✉]), Costin Caval[1], Cédric Dinont[2],
Amal El Fallah Seghrouchni[1], and Patrick Tailliert[1]

[1] Sorbonne Universités, UPMC Univ Paris 06, LIP6, Paris, France
[2] Institut Supérieur de l'Électronique et du Numérique, Lille, France
ferdinand.piette@yncrea.fr

Abstract. Ambient Intelligence (AmI) and Internet of Things (IoT) are promising fields for the application of Multi-Agent Systems (MAS). A specific MAS application, described through a video doorkeeper scenario in this paper, is the deployment and the configuration of distributed applications on a hardware infrastructure in ambient systems. It requires the modelling of the available infrastructure and of the deployable applications, respecting a domain ontology, which can then be used by reasoning tools to find the hardware entities that can support the running of the application in the existing infrastructure. It also requires a distributed architecture that allows this solution to be scalable and to provide mechanisms to enhance privacy. In this paper, we discuss this last point. We describe the use of goal-driven agents and show how the MAS architecture and organisation allow for the privacy of the infrastructure resources to be enhanced.

Keywords: Applicative paper · Multi-agent system · Ambient Intelligence · Goal-driven agents · Agent design · Privacy management · Deployment

1 Deployment of Smart Applications

AmI research focuses on the improvement of human interactions with smart applications [13]. These improvements are made possible by the proposal of frameworks and platforms that facilitate the development of context-aware and dynamic applications. These platforms offer mechanisms to build such applications by handling data and events [16,18] or by wrapping hardware and software capabilities into agents [9,14]. However, it is often assumed that an underlying interoperable hardware and energy infrastructure already exists [22]. Meanwhile, the Internet of Things (IoT) aims to provide a global infrastructure for the information society, enabling advanced services by interconnecting physical and virtual "things" based on existing and evolving interoperable information and communication technologies [17]. The main challenge of the IoT is to achieve full interoperability of interconnected devices while guaranteeing the trust, privacy

© Springer International Publishing AG 2016
M. Baldoni et al. (Eds.): EMAS 2016, LNAI 10093, pp. 156–175, 2016.
DOI: 10.1007/978-3-319-50983-9_9

and security of communications [4]. However, a gap exists between AmI and the IoT. Indeed, because of the heterogeneity of such systems, it is difficult to have horizontal communication between connected devices. Present applications use devices that are vertically connected, from the device to an external server that collects and processes the data. The available commercial products are usually not directly interoperable. Moreover, this approach raises privacy questions: the user does not own his data any more, so privacy cannot be guaranteed. Hence, to fill this gap between IoT and AmI applications, adequate deployment mechanisms are required. We addressed the deployment problem in [23] by proposing to model the available hardware infrastructure and the needs of the applications using graphs that describe the various entities, their relations and properties. For deploying an application on the infrastructure, we proposed an extended graph matching algorithm for finding the hardware entities of the infrastructure that fulfil the requirements of the distributed application. However, this solution was centralised, which makes it unsuitable for real systems that need to take into consideration, among others, privacy and scalability. To address these issues, we propose a multi-agent-based distributed deployment software. Through its modularity, the multi-agent paradigm facilitates the local processing of data and guarantees the autonomy of the different parts of the hardware infrastructure, thus enhancing the privacy and robustness of the software.

This paper is organised as follows. Section 2 shows similar works that use agents for the deployment of applications and privacy management. Section 3 presents a scenario that illustrates the deployment of applications and introduces the different key aspects of our solution. The next sections show that multi-agent systems are a well-adapted paradigm to handle the distributed aspect and ensure resource privacy. We detail this multi-agent architecture of our solution (Sect. 4) and the behaviour of each kind of agent using a goal-directed approach (Sect. 5). At last, Sect. 6 explains some implementation specificities and presents the first results. We conclude by presenting the next steps of this work.

2   Related Work

Several works address the deployment problem. Braubach et al. [6] propose a deployment reference model based on a MAS architecture (e.g. agent services) for deploying MAS applications. As an agent is a software entity, the deployment of agents does not have to deal with the high heterogeneity of hardware entities. Some other works in the service-oriented architectures (SOA) community [3] reason on deployment patterns, that specify the structure and constraints of composite solutions on the infrastructure, in order to compose services. The cited paper refers not to the localisation of resources and installation of software, but rather to the binding of existing resources in order to provide the desired composition of services. This is realised using a centralised pattern-matching algorithm that takes into account the various requirements for the given service. Flissi et al. [15] propose a meta-model for abstracting the concepts of the deployment of software over a grid. All these works have shortcomings when considering their use for deploying AmI applications on the IoT infrastructure. Some do not take into consideration the heterogeneity of the hardware and software, as well as the interaction between the two layers (i.e. software and hardware). Others do not tackle the privacy problem. And some propose centralised solutions that are not scalable for real life AmI applications. Our MAS approach takes these problems into consideration: scalability is handled thanks to the agent structure; the autonomy of agents, organisation and privacy policies provide resource privacy; and heterogeneity is supported by the description of the system and the reasoning mechanisms that find projections of applications on the infrastructure.

Privacy in multi-agent systems has already been well explored. Such et al. [27] categorise research on data privacy on different levels: collection, disclosure, processing and dissemination. Multi-agent system specificities have been used to propose different manners of handling the data privacy. Some works focus on norms [5,20] and privacy policies [12,28,29], checked by agent brokers to control the disclosure of the data. Other works [24,26] use social relationships like trust, intimacy or reputation to select the agents with which data can be shared. Trusted third parties are already used in [1,11,21] in order to anonymise the data or the metadata (e.g. IP address, receiver or sender identity), and also to check disclosure authorisations. At last, some works [2] focus on integrating secure communication in the agent platforms by using well known encryption protocols. All these works use MAS in order to provide data privacy. In our work, as explained in Sect. 4, we take advantage of MAS properties to handle the privacy of the hardware resources and of the structure of the system. The data privacy of the deployed applications is left to the developer who can use one of the cited methods.

3   Scenario

The scenario we use in this paper highlights the dynamic deployment of distributed applications. Mr Snow uses a *video doorkeeper* for dependant persons (e.g. visually impaired) application in his home. When someone rings at the door, the image of the entrance camera is displayed on a screen near Mr Snow, making sure he can properly see the person. He can then discuss with the person and decide whether or not to remotely open the door.

It is Saturday morning and Mr Snow is waiting for a parcel that will be delivered to his home at any time. While he is grooming himself in the bathroom, his neighbour, Mr Den, rings the door. The smart house, aware that Mr Snow is in his bathroom, selects the connected mirror of the bathroom, instead of any of the other display screens of the house, as a support to display the image stream of the entrance camera. Mr Snow, not being able to receive his guest, informs him, thanks to the microphone in the mirror, that he will meet him in an hour. After getting ready, Mr Snow goes to his neighbour. In the middle of their conversation, he is notified on his smartphone that an unkonwn man rings at his door again. He decides to display the image of this man on Mr Den's television to ask him if he recognises the guest since his smartphone screen is to small. By default, Mr Snow does not have the right to use any devices that he does not own, but Mr Den has authorised him to access the television when he is at home. The doorkeeper application is redeployed dynamically to use the requested hardware entities. Neither Mr Snow nor his neighbour know the visitor. Mr Snow decides to activate the microphone of the camera which allows him to learn that the unknown person is the expected transporter, who he can now go and see in person.

The important point in this scenario is not the video doorkeeper application, but the way it is deployed dynamically in the environment, considering the user's context. The scenario shows two deployment situations: (1) the application was deployed for use in the user's own home infrastructure, but in a less usual place: the bathroom; (2) the application was deployed on the infrastructure of another user, as the necessary access rights had been granted. We can isolate five main needs of the system:

1. The system has to find which hardware entities to use in order to launch the desired application. These entities have to respect hardware requirements and contextual constraints such as the user location.
2. Once the hardware entities have been chosen, the system has to deploy the application or some part of it on the infrastructure. In the scenario, the application can be divided into two parts. The first one monitors the door bell of the house and is automatically deployed when a user chooses to launch the video doorkeeper application. When someone rings the door, the second part of the application, the one which will display the image stream of the camera on a screen near the user, is deployed. It is the deployment of the second part that interests us.
3. The system has to undeploy (part of) the applications. In the scenario, when the user ends the communication with the guest, the second part of the video doorkeeper application should be undeployed and the corresponding resources released.
4. The system has to monitor the environment: get contextual information about the user location or the current amount of bandwidth of a communication channel for instance. If an inconsistency between the hardware infrastructure properties and the requirements of an application is detected, another deployment of the application (or some parts of it) should be planned.
5. At last, a user has to manage the hardware entities he owns. He can also use hardware entities of others if he has the required permissions (as described in Sect. 4.2). However, he does not have access to information on the structure of the infrastructure he does not own.

The first need is already discussed in our previous work [23] and later improved in a distributed version of the algorithm that finds the hardware entities of the infrastructure that can support the deployment of an application, based on their descriptions. The second and third needs involve interactions with the real environment in order to configure the hardware entities. The fourth need also involves interactions with the environment to sense its properties and state. At last, the fifth need raises the question of the privacy of hardware resources:

how can the system guarantee that users cannot have information about the hardware entities of others?

The multi-agent system we describe in this paper is used to deploy applications on an available hardware infrastructure, to monitor the system and to maintain its consistency. As we describe below, the agents are in charge of the high level reasoning, while artifacts correspond to tools for interacting with the environment. The decentralisation of MAS is an asset to enhance resource privacy. Indeed, the description of the hardware infrastructure can be split into agents so that no global knowledge exists. Then the agents can be organised to apply sharing policies and guide the deployment of the applications. At last, cooperation between agents allows to find solutions of the deployment even if no local solution exists.

With these observations, we can establish the different roles of the system. These roles will be associated with the different entities of the MAS.

1. Interact with a user
2. Maintain the consistency of an application
3. Find a projection of the requirements of an application on the infrastructure graph
4. Interact with the environment to configure hardware entities and deploy applications
5. Sense the environment properties
6. Update the description of the environment
7. Manage sharing policies and resource privacy

4   Multi-agent Architecture

Our scenario highlights several necessary specificities of the deployment software. This software has to dynamically deploy and undeploy distributed AmI applications in an environment that is also dynamic: when a visitor rings the doorbell, the deployment of the video doorkeeper should start, considering the available hardware entities and the location of the user, in order to choose the most relevant screen for displaying the image of the camera. Given its the distribution and openness that characterize the AmI domain, privacy is a very important characteristic of the deployment software. Privacy is defined by Alan Westin [30] as the claim of individuals, groups or institutions to determine for themselves when, how and to what extent information about them is communicated. In this scenario, we focus on *resource privacy* since the data manipulated by the deployment solution concerns hardware resources. Mr Snow is the owner of the hardware entities in his house and he does not want unauthorised persons to use or even know of the existence of these resources. At last, autonomy and robustness of the system are also very important specificities: if my neighbour's system failed, mine should continue to work normally and should not be impacted.

As the required software demands distribution, privacy, context management, autonomy and robustness, we identified MAS as a suitable solution. Through its modularity, this paradigm facilitates a local processing of the data and guarantees the autonomy of the different parts of the hardware infrastructure, thus handling aspects of privacy and robustness. To solve the dynamic deployment problem, we use the graph representation for the hardware infrastructure from our previous work [23]. Nodes represent hardware entities or relations between these entities and properties can be attached to each node. The requirements of the deployable applications are also described using such graphs. A graph matching algorithm can then be used on the available infrastructure graph to find the entities that can support the running of the application.

In the next sub-sections, we present the modelling of agents and the agent organisation for our deployment solution, while focusing on the encapsulation of resource privacy.

4.1   Agents and Artifacts

The deployment software involves the user deploying applications on an infrastructure. Three types of agent were therefore defined to represent and clearly separate each of the parties in handling the deployment: *User Agent*, *Application Agent* and *Infrastructure Agent*. A fourth type of agent was introduced for providing organisation capabilities and enhancing resource privacy: the *Infrastructure Super Agent*. For each type of agent we identified the main goals, that will be described in Sect. 5:

An **Infrastructure Agent** deals with a part of the global hardware infrastructure. It uses the graph representation of this available infrastructure [23] (hardware entities, relations and properties). This graph representation is never shared with other agents. To deploy an application, an *Infrastructure Agent* has to find a projection (possibly partial) of the hardware requirements of the application on the infrastructure (role 3, as identified above). The agent may need to cooperate with other agents to complete the projection if no local solution can be found. This infrastructure description is updated (role 6) when the agent receives information about the current state and properties of the real infrastructure. At last, as the infrastructure description is not shared with the other agents, the *Infrastructure Agents* have to manage the authorization levels and the sharing policy (role 7).

An **Application Agent** manages an entire application during its runtime (role 2). It has a graph-based description of the application that expresses its hardware requirements and the way the hardware entities should be used (configuration, software deployment, ...). If the hardware requirements of parts of the deployed application are no longer respected during its runtime, then the agent will plan another deployment of these parts by interacting with *Infrastructure Agents*. An example of such graph is represented in Fig. 1: the upper part represents the functionalities of the application and the bottom part shows their hardware requirements.

The **User Agent** is attached to a user and saves his preferences and his context. It is the interface between the user and the other agents (role 1). Each user is represented in the MAS by his own agent. This one handles the user's requests for the deployment or undeployment of applications and creates the associated *Application Agents*.

The *Infrastructure Agents* can be grouped to form sub multi-agent systems. These groups are represented by an **Infrastructure Super Agent**. From an outside point of view, a *Infrastructure Super Agent* is seen as a regular *Infrastructure Agent*. It acts as a proxy between the agents inside and outside of the group. It is then easier to abstract groups of agents and make then invisible from the outside. It results on a multi-scale organisation that helps to enhance resource privacy by hiding information about the structure of it sub-organisations.

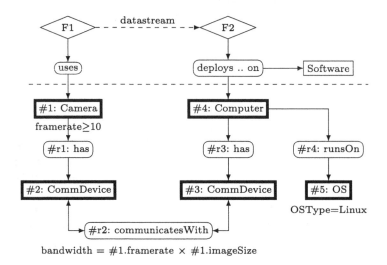

bandwidth = #1.framerate × #1.imageSize

Fig. 1. Example of a basic application graph

In addition to these four classes of agent, we also propose two classes of artifact which are resources and tools that can be instantiated and/or used by agents in order to interact with the environment [25]:

Deployment artifacts [15] can be used by the *Infrastructure Agents* in order to effectively deploy/undeploy some parts of an application, or configure hardware entities so that they can be used by the application (role 4).

Monitoring artifacts provide useful contextual information to the MAS (role 5) such as the location of a user or the current available bandwidth of a communication channel. This information helps the agents keep their application or infrastructure descriptions up to date.

4.2 Sharing Policies

To improve privacy by controlling the use of resources, we also propose sharing policies. *User Agents* can be authorised, by the owner of some hardware infrastructure, to use some parts of its infrastructure, and cooperate with the associated *Infrastructure Agents* or *Super Agents*, to deploy applications. If a

User Agent is not authorised by the *Infrastructure (Super) Agent*, it cannot use the hardware resources proposed by this agent. These authorization levels are defined by the owner of each *Infrastructure (Super) Agent*. The *Administrator level* is defined to identify these owners. With this level, a user can manage the other authorization levels, configure or create sub-organisations of *Infrastructure Agents* (by implicitly instantiating *Infrastructure Super Agents*) and has access to every hardware entity managed by the agent. When an administrator creates a sub-organisation, he is automatically the administrator of the new *Infrastructure Super Agent*.

4.3   Deployment

The deployment is started by a user, through his *User Agent*. The latter then creates an *Application Agent* that will handle the deployment and the monitoring of the application. This agent chooses among the authorized *Infrastructure (Super) Agents* the ones it will ask for the deployment of parts of the application. The concerned *Infrastructure Agents* try to find the hardware entities that will support the deployment of the application. If a partial projection is found, the agent will cooperate with other authorized agents in order to complete the projection. Once such projection is found, the concerned agents effectively deploy the application through the deployment artifacts. The monitoring artifacts provide the *Infrastructure Agents* with information about the environment. When some properties change, these agents notify all the *Application Agents* that have inconsistent applications. These ones can decide to plan another deployment of some parts of the application.

Figures 2 and 3 show the interaction between an *Application Agent* and the *Infrastructure Agents* in order to get a projection of the application and to effectively deploy this application. As stated before, the current *Infrastructure Agent* ("Infra Agent Actor" in the figures) may need to request other agents ("Infra Agent Delegate") to handle a part of the deployment.

4.4   Scenario Illustration

Figure 4 shows the agent structure of the doorkeeper scenario. The description of the infrastructure is split into three *Infrastructure Agents*. The first one manages the hardware entities located in the living room of Mr Snow, like the television set. The second one manages the entities of the bathroom like the connected mirror. These two agents are grouped behind an *Infrastructure Super Agent* representing the house of Mr Snow. And the last one manages the house of the neighbour. Similarly, the *Infrastructure Agent* managing the house of Mr Snow's neighbour can be a super agent, regrouping several *Infrastructure Agents* (or other sub-super agents) to manage more finely the house. The advantage of such organisation is that it is easy to abstract groups of agents and make them invisible from the outside, resulting in a multi-scale organisation that helps improve privacy. Indeed, Mr Snow knows about his own *Infrastructure Agents* (bathroom and living room), but he does not have to know anything about the

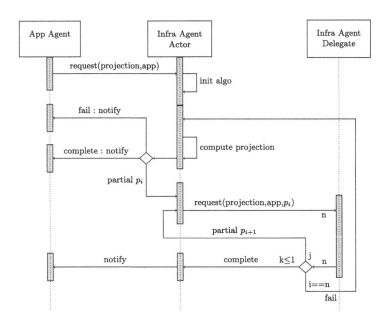

Fig. 2. Infrastructure Agent: get a projection of a part of the application

details of Mr Den's infrastructure organisation. If he wants to interact with his neighbour's house, he has to interact with Mr Den's *Infrastructure Super Agent* – provided that the right access rights were granted, as described below –, without knowing the real number of agents managing Mr Den's house, and reciprocally.

We also find two *Application Agents*. The first one manages the video door-keeper application; when a visitor rings the doorbell, this *Application Agent* triggers the deployment of the video interaction functionality. The second one manages the application which provides the location of the Mr Snow inside his own house to his own *Infrastructure Agents*. The contextual location information is useful for deploying other applications. Indeed, the display screen of the video doorkeeper application has to be chosen near the user. Then, we have two *User Agents*. The first one is the interface between the deployment software and Mr Snow, and the second one is owned by Mr Snow's neighbour. At last, we have a certain number of deployment artifacts that can configure the display screens, the cameras, or deploy software on devices (TV box, connected mirror etc.).

In this scenario, three authorisation levels are defined: the administrator level, the regular user level and the guest level. With the regular user level, the agent has access to the resources of the *Infrastructure (Super) Agent* but it cannot reconfigure authorisation levels or agent organisation. With the guest level, the agent has a restricted access to the resources. Only the resources considered as non critical by an administrator are allowed to be shared. These authorisation levels are not limited to three and can be modified by the administrator of the *Super Agent*. In the video doorkeeper scenario, Mr Snow's *User Agent* is a Regular user for his home *Infrastructure Super Agent*, but it is just a Guest

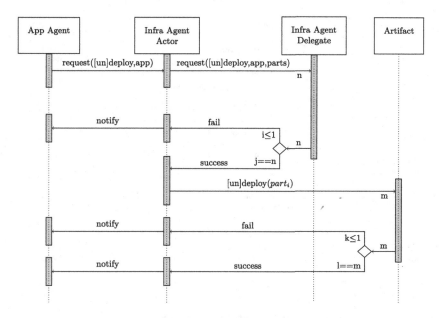

Fig. 3. Infrastructure Agent: deploy a part of an application

to his neighbour's home *Infrastructure Super Agent*. As such, it has only access to the television of Mr Snow's neighbour. This ensures the privacy of the other resources of Mr Den. The *Application Agents* have the same authorisation level as the *User Agent* that creates them. They can interact with the authorised *Infrastructure Agents* in order to effectively deploy their application.

4.5   Summary

In this section, we defined the multi-agent system architecture. *User, Application* and *Infrastructure Agents* were defined in order to provide a clear separation. *Infrastructure Super Agents* were introduced to allow the creation of hierarchical organisations of *Infrastructure Agents*. Sharing policies were defined to control the use of the hardware resources of the infrastructure. The authorizations based on these sharing policies define the organisation and the possible acquaintances for the agents of the MAS.

The agent decomposition encapsulates a part of the privacy mechanism. Indeed, the graph representation of the available hardware infrastructure managed by an *Infrastructure Agent* is only known by this agent and is never shared with others. Moreover, the architecture used helps keep a clear separation between the applicative part, managed by the *Application Agents*, and the hardware part, monitored by the *Infrastructure Agents*. As agents only have a local view of the system, the privacy is enhanced. Privacy policies can allow or prevent the sharing of resources to *User Agents*. This results in privacy by design.

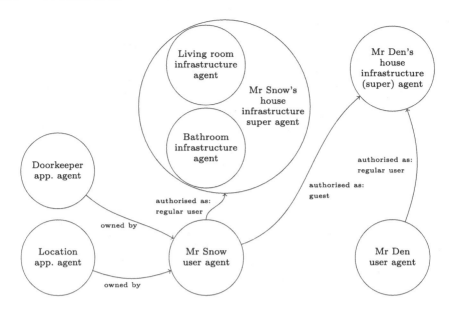

Fig. 4. Agent organisation

5   Agents' Behaviour

The four types of agent presented in the previous section were designed using a goal-based model due to its benefits to the autonomy and robustness of the application [10]. Goals are specified by describing their associated plans: higher level *goal plans* describing relationships between goals and lower level *action plans* for concrete actions. This goal-based representation is based on the Goal-Plan Separation (GPS) approach [8], where each agent has a main goal plan (i.e. plan without any actions, so only decisions, perceptions and goal adoptions) that describes the top level behaviour, which can be pursued using other goal plans or directly action plans (i.e. plan without any goal adoptions). This approach helps handle agent complexity through a multi-level description, from top level abstract behaviours with goals to concrete action plans. Using goal-plans also has the advantage of specifying the relationships between goals in a plan format.

Plans are represented using a flowchart notation we adapted for modelling goal-driven agents (Fig. 5). The notation contains the main elements that allow for the behaviours of agents to be defined. Event perceptions (wait), decision nodes and iterators (ForEach) can be used in any type of plan. Action nodes are specific to action plans and goal adoptions (parallel or synchronous) are specific to goal plan. Parallel executions are launched when adopting goals. For this application, we considered a simple goal model (similar to a *perform* goal [7]) where a goal is successful ("S") when the plan executing for it ends with "End ok". This allowed us to keep a simple goal life-cycle appropriate for using in our application, while still benefiting from the features of the goal-based design.

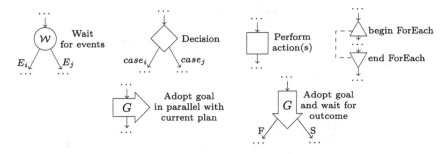

Fig. 5. Flowchart nodes for efficiently describing the plans of goal-driven agents

We continue by describing in detail the agents of the system. Since the *Infrastructure Super Agent* is only a proxy between the agents of the group it represents and the other agents outside this group, its implementation is not detailed here. In what follows, P_{Xi-j} are the plans for a goal G_{Xi}.

5.1 User Agent

The *User Agent* acts as an interface between the user and the deployment MAS. The main goal plan of the *User Agent* (Fig. 6) waits for user input and, depending on the received request, adopts the necessary goal, corresponding to the agent functions identified in Sect. 4.1. The goal plan of G_{U1} (Fig. 7) creates an *Application Agent*, wait for a confirmation and adopt a goal that monitor the *Application Agent*.

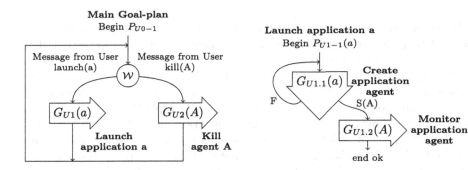

Fig. 6. *User Agent*: main goal plan   **Fig. 7.** *User Agent*: goal plan for G_{U1}

5.2 Application Agent

The *Application Agent* is created by a *User Agent*. It tries to deploy a precise application by cooperating with one or more known *Infrastructure (Super) Agents*, from which it does not need to have any infrastructure details.

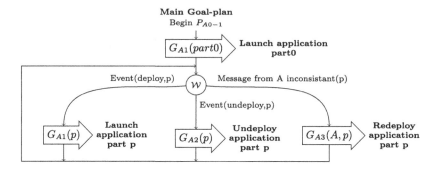

Fig. 8. *Application Agent*: main goal plan

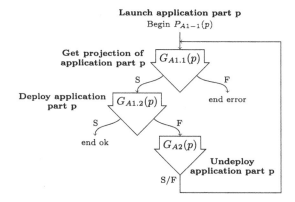

Fig. 9. *Application Agent*: goal plan for G_{A1}: "Launch application part"

Upon its creation, an *Application Agent* execute its main goal plan (Fig. 8). The goal G_{A1} that deploy an initial functionality (Fig. 9) is adopted and the agent waits for internal events for new deployments or undeployments.

The deployment is done in two steps: first the agent obtains a deployment solution from *Infrastructure Agents* via $G_{A1.1}$ and then it requests the deployment according to this solution through $G_{A1.2}$. The *Application Agent* sends a list of the requirements described in the application graph to the *Infrastructure Agent* and the solution it receives contains the list of requirements that could be fulfilled. Note that the reply does not contain any actual infrastructure details, which is important for the privacy of the infrastructure. It can be seen (Fig. 10) that the agent may need to call multiple *Infrastructure Agents* in order to obtain a complete deployment solution. Indeed an *Infrastructure Agent* tries to find in its own infrastructure the hardware entities that match the requirements of the application. However, if these requirements only partially match, the *Infrastructure Agent* will return a partial solution to the *Application Agent*. In this case, the latter will call another *Infrastructure Agent* that will continue to match the requirements of the application. Once a solution has been found, the

Application Agent interacts again with the concerned *Infrastructure Agents* to effectively deploy the functionalities of the application: plan $P_{A1.2}$ simply sends messages and waits for a confirmation (Fig. 11). The plan for the undeployment of a part of the application (G_{A2}) is similar to the plan that deploy a part of the application $(G_{A1.2})$. The plan for the redeployment of a part of the application (G_{A3}) only undeploy this part first and deploy it again. After a functionality was deployed, the agent monitors it through G_{A0} and wait for a message from the *Infrastructure Agents* that tells that a part of the application is inconsistency (e.g. changing infrastructure availability, changing user location).

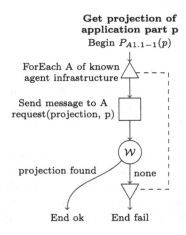 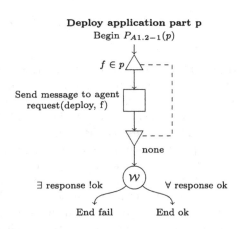

Fig. 10. *Application Agent*: plan for $G_{A1.1}$: "get projection of application part"

Fig. 11. *Application Agent*: plan for $G_{A1.2}$: "deploy application part"

Note here that the *Application Agents* only handle the application deployment. The application itself is in charge of its own actions, data and privacy.

5.3   Infrastructure Agent

An *Infrastructure Agent* receives requests from *Application Agents* that it tries to satisfy (Fig. 12). Only requests originating from known *User Agents* are treated, in other words only applications from agents that were granted one of the levels of authorisation are accepted.

When it receives a request for a deployment solution, the *Infrastructure Agent* uses the graph matching algorithm to determine if it can fulfil the requirements of the request (Fig. 13) using the devices it manages. The algorithm takes into consideration the levels of authorisation of the involved *User Agents*. If it cannot produce a complete solution, the *Infrastructure Agent* requests the help of other agents in its group, but without informing the *Application Agents*. In this way, the components of the infrastructure remain private. If a complete solution is eventually produced and the *Infrastructure Agent* is given the order to deploy

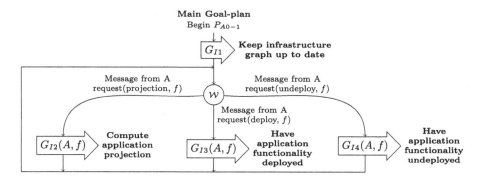

Fig. 12. *Infrastructure Agent*: main goal plan

the application, it will dispatch the deployment tasks to its own deployment artifacts as well as to any other *Infrastructure Agents* that were included in the final solution. In case any of these requests fails (e.g. an artifact malfunctions), the whole application is undeployed and the *Application Agent* is informed, which will cause it to restart the deployment procedure.

In parallel with the request handling, the agent also adopts G_{I1} which listens for agent and artifact information in order to manage the graph the devices corresponding to the *Infrastructure Agent*. In case of an inconsistency (e.g. Mr Snow leaves Mr Den's home, so any display he used there are no longer relevant for the application), the agent informs the *Application Agents* that it will need to redeploy the concerned parts of their applications.

6 Implementation and Experimentations

A demonstration model of the deployment software has been developed in an apartment replica attached to our laboratory. This home replica implements various scenarios applied to home care for dependent persons, including the presented scenario. These scenarios are using commercial connected devices tweaked to be horizontally connected, thanks to the deployment software.

Our goal is to run the MAS on different devices like smartphones or embedded systems with few resources. Most of existing regular MAS platforms like Jade for instance are memory-consuming and Java-oriented platforms [19]. They are not suitable for our purpose. That is why we designed our own MAS platform in JavaScript. Indeed, web technologies are fully interoperable and the agents can easily be run on devices like smartphones or the Raspberry Pi. Visualisation and interfaces are also JavaScript web applications. The agents embed a monitoring and debugging web server that proposes interfaces for interacting with it. The effective deployment is handled by deployment artifacts. The demonstration model handles *ssh* and *puppet* artifacts in order to deploy and run software on UNIX systems (computers, micro-computers, Unix-based devices etc.). We also implemented a specific deployment artifact that configures the frame rate of IP

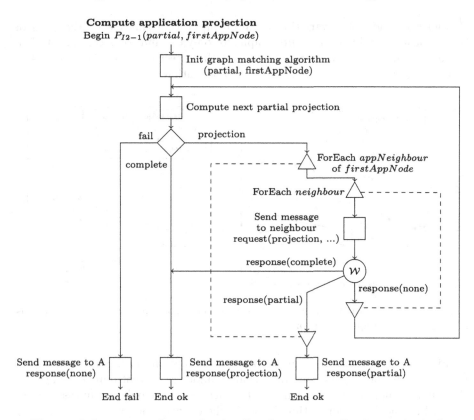

Compute application projection
Begin $P_{I2-1}(partial, firstAppNode)$

Fig. 13. *Infrastructure Agent*: plan for G_{I2}: "compute application projection"

cameras. In this implementation we mostly used IP devices. We also integrated EnOcean devices. These devices, however, are handled by a hard-coded gateway that extends the IP network to EnOcean devices. Next stage will be to handle multiple means of communication by automatically deploying gateways or proxies between the devices when needed. At last, the agent implementation was, in first place, not obvious. The multi-level GPS approach made it intuitive to develop.

For these experiments, we generated random infrastructure and application graphs for which we varied the number of nodes, the average number of edges and the average number of properties each node has. We only considered the infrastructure-application pairs for which at least one complete projection solution exists. In the graphs depicted below, each point is the median execution time obtained by running the algorithm on 100 randomly-generated infrastructure-application pairs. A random graph generation was introduced in order to evaluate the MAS performances independently of the application domain. Then, the properties of the application and infrastructure graph in the context of smart-homes were extracted and correlated with the general results.

Figure 14 shows the variation of the computation times with the sizes of the application and infrastructure graphs for only one infrastructure agent. The execution time shows a moderate increase with respect to the infrastructure size variation. However, it grows fast with the application graph size.

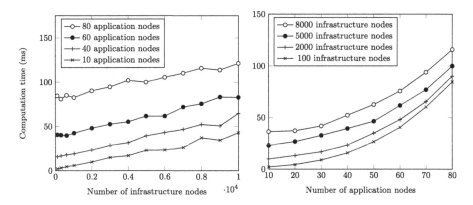

Fig. 14. The execution times of the projection algorithm executed for various infrastructure and application sizes.

Figure 15 represents the variation of the execution times with size of the infrastructure and application graph shared amoung different number of agents. We can note that it is not efficient to let an agent manage only few infrastructure nodes. In that case, a lot of time is lost in the cooperation process.

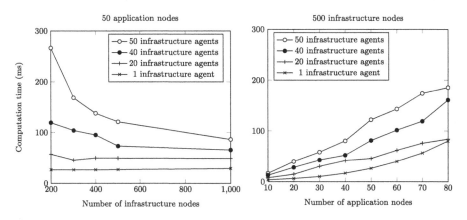

Fig. 15. The execution times of the graph-matching algorithm for various size of infrastructure, application and number of agents.

These experiments show that the algorithm can be used with real applications and smart environments. Indeed, the computation time grows fast with the size of the application graph, however, applications do not have an important number of nodes. Contrariwise, the global infrastructure graph can grow rapidly, but we have seen that the computation time evolves reasonably. For example, the application from the scenario in Sect. 3 contains 23 nodes, while the infrastructure is made of more than 50 nodes shared amoung 3 agents. The average number of edges between the nodes is between 2 and 3.

This realisation helps us to figure out the difficulties of handling the heterogeneity of hardware entities. We are now able to handle applications through an AppStore for Smart Homes. These applications can be automatically deployed in a real environment, using the available hardware devices, and including mechanisms to ensure privacy management of the resources. This provides a concrete base for the implementation of a complete middleware for the deployment of distributed applications in a smart environment.

7   Conclusion and Future Work

In this paper, we presented a multi-agent solution for reasoning on the dynamic deployment of distributed applications in ambient systems. We described the modelling of the system and presented the specifications of the goal-based agents. We illustrated the MAS using a context-aware video doorkeeper scenario. In this scenario, a doorkeeper application is dynamically deployed in order to route the video stream of the entrance hall camera to a relevant screen, near the user, thanks to contextual information about his location. Even if smartphones are nowadays the favorite interface of the users, we are convainced that multimodal interactions have to be proposed. The devices and the interfaces has to be selected considering the context. Other scenarios to help people with reduce mobility has been inplemented using the apartment replica we used.

The MAS proposed in this paper contains four classes of goal-directed agent to handle a clear separation between the hardware and software layers and to ensure resource privacy in ambient systems. In order to preserve the privacy of the resources, the graph models of the infrastructure are handled locally by the concerned agents. The use of MAS made it possible to introduce privacy measures at architecture and organisation level, on top of which we were able to add a user-defined privacy policy mechanism. This was an important criterion for the choice of the agent paradigm since in the domain of Ambient Intelligence there are often different infrastructure owners that need to ensure the privacy of their resources. The separation between the applicative and the infrastructure layers, together with the decentralised approach also enhance the robustness of the solution. The clearly delimited entities, with either virtual (the applications) or physical (users, infrastructure elements) correspondents, guided the agentification. The use of a goal-based representation for agents together with the Goal-Plan Separation approach facilitated the modelling task. The specific plan notation was efficient in describing the agent plans both during design and for presentation purposes.

In terms of future work, for the deployment software, data privacy in the deployed applications should also be taken into consideration in addition to the resource privacy discussed here. We would like to facilitate the local processing and storage of the data by defining data privacy policies which should be facilitated by the modularity of the MAS. This would impact the reasoning on the deployment: the hardware entities would have to be filtered with respect to this new data privacy policy. In the interest of the engineering of multi-agent systems, we are studying the goal-based modelling approach with GPS agents and the plan notation for the extension towards a development methodology for robust software.

References

1. Aïmeur, E., Brassard, G., Fernandez, J.M., Onana, F.S.M.: Privacy-preserving demographic filtering. In: Proceedings of the 2006 ACM Symposium on Applied Computing, SAC 2006, pp. 872–878. ACM, New York (2006)
2. Alberola, J., Such, J., Garcia-Fornes, A., Espinosa, A., Botti, V.: A performance evaluation of three multiagent platforms. Artif. Intell. Rev. **34**(2), 145–176 (2010)
3. Arnold, W., Eilam, T., Kalantar, M., Konstantinou, A.V., Totok, A.A.: Automatic realization of SOA deployment patterns in distributed environments. In: Bouguettaya, A., Krueger, I., Margaria, T. (eds.) ICSOC 2008. LNCS, vol. 5364, pp. 162–179. Springer, Heidelberg (2008). doi:10.1007/978-3-540-89652-4_15
4. Atzori, L., Iera, A., Morabito, G.: The internet of things: a survey. Comput. Netw. **54**(15), 2787–2805 (2010)
5. Barth, A., Datta, A., Mitchell, J., Nissenbaum, H.: Privacy and contextual integrity: framework and applications. In: 2006 IEEE Symposium on Security and Privacy, pp. 15–198, May 2006
6. Braubach, L., Pokahr, A., Bade, D., Krempels, K.-H., Lamersdorf, W.: Deployment of distributed multi-agent systems. In: Gleizes, M.-P., Omicini, A., Zambonelli, F. (eds.) ESAW 2004. LNCS (LNAI), vol. 3451, pp. 261–276. Springer, Heidelberg (2005). doi:10.1007/11423355_19
7. Braubach, L., Pokahr, A., Moldt, D., Lamersdorf, W.: Goal representation for BDI agent systems. In: Bordini, R.H., Dastani, M., Dix, J., Fallah Seghrouchni, A. (eds.) ProMAS 2004. LNCS (LNAI), vol. 3346, pp. 44–65. Springer, Heidelberg (2005). doi:10.1007/978-3-540-32260-3_3
8. Caval, C., El Fallah Seghrouchni, A., Taillibert, P.: Keeping a clear separation between goals and plans. In: Dalpiaz, F., Dix, J., Riemsdijk, M.B. (eds.) EMAS 2014. LNCS (LNAI), vol. 8758, pp. 15–39. Springer, Heidelberg (2014). doi:10.1007/978-3-319-14484-9_2
9. Chen, H., Finin, T.W., Joshi, A., Kagal, L., Perich, F.: Intelligent agents meet the semantic web in smart spaces. IEEE Internet Comput. **8**(6), 69–79 (2004)
10. Cheong, C., Winikoff, M.: Hermes: designing goal-oriented agent interactions. In: Müller, J.P., Zambonelli, F. (eds.) AOSE 2005. LNCS, vol. 3950, pp. 16–27. Springer, Heidelberg (2006). doi:10.1007/11752660_2
11. Cissée, R., Albayrak, S.: An agent-based approach for privacy-preserving recommender systems. In: Proceedings of the 6th International Joint Conference on Autonomous Agents and Multiagent Systems, AAMAS 2007, pp. 182:1–182:8. ACM, New York (2007)
12. Crépin, L., Demazeau, Y., Boissier, O., Jacquenet, F.: Sensitive data transaction in hippocratic multi-agent systems. In: Artikis, A., Picard, G., Vercouter, L. (eds.) ESAW 2008. LNCS (LNAI), vol. 5485, pp. 85–101. Springer, Heidelberg (2009). doi:10.1007/978-3-642-02562-4_5

13. Ducatel, K., Bogdanowicz, M., Scapolo, F., Leijten, J., Burgelman, J.: Scenarios for ambient intelligence in 2010 (2001)
14. Fallah Seghrouchni, A., Olaru, A., Nguyen, N.T.T., Salomone, D.: Ao dai: agent oriented design for ambient intelligence. In: Desai, N., Liu, A., Winikoff, M. (eds.) PRIMA 2010. LNCS (LNAI), vol. 7057, pp. 259–269. Springer, Heidelberg (2012). doi:10.1007/978-3-642-25920-3_18
15. Flissi, A., Dubus, J., Dolet, N., Merle, P.: Deploying on the grid with deployware. In: 8th IEEE International Symposium on Cluster Computing and the Grid, CCGRID 2008, pp. 177–184, May 2008
16. Hellenschmidt, M., Kirste, T.: A generic topology for ambient intelligence. In: Markopoulos, P., Eggen, B., Aarts, E., Crowley, J.L. (eds.) EUSAI 2004. LNCS, vol. 3295, pp. 112–123. Springer, Heidelberg (2004). doi:10.1007/978-3-540-30473-9_12
17. ITU-T: Overview of the internet of things, recommendations (2012)
18. Johanson, B., Fox, A., Winograd, T.: The interactive workspaces project: experiences with ubiquitous computing rooms. IEEE Pervasive Comput. 1(2), 67–74 (2002)
19. Kravari, K., Bassiliades, N.: A survey of agent platforms. J. Artif. Soc. Soc. Simul. 18(1), 11 (2015)
20. Krupa, Y., Vercouter, L.: Contextual integrity and privacy enforcing norms for virtual communities. In: Boissier, O., El Fallah Seghrouchni, A., Hassas, S., Maudet, N. (eds.) MALLOW. CEUR Workshop Proceedings, vol. 627 (2010). CEUR-WS.org
21. Menczer, F., Street, W., Vishwakarma, N., Monge, A., Jakobsson, M.: IntelliShopper: a proactive, personal, private shopping assistant. In: Proceeding 1st ACM International Joint Conference on Autonomous Agents and MultiAgent Systems (AAMAS) (2002)
22. O'Hare, G.M.P., Collier, R., Dragone, M., O'Grady, M.J., Muldoon, C., Montoya, J.A.: Embedding agents within ambient intelligent applications. In: Bosse, T. (ed.) Agents and Ambient Intelligence, Ambient Intelligence and Smart Environments, vol. 12, pp. 119–133. IOS Press (2012)
23. Piette, F., Dinont, C., El Fallah Seghrouchni, A., Taillibert, P.: Deployment and configuration of applications for ambient systems. In: The 6th International Conference on Ambient Systems, Networks and Technologies (ANT-2015), Procedia Computer Science, vol. 52, pp. 373–380 (2015)
24. Ramchurn, S.D., Huynh, D., Jennings, N.R.: Trust in multi-agent systems. Knowl. Eng. Rev. 19(1), 1–25 (2004)
25. Ricci, A.: Agents and coordination artifacts for feature engineering. In: Ryan, M.D., Meyer, J.-J.C., Ehrich, H.-D. (eds.) Objects, Agents, and Features. LNCS, vol. 2975, pp. 209–226. Springer, Heidelberg (2004). doi:10.1007/978-3-540-25930-5_13
26. Such, J.M., Espinosa, A., GarcíA-Fornes, A., Sierra, C.: Self-disclosure decision making based on intimacy and privacy. Inf. Sci. 211, 93–111 (2012)
27. Such, J.M., Espinosa, A., Garca-Fornes, A.: A survey of privacy in multi-agent systems. Knowl. Eng. Rev. 29, 314–344 (2014)
28. Tentori, M., Favela, J., Rodriguez, M.D.: Privacy-aware autonomous agents for pervasive healthcare. IEEE Intell. Syst. 21(6), 55–62 (2006)
29. Udupi, Y.B., Singh, M.P.: Information sharing among autonomous agents in referral networks. In: Joseph, S.R.H., Despotovic, Z., Moro, G., Bergamaschi, S. (eds.) AP2PC 2007. LNCS (LNAI), vol. 5319, pp. 13–26. Springer, Heidelberg (2010). doi:10.1007/978-3-642-11368-0_2
30. Westin, A.F.: Privacy and Freedom. Atheneum, New York (1967)

Reasoning About the Executability
of Goal-Plan Trees

Yuan Yao[1], Lavindra de Silva[2], and Brian Logan[1(✉)]

[1] School of Computer Science, University of Nottingham, Nottingham, UK
{yvy,bsl}@cs.nott.ac.uk
[2] Faculty of Engineering, Institute for Advanced Manufacturing,
University of Nottingham, Nottingham, UK
lavindra.desilva@nottingham.ac.uk

Abstract. User supplied domain control knowledge in the form of hierarchically structured agent plans is at the heart of a number of approaches to reasoning about action. This knowledge encodes the "standard operating procedures" of an agent for responding to environmental changes, thereby enabling fast and effective action selection. This paper develops mechanisms for reasoning about a set of hierarchical plans and goals, by deriving "summary information" from the conditions on the execution of the basic actions forming the "leaves" of the hierarchy. We provide definitions of necessary and contingent pre-, in-, and postconditions of goals and plans that are consistent with the conditions of the actions forming a plan. Our definitions extend previous work with an account of both deterministic and non-deterministic actions, and with support for specifying that actions and goals within a (single) plan can execute concurrently. Based on our new definitions, we also specify requirements that are useful in scheduling the execution of steps in a set of goal-plan trees. These requirements essentially define conditions that must be protected by any scheduler that interleaves the execution of steps from different goal-plan trees.

1 Introduction

User supplied domain control knowledge in the form of hierarchically structured agent plans is at the heart of a number of approaches to reasoning about action. This knowledge encodes the "standard operating procedures" of an agent for responding to environmental changes, thereby enabling fast and effective action selection. Various lines of previous work have exploited such control knowledge, including multi-agent coordination [6,7], interleaved plan execution in single-agent systems [16,17], heuristic approaches to speeding up classical planning [2,4,11], and approaches to synthesising desirable primitive and abstract plans [8,12].

This paper develops mechanisms for reasoning about a set of hierarchical plans and goals, by deriving "summary information" from the conditions on the execution of the basic actions forming the "leaves" of the hierarchy. We provide

M. Baldoni et al. (Eds.): EMAS 2016, LNAI 10093, pp. 176–191, 2016.
DOI: 10.1007/978-3-319-50983-9_10

definitions of necessary and contingent pre-, in-, and postconditions of goals and plans that are consistent with the conditions of the (possibly nondeterministic) actions forming a plan. Such information is useful when writing agent programs, e.g. when deciding which goal-plan tree is the minimally interfering "building block" to include within a new plan in order to bring about a desired postcondition. In addition to summarising the "static" properties of a single goal-plan tree, we also define requirements that are useful in scheduling the execution of steps in a set of goal-plan trees. While goal-plan trees are most commonly used to represent a BDI agent's domain knowledge, the mechanisms we present could equally be used to represent and reason about the executability of Hierarchical Task Network (HTN) planning [10] structures, e.g., to synthesise new HTN recipes from existing task networks. HTN and BDI systems are closely related in terms of syntax and semantics, making it possible to translate between the two representations [14].

The paper extends the most closely related strands of work in the literature, i.e., [6,7,16,17] in two main ways. Like us, these authors also derive summary information from a set of hierarchical plans, and use that information to find a schedule for the concurrent execution of a given set of top-level goals. Our first extension is an account of both deterministic and non-deterministic primitive actions, and the second is the ability to specify that actions and goals within a (single) plan can execute concurrently. We also contribute novel corresponding definitions for the conditions that must be protected by any scheduler that interleaves the execution of steps from different goal-plan trees.

The remainder of this paper is organised as follows. In Sect. 2 we discuss closely related work from the literature. In Sect. 3, we define the 'static', necessary and contingent conditions of actions, plans and goals. Then, in Sect. 4 we define the corresponding 'dynamic' notions, which specify the conditions that must be taken into account when scheduling. Finally, in Sect. 5, we conclude and identify directions for future work.

2   Related Work

Our approach is closely related to two previous strands of work in the literature. The first is that of Clement et al. [6,7], where algorithms are presented for deriving "summary" information from developer-defined hierarchical plans belonging to the agents in a multi-agent system. The derived knowledge is then used to find a schedule that coordinates the activities of the agents at run time. The work of Thangarajah et al. [15–17] is similar, though they focus on the single-agent case. They describe an approach based on summary information that coordinates the various goal-plan trees of a single agent, in order to exploit positive interactions between them and to avoid negative interactions, both of which involve reasoning about necessary and possible (summary) conditions of different ways of achieving a goal. They give algorithms for scheduling goal-plan trees, e.g., to determine whether a newly adopted (sub)goal will definitely be safe to execute without conflicts, or will definitely result in conflicts. In the latter case, Thangarajah et al. suspend the goal until it is safe to execute it.

An important difference between the work of Thangarajah et al. and that of Clement et al., is that Thangarajah et al. define the necessary post-condition of a goal or plan as the effects that are necessarily brought about at any (even an intermediate) stage during the goal's or plan's possible executions, whereas Clement et al. define a necessary post-condition as those effects that necessarily hold at the end of all executions. We incorporate both these notions in our approach: our definition of a necessary postcondition of a plan or goal in Sect. 3 is similar to the necessary postconditions of Clement et al., and the notion of execution conditions that must hold for the successful execution of a set of goal-plan trees we present in Sect. 4 is similar to the necessary postconditions of Thangarajah et al. Another important difference involves the treatment of cases where a plan step makes a 'descendant' (sub)plan associated with a later plan step inapplicable. Clement et al. assume that such conflicts can be resolved during the scheduling phase, by inserting an available (concurrent) plan—possibly one belonging to a different agent—that asserts a suitable post-condition.[1] We disallow such conflicts, and define a "local" notion of a contingent condition which does not rely on other concurrent plans.

Our work is also related to that of de Silva et al. [9], who focus on how summary information could be used for the synthesis of "abstract plans". In [9], the authors describe how both the strands of work described above could be extended to support agent programs that include variables, i.e., to a restricted first-order language. While the approach of de Silva et al. also supports basic actions, the actions they consider are deterministic and cannot be executed in parallel with other actions. In contrast, our approach is sufficiently general to allow the parallel execution of (nondeterministic) actions and subgoals.

3   Goal-Plan Trees

As in [15,17] we use *goal-plan trees* to represent the relations between goals, plans and actions, and to reason about the interactions between intentions. The root of a goal-plan tree is a top-level goal[2] (goal node), and its children are the plans that can be used to achieve the goal (plan nodes). Plans may in turn contain subgoals (goal nodes), giving rise to a tree structure representing all possible ways an agent can achieve the top-level goal.

In [15,17] goal-plan trees contain only goals and plans. We extend their definition of goal-plan trees to allow primitive actions in plans in addition to subgoals as in [21,23,24]. Plans thus consist of a sequence of steps, where a step is either a primitive action or a subgoal, or a parallel composition of plan steps.[3] Parallel

---

[1] This assumption is related to the Modal Truth Criterion [5]. See also [24], where scheduling the concurrently executing plans of a single agent is used to recover from action failures.

[2] We assume a procedural interpretation of goals ('goals to do' rather than goals to achieve a state). It is straightforward to adapt the definitions below for declarative goals.

[3] The goal-plan trees in [21,23,24] do not include parallel constructs.

⟨GoalType⟩ ::= ⟨GoalTypeName⟩ ⟨Precondition⟩ ⟨In-condition⟩ ⟨Postcondition⟩
⟨Plans⟩

⟨GoalTypeName⟩ ::= ⟨Label⟩

⟨Plans⟩ ::= ⟨PlanTypeName⟩ (, ⟨PlanTypeName⟩)*

⟨PlanType⟩ ::= ⟨PlanTypeName⟩ ⟨Precondition⟩ ⟨In-condition⟩ ⟨Postcondition⟩
⟨PlanBody⟩

⟨PlanTypeName⟩ ::= ⟨Label⟩

⟨PlanBody⟩ ::= ⟨ExecutionStep⟩ (; ⟨ExecutionStep⟩)*

⟨ExecutionStep⟩ ::= ⟨ActionTypeName⟩ | ⟨GoalTypeName⟩
| (⟨ExecutionStep⟩ || ⟨ExecutionStep⟩)

⟨ActionType⟩ ::= ⟨ActionTypeName⟩ ⟨Precondition⟩ ⟨In-condition⟩ ⟨Postcondition⟩

⟨ActionTypeName⟩ ::= ⟨Label⟩

⟨Precondition⟩ ::= ε | ⟨Condition⟩ (, ⟨Condition⟩)*

⟨In-condition⟩ ::= ε | ⟨Condition⟩ (, ⟨Condition⟩)*

⟨Postcondition⟩ ::= ε | ⟨Condition⟩ (, ⟨Condition⟩)*

⟨Condition⟩ ::= ⟨Statement⟩ | *NOT* ⟨Statement⟩

⟨Statement⟩ ::= *string* | ⟨Variable⟩ = ⟨Value⟩

⟨Label⟩ ::= *unique string*

⟨Variable⟩ ::= *unique string*

⟨Value⟩ ::= *string*

⟨GoalInstance⟩ ::= ⟨InstanceName⟩ ⟨GoalType⟩

⟨PlanInstance⟩ ::= ⟨InstanceName⟩ ⟨PlanType⟩

⟨ActionInstance⟩ ::= ⟨InstanceName⟩ ⟨ActionType⟩

⟨InstanceName⟩ ::= ⟨Label⟩

Fig. 1. BNF Syntax of goal-plan trees with actions

composition is supported by BDI agent systems such as JACK [20] and HTN-like planning systems such as RETSINA [13].

Figure 1 shows the BNF syntax of our extended goal-plan trees. A *GoalType* is a template for a goal. A *GoalInstance* is created when an agent chooses to pursue a particular instance of goal-type. Similarly, a *PlanType* is a template for a plan, and a *PlanInstance* is created when the agent executes a particular plan. In addition, we introduce an *ActionType* as a template for an action, and an *ActionInstance* is created when a particular action is chosen for execution by the agent. *GoalTypeName*, *PlanTypeName* and *ActionTypeName* are labels that indicate the type of the goal, the plan or the action respectively. *Plans* represents the set of plan-types that may be used to satisfy a goal of the corresponding *GoalType*.

Goals, plans and actions have pre-, in-, and postconditions. Pre- and postconditions specify respectively the states of the environment which must hold immediately before the action, plan, or goal is executed, and which are brought about by executing the action, plan, or goal. In-conditions specify the states of the environment which must hold for the duration of the execution of the action, plan, or goal. In-conditions of plans and goals are thus relevant when their associated actions are interleaved or overlapped, and in-conditions of actions are relevant when they are overlapped.

We model the environment using a set of propositions Φ, and define pre-, in- and postconditions of a goal-plan tree node η (an action, plan or goal) as sets of literals (elements of $\Phi^+ = \Phi \cup \{\neg p \mid p \in \Phi\}$) as follows.

Precondition: a precondition is a set of literals $\phi = pre(\eta)$, $\phi \subseteq \Phi^+$ that must be true for η to begin execution (where η is an action or plan), or for η to be achieved (where η is a goal).

In-condition: an in-condition is a set of literals $v = in(\eta)$, $v \subseteq \Phi^+$ that must hold during the execution of η (where η is an action or plan), or during the pursuit of η (where η is a goal); if any of the literals in v becomes false during execution, the action, plan or goal is aborted with failure.

Postcondition: a postcondition (or effect) is a set of literals $\psi = post(\eta)$, $\psi \subseteq \Phi^+$ that are or may be made true by executing η (where η is an action or plan), or by achieving η (where η is a goal).

We distinguish two types of pre-, in- and postconditions: necessary and contingent. A *necessary* (or universal) condition must hold for all executions of an action or plan or for all ways of achieving a goal, while a *contingent* (or existential) condition must hold for some executions of the action or plan or some ways of achieving the goal. We denote the necessary and contingent preconditions as $pre_n(\eta)$ and $pre_c(\eta)$, where η is an action, plan or goal, and stipulate that $pre(\eta) = pre_n(\eta) \cup pre_c(\eta)$. Similarly, we denote necessary and contingent in-conditions as $in_n(\eta)$ and $in_c(\eta)$, and necessary and contingent postconditions as $post_n(\eta)$ and $post_c(\eta)$, and stipulate that $in(\eta) = in_n(\eta) \cup in_c(\eta)$ and $post(\eta) = post_n(\eta) \cup post_c(\eta)$. The necessary and contingent postconditions of an action, plan, or goal are always disjoint, and the same applies to necessary and contingent in-conditions, and to necessary and contingent preconditions.

While the relevant pre-, in- and postconditions form part of the definition of an action, the conditions of plans and goals are derived from the conditions of their actions and subgoals (in the case of plans) and from plans to achieve the goal (in the case of goals). We give formal definitions of necessary and contingent conditions for actions, plans, and goals in the sections below.

3.1   Actions

Actions are the basic steps an agent can perform in order to change its environment. Actions may be deterministic or non-deterministic. Deterministic actions have a single outcome (postcondition), while the execution of a non-deterministic action results in one of a set of possible outcomes (set of postconditions).

The precondition of an action α, $pre_n(\alpha) = \phi$, is always necessary (and $pre_c(\alpha) = \emptyset$). The in-condition of an action, $in_n(\alpha) = v$, is also necessary (and $in_c(\alpha) = \emptyset$). Deterministic actions have a single postcondition ψ. The necessary postcondition of a deterministic action α is defined as $post_n(\alpha) = \psi$, and the contingent postcondition is defined by $post_c(\alpha) = \emptyset$. The execution of a non-deterministic action results in one of a set of possible postconditions $\{\psi_1, \ldots, \psi_n\}, \psi_i \subseteq \Phi^+$. The necessary postcondition of a non-deterministic action α is defined as $post_n(\alpha) = \bigcap \psi_i \in \{\psi_1, \ldots, \psi_n\}$, and the contingent postcondition is defined by $post_c(\alpha) = \bigcup \psi_i \in \{\psi_1, \ldots, \psi_n\} \backslash post_n(\alpha)$.[4] We assume that action specifications are consistent in the sense that each possible outcome of an action is itself consistent, i.e., that $\psi_i \not\models \perp, 1 \leq i \leq n$, and that execution of an action does not invalidate the in-condition of the action, i.e., $in_n(\alpha) \cup post_n(\alpha) \cup post_c(\alpha) \not\models \perp$.[5]

3.2   Plans

A plan π consists of a sequence of actions, subgoals, and parallel compositions of actions and subgoals. That is, a plan is of the form $\pi = \alpha_1; \ldots; \alpha_m$, where each α_i is either an action, a subgoal or a parallel composition $\beta_1 \| \ldots \| \beta_k$, where each β_i is either an action or a subgoal. In the interests of generality, we make no assumptions about the execution of a parallel composition of actions and subgoals: steps $\beta_1, \ldots, \beta_k$ may be executed in parallel, i.e., they may overlap in any of the ways defined in [1], or their execution may be arbitrarily interleaved. For example, if β_i is an action and β_j a subgoal, then β_i may be interleaved with the actions appearing in the goal-plan tree for β_j. However, we require that there are no conflicts between the pre-, in- and postconditions of $\beta_1, \ldots, \beta_k$ and, as a result, the overall postcondition of the parallel composition is "stable", i.e., for each $\beta_i, \beta_j, 1 \leq i \leq k, 1 \leq j \leq k, i \neq j$, the necessary and contingent postconditions of β_i must be consistent with the necessary and contingent pre- in- and postconditions β_j.

More precisely, the necessary postcondition of a parallel composition $\alpha = \beta_1 \| \ldots \| \beta_k$ is defined as the union of the necessary postconditions of each of its parallel steps (which, as above, are assumed to be "non-conflicting"):

$$post_n(\alpha) = \bigcup_{i=1}^{k} post_n(\beta_i).$$

The contingent postcondition of a parallel composition is defined similarly, except that we exclude any contingent postcondition literal of a step if it is also a necessary postcondition of some other step, i.e.,

$$post_c(\alpha) = \bigcup_{i=1}^{k} post_c(\beta_i) \backslash post_n(\alpha).$$

However, the definition of the necessary pre- and in-conditions of a parallel composition must to take into account the necessary and contingent postcondi-

---

[4] Note that this means the necessary conditions of an action may differ from its contingent conditions.

[5] For entailment, we sometimes treat a a set of literals as the conjunction of the literals in the set.

tions of steps that may establish—by virtue of how steps may be interleaved or overlapped—the pre- and in-conditions of other steps, i.e.,

$$con_n(\alpha) = \bigcup_{i\in\{1,\dots,k\}} \Big(con_n(\beta_i)\backslash \bigcup_{j\in\{1,\dots,k\}\backslash\{i\}} (post_n(\beta_j) \cup post_c(\beta_j))\Big),$$

where con is either pre or in. That is, the necessary in-conditions of steps that may be established by interleaving of other steps in the parallel composition are not considered necessary. Finally, the contingent pre- (resp. in-) conditions of a parallel composition are the contingent pre- (resp. in-) conditions of the parallel steps, together with the necessary pre- (resp. in-) conditions of its steps that may be established by other steps. That is, necessary in-conditions that may be established by interleaving of other steps in the parallel composition become contingent. Formally, we define

$$con_c(\alpha) = \bigcup_{i=1}^{k} \Big(con_c(\beta_i) \cup con_n(\beta_i)\Big)\backslash con_n(\alpha),$$

where con is either pre or in.

We can now define the necessary and contingent pre-, in- and postconditions of plans. The necessary precondition of a plan $\pi = \alpha_1;\dots;\alpha_m$ is defined as

$$pre_n(\pi) = pre_n(\alpha_1) \cup \bigcup_{i=2}^{m}\left[pre_n(\alpha_i)\backslash \bigcup_{j=1}^{i-1} post_n(\alpha_j) \cup post_c(\alpha_j)\right],$$

that is, the necessary preconditions of steps that are not established by the necessary or contingent postconditions of previous steps. Necessary preconditions must hold for all executions of π.[6] Note that we do not assume that a plan establishes all the preconditions of the steps in the plan. For example, a plan to make coffee may assume that the agent is in the kitchen and that there is coffee in the kitchen. However, we do assume that each plan π ensures a 'free-choice' among its 'descendant' plans (plans that achieve the subgoals of π). For example, a plan to make coffee should not cause the agent to leave the kitchen before the coffee is made, as that would then invalidate one or more subplans, e.g. one that grinds the coffee. More precisely, for any step α_k in a plan $\pi = \alpha_1;\dots;\alpha_n$, if there is an earlier step α_i ($i < k$) and a literal $l \in post_n(\alpha_i)$ such that $\sim l \in pre_c(\alpha_k) \cup pre_c(\alpha_k) \cup in_n(\alpha_k) \cup in_c(\alpha_k)$, then there is also an intermediate step α_j ($i < j < k$) with $\sim l \in post_n(\alpha_j) \cup post_c(\alpha_j)$, where $\sim l = \neg p$ if $l = p$ and $\sim l = p$ if $l = \neg p$.

If π contains non-deterministic actions or subgoals, it may also have contingent preconditions, i.e., preconditions which may have to be established depending on the outcome of a non-deterministic action (if the outcome of the action

---

[6] As we are concerned with the executability of plans rather than their applicability in a particular context, we do not include the context condition (belief context) of a plan specified by a developer to be part of its precondition. However, in a well-formed plan, the necessary precondition should form (part of) the context condition of the plan.

fails to achieve the precondition of a later action in the plan) or the choice of plan to achieve a subgoal. Thus, the contingent precondition of a plan $\pi = \alpha_1; \ldots; \alpha_m$ is defined as $prec_c(\pi) = prec_c(\alpha_1) \cup$

$$\bigcup_{i=2}^{m} \left[\left(prec_c(\alpha_i) \setminus \bigcup_{j=1}^{i-1} post_n(\alpha_j) \right) \cup \left(\left(pre_n(\alpha_i) \setminus \bigcup_{j=1}^{i-1} post_n(\alpha_j) \right) \cap \bigcup_{j=1}^{i-1} post_c(\alpha_j) \right) \right].$$

That is, the possible preconditions of each step not established by necessary postconditions of previous steps, and the necessary preconditions of each step that are (possibly) established by contingent postconditions of previous steps, but not by their necessary postconditions. Observe that sets $pre_n(\pi)$ and $pre_c(\pi)$ are mutually exclusive by definition.

The necessary in-condition of a plan $\pi = \alpha_1; \ldots; \alpha_m$ is defined as

$$in_n(\pi) = \bigcup_{i=1}^{m-1} (in_n(\alpha_i) \cap in_n(\alpha_{i+1})).$$

That is, a necessary in-condition of a plan π is an in-condition that is necessary for two or more consecutive steps in π. The rationale for this definition arises from the role of in-conditions in scheduling. The in-condition of an action α specifies which other actions may be scheduled in a parallel with the action without negative interactions—only actions α' whose postcondition does not result in a negative interaction with the in-condition of α may be scheduled in parallel with α. When reasoning with summary information at the plan level, we seek to detect situations where the parallel or interleaved execution of actions in a plan π' may result in a negative interaction between the postcondition of an action in π' and the in-condition of actions in π'.

The contingent in-condition of a plan $\pi = \alpha_1; \ldots; \alpha_m$ is defined as

$$in_c(\pi) = \bigcup_{i=1}^{m} (in_c(\alpha_i) \cup in_n(\alpha_i)) \setminus in_n(\pi).$$

Finally, we define the necessary and contingent postconditions of a plan. The necessary postconditions of a plan $\pi = \alpha_1; \ldots; \alpha_m$ is defined as

$$post_n(\pi) = \{l \mid \exists i : l \in post_n(\alpha_i) \wedge \forall j \in \{i, \ldots, m\} :\sim l \notin post_n(\alpha_j) \cup post_c(\alpha_j)\}.$$

That is, the necessary postconditions of each step not 'undone' by the necessary or contingent postconditions of later steps. The contingent postcondition of a plan $\pi = \alpha_1; \ldots; \alpha_m$ is defined as $post_c(\pi) = post_c^1(\pi) \cup post_c^2(\pi)$, where

$$post_c^1(\pi) = \{l \mid \exists i : l \in post_c(\alpha_i) \wedge \forall j \in \{i, \ldots, m\} :\sim l \notin post_n(\alpha_j)\}$$

and

$$post_c^2(\pi) = \{l \mid \exists i : l \in post_n(\alpha_i) \wedge$$
$$\exists j \in \{i, \ldots, m\} :\sim l \in post_c(\alpha_j) \wedge$$
$$\forall j \in \{i, \ldots, m\} :\sim l \notin post_n(\alpha_j)\}.$$

That is, the contingent postcondition of a plan is either a contingent post-condition of a step that is not 'undone' by the necessary postcondition of a later step, or a necessary postcondition of a step that may be 'undone' by a contingent postcondition of a later step. Observe that sets $post_n(\pi)$ and $post_c(\pi)$ are mutually exclusive by definition.

3.3   Goals

A goal γ is associated with a set of plans $\pi_1, \ldots, \pi_n$ that achieve γ, and the pre-, in- and postconditions of γ are derived from this set of associated plans. For simplicity, we stipulate that goals with the same *GoalType* as γ do not appear in the goal-plan tree rooted at γ.[7]

The necessary pre-, in- and postconditions of a goal γ associated with plans $\pi_1, \ldots, \pi_n$ is defined as

$$con_n(\gamma) = \bigcap_{i=1}^{n} con_n(\pi_i),$$

where *con* is either *pre*, *in* or *post*. That is, necessary pre-, in-, or postconditions must hold respectively before, during, or after all ways of achieving γ.

The contingent pre-, in-, and postconditions of a goal γ associated with plans $\pi_1, \ldots, \pi_n$ is defined as

$$con_c(\gamma) = \bigcup_{i=1}^{n} con_c(\pi_i) \cup \left[\bigcup_{j=1}^{n} con_n(\pi_j) \backslash con_n(\gamma) \right]$$

where *con* is either *pre*, *in* or *post*. That is, a pre-, in-, or postcondition is contingent for γ if it is a contingent condition of a plan π_i to achieve γ, or if it is a necessary condition for a plan π_j but not for γ itself (i.e., it is a necessary condition of some but not all plans for γ).

The definitions above capture the relationship between the pre-, in- and postconditions of actions, plans and goals in a goal-plan tree. The conditions for actions define which propositions must be true before, during and after either all executions of an action (necessary conditions), or some execution of the action (contingent conditions). The conditions for plans define which propositions must be true before, during and after either all executions of a plan, or some execution of the plan. The necessary preconditions of a plan specify the states in which the plan is applicable. The conditions for goals define which propositions must be true before, during and after either all means of achieving a goal or some means of achieving a goal.

---

[7] This is a standard assumption in computing summary information e.g., [6,7,16,17]. The assumption can be relaxed, but the definitions of conditions below become more complex.

4   Execution Conditions

In the previous section, we defined the necessary and contingent conditions for the execution of a single goal-plan tree. In this section, we consider information relevant to the execution of a *set* of goal plan trees.

If an agent always executes at most one goal-plan tree at a time, e.g., it executes its intentions in first-in-first-out order, then the execution conditions are the same as those given in Sect. 3. However, in many application domains, an agent's goal-plan trees comprising a system or an agent's user supplied domain knowledge are executed in parallel. For example, in many BDI agent architectures, the plans comprising the agent's intentions are executed in parallel, e.g., by executing one step of an intention at each cycle in a round robin fashion [3, 20]. Interactions between interleaved steps in plans in different goal-plan trees may result in conflicts, i.e., the execution of a step in one plan makes the execution of a step in another concurrently executing plan impossible.

Given a set of goal-plan trees, the *scheduling problem* is to determine which step of which goal-plan tree to execute next, so as to minimise the number of execution conflicts.[8] Scheduling aims to minimise the number of plan failures resulting from choices made by the agent regarding the order of execution of a set of goal-plan trees, thus allowing the largest number of goals to be achieved.[9] Our aim here is not to solve the scheduling problem; for example, we do not consider the problem of which plan an agent should adopt for a given (sub)goal—this is the concern of deliberation scheduling. Rather, we focus on defining conditions that must or may hold on all possible future executions of a set of goal-plan trees. As such, the conditions we define should be taken into account by any scheduler, but are neutral with respect to the actual form of deliberation scheduling adopted. It turns out that, in our setting, the information relevant for scheduling differs from the conditions on the wellformedness of a goal-plan tree defined in the previous section. The definitions of execution conditions below therefore depart from those in, e.g., [15, 16].

To define the execution conditions for a goal-plan tree, we need some auxiliary notions. Given a set of goal-plan trees $T = \{\tau_1, \ldots, \tau_n\}$, an *execution context* for T is a set of pairs $I = \{(\tau_1, \rho_1), \ldots (\tau_n, \rho_n)\}$, where each ρ_i defines the set of possible future execution paths for τ_i. Each ρ_i corresponds to the point execution has reached in the goal-plan tree τ_i, and hence the possible paths future execution of τ_i may follow. (I essentially corresponds to the intentions of a BDI agent.) Initially, each ρ_i points to the top-level goal of the corresponding

---

[8] Scheduling may also be used to maximise the number of positive interactions between goal-plan trees, as in, e.g., [17, 24]; we do not consider positive interactions here.

[9] Plans may fail for reasons that are outside the control of the agent, e.g., due to changes in the environment, or actions of other agents violating the conditions of a plan. Several approaches, e.g., [18, 19, 21] have been proposed which attempt to avoid such failures. However, the information about goal-plan trees required by these approaches (essentially the the percentage of world states for which there is some applicable plan for any subgoal within an intention) is different from that required for scheduling, and we do not consider them further here.

goal-plan tree τ_i. As execution of τ_i proceeds, plans are selected, restricting the possible future execution paths to a subtree of τ_i captured by ρ_i. In the interests of brevity, and where no confusion can arise, we shall refer to possible future execution paths simply as possible execution paths.

An initial set of possible execution paths ρ_0 for a goal-plan tree τ is a sequence $(\pi_i, \alpha_1), \ldots, (\pi_i, \alpha_k)$, where $\pi_i = \alpha_1; \ldots; \alpha_k$ is the selected plan for the top-level goal of τ. As execution progresses, a set of possible execution paths $\rho = (\pi_1, \alpha_1), (\pi_2, \alpha_2), \ldots, (\pi_m, \alpha_m)$ evolves as follows. The successor set of possible execution paths ρ' of ρ is $(\pi_2, \alpha_2), \ldots, (\pi_m, \alpha_m)$ if α_1 is an action, and $\rho' = (\pi_1', \alpha_1'), \ldots, (\pi_1', \alpha_n'), (\pi_2, \alpha_2), \ldots, (\pi_m, \alpha_m)$ if α_1 is a subgoal γ_1 and $\pi_1' = \alpha_1'; \ldots; \alpha_n'$ is the plan selected for γ_1. Only sets of possible execution paths which are the initial set of possible execution paths in τ (corresponding to the top-level of goal of τ) or are obtained by the progression step described above are sets of possible execution paths in τ.

We can now define the necessary and contingent execution conditions of an execution context. Informally, the necessary execution conditions of a set of possible execution paths ρ_i, are those conditions that must hold or be achieved at some point in all possible future executions of a goal-plan tree τ_i starting from ρ_i, and the contingent execution conditions are those conditions that must hold or be achieved at some point of time in at least one possible future execution (but not all executions) of τ_i starting from ρ_i. When executing the set of goal-plan trees in T in parallel, such execution conditions must be protected—if the execution conditions of two sets of possible execution paths ρ_i and ρ_j intersect, then interleaving steps in ρ_i and ρ_j may result in conflicts.

4.1 Actions

As actions are atomic, the necessary and contingent execution conditions of an action α are identical to the corresponding necessary and contingent conditions for α (we denote execution conditions with a $*$):

$$con_n^*(\alpha) = con_n(\alpha) \qquad con_c^*(\alpha) = con_c(\alpha)$$

where con_n^* and con_n are either pre_n^* and pre_n, in_n^* and in_n or $post_n^*$ and $post_n$ respectively, and similarly con_c^* and con_c are either pre_c^* and pre_c, in_c^* and in_c or $post_c^*$ and $post_c$.

4.2 Plans

The necessary and contingent execution conditions of a plan π differ from the corresponding necessary and contingent conditions for π. As steps in plans in different goal-plan trees may be arbitrarily interleaved, we need to protect *all* the preconditions in a plan, even if they are established by a preceding step in the same plan, as the condition may be invalidated by a step in a plan in another goal-plan tree.

The necessary execution pre-, in- and postcondition of a parallel composition $\alpha = \beta_1 \| \ldots \| \beta_k$ is therefore the union of the necessary execution conditions of each β_i, i.e.,

$$con_n^*(\alpha) = \bigcup_{i=1}^{k} con_n^*(\beta_i)$$

where con_n^* is either pre_n^*, in_n^* or $post_n^*$.

The contingent pre-, in- and post- execution conditions of a parallel composition is also defined as the union of contingent execution conditions of each β_i, except that we exclude any contingent postcondition literal of a step if it is also a necessary postcondition of some other step, i.e.,

$$con_c^*(\alpha) = \bigcup_{i=1}^{k} con_c^*(\beta_i) \backslash con_n^*(\alpha).$$

The necessary and contingent execution preconditions of a plan (or plan suffix) $\pi = \alpha_1; \ldots; \alpha_m$ are therefore given by

$$pre_n^*(\pi) = \bigcup_{i=1}^{m} pre_n^*(\alpha_i) \qquad pre_c^*(\pi) = \bigcup_{i=1}^{m} pre_c^*(\alpha_i) \backslash pre_n^*(\pi).$$

Similarly, the postconditions of interest are no longer the 'eventual' postconditions of the plan, since the postcondition of an action α_i 'undone' by a later step $\alpha_j, i < j$ in π may be 'visible' to a step in a plan in another goal-plan tree. The necessary and contingent execution postconditions of π are therefore given by

$$post_n^*(\pi) = \bigcup_{i=1}^{m} post_n^*(\alpha_i) \qquad post_c^*(\pi) = \bigcup_{i=1}^{m} post_c^*(\alpha_i) \backslash post_n^*(\pi).$$

In contrast, the necessary and contingent execution in-conditions of π are the same as the necessary and contingent in-conditions of π: $in_n^*(\pi) = in_n(\pi)$, $in_c^*(\pi) = in_c(\pi)$. (Since $in_n(\pi)$ and $in_c(\pi)$ define conditions that must hold between the execution of steps in π, they also apply to the interleaving of plan steps.)

4.3   Goals

As with plans, the necessary and contingent execution conditions of a goal γ associated with plans $\pi_1, \ldots, \pi_n$ differ from the corresponding necessary and contingent conditions for γ. (The conditions of goals are defined in terms of the conditions of their associated plans.)

The necessary pre-, in- and post- execution conditions of a goal γ associated with plans $\pi_1, \ldots, \pi_n$ is defined as

$$con_n^*(\gamma) = \bigcap_{i=1}^{n} con_n^*(\pi_i),$$

where *con* is either *pre*, *in* or *post*. That is, necessary pre-, in-, or post- execution conditions must hold respectively before, during, or after all ways of achieving γ.

The contingent pre-, in-, and post- execution conditions of a goal γ associated with plans $\pi_1, \ldots, \pi_n$ is defined as

$$con_c^*(\gamma) = \bigcup_{i=1}^n con_c^*(\pi_i) \cup \left[\bigcup_{j=1}^n con_n^*(\pi_j) \backslash con_n^*(\gamma) \right],$$

where *con* is either *pre*, *in* or *post*. That is, a pre-, in-, or postcondition is contingent for γ if it is a contingent condition of a plan π_i to achieve γ, or if it is a necessary condition for a plan π_j but not for γ itself (i.e., it is a necessary condition of some but not all plans for γ).

4.4   Sets of Execution Paths

We can now define the necessary and contingent execution conditions of a set of possible execution paths $\rho = (\pi_1, \alpha_1), \ldots, (\pi_k, \alpha_k)$ of a goal-plan tree τ. These conditions can be used to reason about possible conflicts that may arise in the execution of each pair of goal-plan trees in a set of goal-plan trees.

The necessary execution precondition of a set of possible execution paths ρ is given by

$$pre_n^*(\rho) = \bigcup_{i=1}^k pre_n^*(\alpha_i).$$

That is, we must protect the necessary preconditions of all steps in ρ. The contingent execution precondition of ρ is given by

$$pre_c^*(\rho) = \bigcup_{i=1}^k pre_c^*(\alpha_i) \backslash pre_n^*(\rho).$$

Contingent preconditions are those that may need to be established during execution, depending on the choice of plan to achieve a goal.

The necessary execution in-condition of a set of possible execution paths ρ is given by

$$in_n^*(\rho) = \bigcup_{i=1}^k in_n^*(\alpha_i) \cup \bigcup_{i=1}^k in_n(\pi_i).$$

That is, we must protect the in-conditions of all steps in ρ, and in addition we also need to protect the in-conditions of all currently executing plans in ρ. The contingent execution in-condition of ρ is given by

$$in_c^*(\rho) = \bigcup_{i=1}^k in_c^*(\alpha_i) \cup \bigcup_{i=1}^k in_c(\pi_i) \backslash in_n^*(\rho).$$

The necessary and contingent execution postconditions of a set of possible execution paths ρ is given by

$$post_n^*(\rho) = \bigcup_{i=1}^{k} post_n^*(\alpha_i) \qquad post_c^*(\rho) = \bigcup_{i=1}^{k} post_c^*(\alpha_i) \backslash post_n^*(\rho).$$

Finally, the necessary execution conditions of a set of possible execution paths ρ are given by

$$cond_n^*(\rho) = pre_n^*(\rho) \cup in_n^*(\rho) \cup post_n^*(\rho),$$

and the contingent execution conditions of ρ are given by

$$cond_c^*(\rho) = pre_c^*(\rho) \cup in_c^*(\rho) \cup post_c^*(\rho).$$

Conflicts may occur when we have complementary literals in the execution conditions of two sets of possible execution paths, ρ_i and ρ_j, i.e., when

$$\exists l \in cond_x^*(\rho_i) \land \sim l \in cond_x^*(\rho_j),$$

where $cond_x^*$ is either $cond_n^*$ or $cond_c^*$. Clearly, there are different cases. For example, conflicts between the necessary execution conditions of two execution paths may be a more serious problem than conflicts between contingent execution conditions.

If no conflicts (as defined above) occur between two sets of possible execution paths ρ_i and ρ_j, then the next step in either (or both) ρ_i and ρ_j may be safely executed. On the other hand, if there are conflicts between the two sets of possible execution paths, then we could still interleave their execution such that they do not interfere with one another, e.g., by borrowing techniques from [16]. For example, if the conflict between ρ_i and ρ_j is due to complementary literals in $in_n^*(\rho_i)$ and $post_n^*(\rho_j)$, then we could delay the execution of ρ_j until ρ_i progresses to a point where there is no longer a conflict with ρ_j. This is because ρ_j might otherwise interfere with the in-condition of a plan that is currently being pursued.[10] If the conflict between ρ_i and ρ_j is due to complementary literals in $pre_c^*(\rho_i)$ and $post_c^*(\rho_j)$, an optimistic approach would be to first execute ρ_j until it progresses to a point where a conflict no longer occurs with ρ_i, and only then begin executing ρ_i. This assumes that either execution of ρ_j does not actually bring about the conflicting literal, or that if it is brought about, execution of ρ_i is such that the conflicting contingent precondition is not required, or a step within ρ_i itself asserts the negation of the conflicting literal.

---

[10] Note that if ρ_i and ρ_j are considered in order of the priority of the associated top-level goal (or ties are broken arbitrarily), deadlock (as defined in [15,16]) cannot arise, even if there are complementary literals in $in_n^*(\rho_j)$ and $post_n^*(\rho_i)$. However, this may result in conditions of the lower priority set of possible execution paths being violated. In such cases, more sophisticated intention scheduling techniques, e.g., [21,22] may be able to find an interleaving that protects the conditions of both sets of possible execution paths.

5   Conclusion and Future Work

This paper has provided definitions of pre-, in-, and postconditions of actions, plans, and goals, for an extended goal-plan tree that supports the execution of steps (goals and actions) in parallel, as well as the specification of both deterministic and non-deterministic actions. Our definitions essentially capture 'static' and 'dynamic' notions of conditions, which are derived from the primitive ones specified within the basic actions that form plans. We believe that 'static' properties defined by our notions will facilitate authoring agent programs, particularly because it is important to know the properties of the individual "building blocks" (goal-plan trees) that are available when composing a new plan. Our 'dynamic' notion of execution conditions specify those conditions that must be protected by any scheduler when interleaving two or more goal-plan trees.

We foresee two main directions for future work. First, we could allow for a step in a plan to necessarily invalidate one or more (though not all) 'descendant' (sub)plans of a later step, and accordingly extend our notions of the necessary and contingent postconditions of a plan. This extension would involve identifying which postconditions in the later step are never asserted due to the conflict (and are thereby neither necessary nor contingent postconditions), and which ones are always asserted due to the conflict, by virtue of certain descendant plans always being inapplicable. Second, we could explore how to generate a schedule for interleaving two or more goal-plan trees while respecting execution conditions.

References

1. Allen, J.F.: Maintaining knowledge about temporal intervals. Commun. ACM **26**(11), 832–843 (1983)
2. Baier, J.A., Fritz, C., McIlraith, S.A.: Exploiting procedural domain control knowledge in state-of-the-art planners. In: Proceedings of the Seventeenth International Conference on Automated Planning and Scheduling (ICAPS-07), pp. 26–33 (2007)
3. Bordini, R.H., Hübner, J.F., Wooldridge, M.: Programming multi-agent systems in AgentSpeak using Jason. Wiley Series in Agent Technology. Wiley, Chichester (2007)
4. Botea, A., Enzenberger, M., Müller, M., Schaeffer, J.: Macro-FF: improving AI planning with automatically learned macro-operators. J. Artif. Intell. Res. (JAIR) **24**, 581–621 (2005)
5. Chapman, D.: Planning for conjunctive goals. Artif. Intell. **32**(3), 333–377 (1987)
6. Clement, B.J., Durfee, E.H.: Theory for coordinating concurrent hierarchical planning agents using summary information. In: Proceedings of the Sixteenth National Conference on Artificial Intelligence (AAAI-1999), pp. 495–502 (1999)
7. Clement, B.J., Durfee, E.H., Barrett, A.C.: Abstract reasoning for planning and coordination. J. Artif. Intell. Res. (JAIR) **28**, 453–515 (2007)
8. de Silva, L., Sardina, S., Padgham, L.: First principles planning in BDI systems. In: Proceedings of the Eighth International Joint Conference on Autonomous Agents and Multiagent Systems (AAMAS-2009), pp. 1105–1112 (2009)
9. de Silva, L., Sardina, S., Padgham, L.: Summary information for reasoning about hierarchical plans. In: Proceedings of the 22nd European Conference on Artificial Intelligence (ECAI-2016), pp. 1300–1308 (2016)

10. Erol, K., Hendler, J., Nau, D.S.: HTN planning: complexity and expressivity. In: Proceedings of the Twelfth National Conference on Artificial Intelligence (AAAI-1994), pp. 1123–1128 (1994)

11. Fritz, C., Baier, J.A., McIlraith, S.A.: ConGolog, Sin Trans: Compiling ConGolog into Basic Action Theories for planning and beyond. In: Proceedings of the 11th International Conference on Principles of Knowledge Representation and Reasoning (KR-2008), pp. 600–610 (2008)

12. Kambhampati, S., Mali, A.D., Srivastava, B.: Hybrid planning for partially hierarchical domains. In: Proceedings of the Fifteenth National Conference on Artificial Intelligence (AAAI-1998), pp. 882–888 (1998)

13. Paolucci, M., Shehory, O., Sycara, K., Kalp, D., Pannu, A.: A planning component for RETSINA agents. In: Jennings, N.R., Lespérance, Y. (eds.) ATAL 1999. LNCS (LNAI), vol. 1757, pp. 147–161. Springer, Heidelberg (2000). doi:10.1007/10719619_11

14. Sardina, S., de Silva, L., Padgham, L.: Hierarchical planning in BDI agent programming languages: a formal approach. In: Proceedings of the Fifth International Joint Conference on Autonomous Agents and Multiagent Systems (AAMAS-2006), pp. 1001–1008 (2006)

15. Thangarajah, J., Padgham, L.: Computationally effective reasoning about goal interactions. J. Autom. Reasoning **47**(1), 17–56 (2011)

16. Thangarajah, J., Padgham, L., Winikoff, M.: Detecting and avoiding interference between goals in intelligent agents. In: Proceedings of the Eighteenth International Joint Conference on Artificial Intelligence (IJCAI-2003), pp. 721–726 (2003)

17. Thangarajah, J., Padgham, L., Winikoff, M.: Detecting and exploiting positive goal interaction in intelligent agents. In: Proceedings of the Second International Joint Conference on Autonomous Agents and Multiagent Systems (AAMAS-2003), pp. 401–408 (2003)

18. Thangarajah, J., Sardina, S., Padgham, L.: Measuring plan coverage and overlap for agent reasoning. In: Proceedings of the Eleventh International Joint Conference on Autonomous Agents and Multiagent Systems (AAMAS-2012), pp. 1049–1056 (2012)

19. Waters, M., Padgham, L., Sardina, S.: Evaluating coverage based intention selection. In: Proceedings of the 13th International Joint Conference on Autonomous Agents and Multi-agent Systems (AAMAS-2014), pp. 957–964 (2014)

20. Winikoff, M.: JACK intelligent agents: an industrial strength platform. In: Bordini, R.H., Dastani, M., Dix, J., Seghrouchni, A.E.F. (eds.) Multi-agent Programming, pp. 175–193. Springer, New York (2005)

21. Yao, Y., Logan, B.: Action-level intention selection for BDI agents. In: Proceedings of the 15th International Conference on Autonomous Agents and Multiagent Systems (AAMAS 2016), pp. 1227–1235 (2016)

22. Yao, Y., Logan, B., Thangarajah, J.: SP-MCTS-based intention scheduling for BDI agents. In: Proceedings of the 21st European Conference on Artificial Intelligence (ECAI-2014), pp. 1133–1134 (2014)

23. Yao, Y., Logan, B., Thangarajah, J.: Intention selection with deadlines. In: Proceedings of the 22nd European Conference on Artificial Intelligence (ECAI-2016), pp. 1700–1701 (2016)

24. Yao, Y., Logan, B., Thangarajah, J.: Robust execution of BDI agent programs by exploiting synergies between intentions. In: Proceedings of the Thirtieth AAAI Conference on Artificial Intelligence (AAAI-2016), pp. 2558–2564 (2016)

Augmenting Agent Computational Environments with Quantitative Reasoning Modules and Customizable Bridge Rules

Stefania Costantini[1] and Andrea Formisano[2(✉)]

[1] GNCS-INdAM and DISIM, Università di L'Aquila, L'Aquila, Italy
[2] GNCS-INdAM and DMI, Università di Perugia, Perugia, Italy
`formis@dmi.unipg.it`

Abstract. There are many examples where large amount of data might be potentially accessible to an agent, but the agent is constrained by the available budget since access to knowledge bases is subject to fees. There are also several activities that an agent might perform on the web where one or more stages imply the payment of fees: for instance, buying resources in a cloud computing context where the objective of the agent is to obtain the best possible configuration of a certain application withing given budget constraints. In this paper we consider the software-engineering problem of how to practically empower agents with the capability to perform such kind of reasoning in a uniform and principled way. To this aim, we enhance the ACE component-based agent architecture by means of a device for practical and computationally affordable quantitative reasoning, whose results actually determine one or more courses of agent's actions, also according to policies/preferences.

1 Introduction

There are many examples where large amount of data might be potentially accessible to an agent, but the agent is constrained by the available budget since access to knowledge bases is subject to fees. There are also several activities that an agent may perform on the web on behalf of an user where one or more stages imply the payment of fees. An important example is that of buying resources in a cloud-computing context, where the objective of the agent is to obtain the best possible configuration for performing certain tasks in the sense of maximizing performance and minimizing costs, that can anyway stay withing given budget constraints. The work [33] identifies the problem that an agent faces when it has limited budget and costly queries to perform. In order to model such situations,

This paper has originally been published in N. Osman and C. Sierra (Eds.), AAMAS 2016 WS, Visionary Papers, LNAI 10003, 2016.

N. Osman and C. Sierra (Eds.): AAMAS 2016 WS, Visionary Papers, LNAI 10003, pp. 104–121, 2016.
DOI: 10.1007/978-3-319-46840-2_7

M. Baldoni et al. (Eds.): EMAS 2016, LNAI 10093, pp. 192–209, 2016.
DOI: 10.1007/978-3-319-50983-9_11

the authors propose a special resource-aware modal logic so as to be able to represent and reason about what is possible to do with a certain available budget. The logic can be adapted to reason separately about cost and time limitation, though an integration is envisaged. Interesting as it is, this work constitutes a good starting point but it presents two problems: (i) such kind of modal logic is computationally hard (though this aspect is not discussed in the aforementioned paper) and thus it can hardly constitute the basis for practical tools; (ii) the axiomatic system of [33] allows one to prove that something can or cannot be achieved within a certain cost. However, an agent needs, in general, to become aware of how goals might possibly be achieved, and should be enabled to choose the best course of action according to its own policies/preferences.

In this paper we tackle some issues related to this problem. First, we consider the software-engineering problem of how to practically empower agents with the capability to perform such kind of reasoning in a uniform and principled way. Second, we consider the adoption of a reasoning device that enables an agent, which may have several costly objectives, to establish which are the alternative possibilities within the available budget, and to select, based upon its preferences, the goals to achieve and the resources to spend, and finally to implement its choice.

Concerning the first aspect, we enhance the Agent Computational Environment (ACE) framework [13], which is a software engineering methodology for designing intelligent logical agents in a modular way. Therefore, in this paper we refer to agent-oriented languages and frameworks which are rooted in Computational Logic. Modules composing an agent interact, in ACE, via *bridge rules* in the style of the Multi-Context Systems (MCS) approach [7,8,10]. Such rules take the form of conjunctive queries where each conjunct constitutes a subquery which is posed to a specific module. Thus, the result is obtained by combining partial results obtained from different sources. The enhancements that we propose here for ACE are based upon the flexible agent-tailored modalities for bridge rules application and for knowledge elaboration defined for the DACMACS framework (Data-Aware Commitment-based managed Multi-Agent-Context Systems), which is aimed at designing data-aware multi-agent-context systems [14,15]. There, bridge rules are proactively triggered upon specific conditions and the obtained knowledge is reactively elaborated via a *management function* which generalizes the analogous MCS concept.

Second, we extend ACEs so as to include modules for specialized forms of reasoning, including quantitative reasoning. For this kind of reasoning we suggest to adopt the RASP framework [16,17,19], which is based upon Answer Set Programming (ASP) and hence it is computationally affordable and reasonably efficient. We show the suitability of such approach by discussing a case study, that will constitute the leading example throughout the paper.

A strong innovation that this paper proposes is that, after obtaining from a reasoning module the description of possible courses of actions, bridge rules "patterns" can be specialized and activated so as to put them into action. This feature is made possible by an enhanced flexible ACE semantics.

The resulting framework can be seen as a creative blend of existing technologies, with some relevant formal and practical extensions. Partially specified bridge rules and their dynamic customization and activation is an absolute novelty and constitutes a relevant advance over MCSs versions, applications and extensions: in fact, bridge rules have been so far conceived as predefined, ground and not amenable to any adaptation. Beyond quantitative reasoning, such more general bridge rules may constitute a powerful flexible device in many applications.

The paper is organized as follows. Section 2 presents a case study that will constitute the leading example throughout the paper. In Sect. 3 we discuss the quantitative reasoning device we suggest to exploit. Sections 4 and 5 present the enhanced ACE framework and illustrate, on the case study, the dynamic customization of bridge rules. Section 6 introduces the extended ACE semantics and for completeness we provide in Sect. 7 an actual RASP formalization. Concluding remarks are given in Sect. 8.

2   Specification of the Case Study

In this section we provide the specification of a case study which we will adopt in the rest of the paper for the illustration of the proposed enhancements to the ACE framework. In Sect. 7 we will present a realistic implementation in a specific existing approach for quantitative reasoning, shortly introduced in the next section.

We consider a student, that will be represented by an agent which can be seen as her "personal assistant agent". Upon completing the secondary school, she wishes to apply for enrollment to an US university. Each application has a cost, and the tuition fee will have to be paid in case of admission and enrollment. The student has an allotted maximum budget for both. Thus the agent, on behalf of the student, has to reason about: (i) the universities to which an application will be sent; (ii) the university where to enroll, in case a choice can be made.

Actually, the proposed case study is seen as a prototype of a wide number of situations where two kinds of quantitative reasoning are required:

1. The cost of knowledge, as in practical terms a student applies in order to know whether she is admitted.
2. Reasoning under budget limits, as a student may send an application only if: (i) she can afford the fees related to the application; (ii) in case of admission, she can then afford the tuition fees.

If a solution is found considering her preferences and her budget, she will then be able to apply and, if admitted, to enroll. In case more than an option is available, a choice is required so as to select the "best" one according to some criteria.

Without any pretension to precision, we consider the steps that a student has to undergo in order to apply for admission:

1. Pass the general SAT test.

2. Pass the specific SAT test for the subject of interest (such as Literature, Mathematics, Chemistry, etc.)
3. In case of foreign students, pass the TOEFL test.
4. Fill the general application on the application website (that we call collegeorg).
5. Send the SAT results to the universities of interest.
6. Complete the application for the universities of interest.

All these steps are subject to the payment of fees, which are fixed (the fee is independent of the university) for steps 1–4 and depend upon the selected university for steps 5–6. In the example we assume that the student has a budget for the application (say 1500 US dollars) and a limit about the tuition fee she is able to pay (say 22000 US dollars per year). However, she has a list of preferred universities, and within such list she would apply only to universities whose ranking is higher than a threshold. Additionally, since she likes basketball, all other things being equal (*ceteris paribus*) she would prefer universities with the best rankings of the basketball team.

3   Resource-Based Reasoning

In the case study, the student's personal assistant agent needs the support of some kind of quantitative reasoning module. Such module should in general be able to provide the agent, given one or more objectives, with a description of the different ways of achieving the objectives while staying within a budget. A desirable property of the reasoner would be that of allowing preferences and constraints to be expressed about objectives to achieve and modalities for achieving them. A mandatory requisite is the ability to perform such reasoning in a computationally affordable way.

In knowledge representation and reasoning, forms of quantitative reasoning are possible, for example, in Linear Logics and Description Logics. For Linear Logic in particular, several programming languages and theorem provers based on its principles exist (cf. [16] for a discussion). In this paper we adopt RASP (Resource-based ASP) [17,19], which has in fact been proven in [18] to be equivalent to an interesting fragment of Linear Logic, specifically, to an empowered Horn fragment allowing for a default negation that Linear Logic does not provide (though still remaining within an NP-complete framework). RASP extends ASP, which is a well-known logic programming paradigm where a program may have several "models", called "answer sets", each one representing a possible interpretation of the situation described by the program (cf., among many, [29]). In particular, RASP explicitly introduces in ASP the notion of *resource*, and supports both formalization and quantitative reasoning on consumption and production of resources. RASP also provides complex preferences about spending resources (and in this it is different from the several approaches to preferences that have been defined for ASP, see e.g., [2,6,11,25] and the references therein). Compared with the "competitors", RASP represents possible different uses of a resource and non-determinism in general by means of different answer sets, rather than exploring the various possibilities via backtracking in a Prolog-like fashion. The RASP inference engine is based upon publicly available ASP solvers [35] that are remarkably well-performing and subject of intensive research and development. After the seminal work of [34] one can mention [1,22,26,28,31,32], among the most recent developments. Specifically, RASP execution is based upon a front-end module called *Raspberry* which translates RASP programs (via a non-trivial process, see [19] for the details) into ASP. The resulting program can be executed by common ASP solvers.

As a side note, we observe that the clasp ASP solver allows one to add external functions to ASP programs. This is done by defining deterministic functions in a scripting language such as lua or python. Relying on this possibility, one might envisage a re-implementation of the RASP framework exploiting such feature of this specific ASP solver, instead of performing a translation from RASP into ASP, as done in Raspberry. Another recently proposed extension of ASP is H-ASP [12], where propositional reasoning is combined with external sources of numerical computation. The main aim of H-ASP is to allow users to reason about a dynamical system by simulating its possible evolutions along a discretized time-line. The external computations are used to compute the system transitions and may involve both continuous and discrete numerical variables. The expressive power of the resulting framework directly depends on the kind of numerical tasks one integrates, and the computational complexity can exceed NP. Clearly, thanks to the generality of ACE, one could integrate modules based on H-ASP in the ACE framework, similarly to what done for RASP. However, in the case of RASP we stay within NP and directly rely on common "pure-ASP" engines without the need of integrating (and encoding) further computational services.

We are not aware of other reasoning frameworks that combine logic and quantitative techniques, apart from the one proposed in [33], which however is not implemented and, as mentioned, in its present form can hardly admit a computationally affordable version. So, there is nowadays no competitor approach to RASP in practical logic-based quantitative reasoning and its applications in agent systems.

4   Enhancing the ACE Framework

The ACE framework as defined in [13] considers an agent as composed of:
(1) the "main" agent program;
(2) a number of Event-Action modules for Complex Event Processing;
(3) a number of external contexts the agent can access in order to gather information.

ACE is therefore a highly modular architecture, where the composing modules communicate via *bridge rules* (to be seen below) in the style of Multi-Context Systems (MCSs) [7,8,10]. MCSs constitute in fact a particularly interesting approach for modeling information exchange among heterogeneous sources because, within a neat formal definition, it is able to accommodate real heterogeneity of sources by explicitly representing their different representation languages and semantics. The same holds for ACEs, where: external contexts are understood as in MCS, i.e., they can be queried but cannot be accessed in any other way; and where "local" agent's modules (main agent program and event-action modules) can be defined in any agent-oriented computational-logic-based programming language, such as, e.g., DALI, AgentSpeak, GOAL, 3APL, METATEM, KGP, etc. (see [3–5,20,21,24,27,30] and the references therein), or also in other logic formalisms such as, e.g., ASP (see [29] and the references therein).

In the present setting, we augment the framework with a set of *Reasoning Modules*, say $R_1, \ldots, R_q$, $q \geq 0$, that we see as specialized modules which are able to perform specific forms of reasoning by means of the best suitable formalism/technique/device. Among such modules we may have quantitative reasoning modules. Therefore, an (enhanced) Agent Computational Environment $\mathcal{A}$ is now defined as a tuple

$$\langle A, M_1, \ldots, M_r, C_1, \ldots, C_s, R_1, \ldots, R_q \rangle$$

where module A is the "basic agent", i.e., an agent program written in any agent-oriented language. The "overall" agent is obtained by equipping the basic agent with the following facilities. The M_is are "Event-Action modules", which are special modules aimed at Complex Event Processing, that allow the agent to flexibly interact with a complex changing environment. The R_js are "Reasoning modules", which are specialized in specific reasoning tasks. The C_ks are contexts in the sense of MCSs, i.e., external data/knowledge sources that the agent is able to query about some subject, but upon which it has no further knowledge and no control: this means that the agent is aware of the "role" of contexts in the sense of the kind of knowledge they are able to provide, but is unable in general to provide a description of their behavior/contents or to affect/modify them in any way.

Interaction among ACE's components occurs via *bridge rules*, inspired by those in MCS. They can be seen as Datalog-like queries where however each sub-query can be posed to a different module. In MCS, bridge rules have, in general, the following form:

$$s \leftarrow (c_1 : p_1), \ldots, (c_j : p_j), not\,(c_{j+1} : p_{j+1}), \ldots, not\,(c_m : p_m).$$

The meaning is that the rule is *applicable* and s can thus be added to the consequences of a module's knowledge base whenever each atom p_r, $r \leq j$, belongs to the consequences of module c_r (that can be a context or an event-action module, or the basic agent), while instead each atom p_w, $j < w \leq m$, does not belong to the consequences of c_w. Practical run-time bridge-rule applicability will consist in posing query p_i to context c_i. In case for some of the c_is the context is omitted, then the agent is querying its own knowledge base. The part $(c_1 : p_1), \ldots, (c_j : p_j)$ is the *positive body* of the rule, while the remaining part is the *negative body*.

We introduce the following restriction on bridge rules bodies: the basic agent A can query any other module (and, clearly, if it is situated in a MAS context it can communicate with other agents according to some kind of protocol). The

M_is and the R_is can query external contexts and the basic agent. Contexts can only query other contexts, i.e., they cannot access agent's knowledge. We also assume (for simplicity and without loss of generality) that bridge-rule heads are unique, i.e., there are never two bridge rules with the same head.

In Managed MCSs the conclusion s, which represents the "bare" result of the application of the bridge rule, becomes $o(s)$ where o is a special operator, whose semantics is provided by a module-specific *management function*. The meaning is that the result computed by a bridge rule is not blindly incorporated into the "target" module knowledge base. Rather, it is filtered, adapted, modified and elaborated by an operator that can possibly perform any elaboration, e.g. evaluation, format conversion, belief revision. To the extreme, the new knowledge item can even be discarded if not deemed to be useful.

In the basic agent we adopt, with suitable adaptations, the special agent-oriented modalities introduced in DACMACS. There, bridge-rule activation and management-function application has been adapted to the specific nature of agent systems. First, while bridge rules in MCSs are conceived to be applied whenever applicable (they can be seen, therefore, as a reactive device), DAC-MACS provides a proactive application upon specific conditions. Second, the incorporation of bridge rule results via the management function is separated from bridge-rule application. In particular, bridge-rule application is determined by a *trigger rule* of the form

$$Q \text{ enables } A(\hat{x})$$

where: Q is a query to agent's internal knowledge-base and $A(\hat{x})$ is the conclusion of one of agent's bridge rules. If query Q (the "trigger") evaluates to true, then the bridge rule is allowed to be applied. A trigger rule is proactive in the sense that the application of a bridge rule is enabled only if and when the agent during its operation concludes Q. The bridge rule will be actually applied according to agent's internal control modalities, and will return its results in $\hat{x}$. The result(s) $\hat{x}$ returned by a bridge rule with head $A(\hat{x})$ will then be exploited via a *bridge-update rule* of the following form (where $\beta(\hat{x})$ specifies the operator, management function and actions to be applied to $\hat{x}$):

$$\text{upon} \quad A(\hat{x}) \text{ then } \beta(\hat{x})$$

We propose a relevant improvement concerning bridge rules. In particular, in MCSs bridge rules are by definition ground, i.e., they do not contain variables: in [9], it is literally stated that [in their examples] they *"use for readability and succinctness schematic bridge rules with variables (upper case letters and '_' [the 'anonymous' variable]) which range over associated sets of constants; they stand for all respective instances (obtainable by value substitution)"* where however such "placeholder" variables occur only in the p_is while instead the c_is (contexts' names) are constants. This is a serious expressive limitation, that we have tackled in related work. In fact, we admit variables in both the p_is in bridge-rule bodies and in the head s, to be instantiated at run-time by the queried contexts. We also admit contexts in the body to be selected from a directory according to their *role*. Here, we propose a further relevant enhancement: we allow contexts occurring in the body of the bridge rules of the main agent A to be instantiated via results returned by ACE's other modules. Such bridge rules will have this form:

$$s \leftarrow (\mathcal{C}_1 : p_1), \ldots, (\mathcal{C}_j : p_j), not\,(\mathcal{C}_{j+1} : p_{j+1}), \ldots, not\,(\mathcal{C}_m : p_m).$$

where each $\mathcal{C}_i$ can be either a plain constant (as before) or an expression of the form $m_i(k_i)$ that we call *context designator*, which is a term where m_i can be seen as a(n arbitrary) meta-function indicating the required instantiation, and k_i is a constant that can be seen as analogous to a Skolem constant. Such term indicates the kind of context to which it must be substituted before bridge-rule execution, so it might be, for instance, *university*(u), *student_data*(sd), *treatment_database*(d), *diagnostic_expert_system*(de). There is no fixed format, rather it is intended as a designation of the required-for knowledge source, that can be either a knowledge repository or a reasoning module.

A bridge rule including context designators will be indicated as a *bridge rule pattern*, as it stands for its versions obtained by substituting the designators with actual contexts' names. Bridge-rule instantiation may be performed by an agent also by means of bridge-update rules, that are in charge of replacing designators with actual suitable knowledge sources. We assume that bridge-update rules' conclusions $\beta(\hat{x})$ are, in general, conjunctions, possibly including actions of the following distinguished forms:

(i) *record*(*Item*), which simply adds *Item* to A's knowledge base; *Item* can be either the "plain" bridge-rule result, or it can be obtained by processing such result via the evaluation of other atoms in $\beta(\hat{x})$;

(ii) *incorporate*(*Item*), which performs some more involved elaboration for incorporating *Item* into A's knowledge base. Notice that *incorporate* is meant as a distinguished predicate, to be defined according to the specific application domain; in particular, it is intended to implement some proper form of belief revision.

(iii) *instantiate*($S, m_i(k_i), L$) which, for every bridge rule ρ with head matching with S, considers the context designator $m_i(k_i)$ and a list L of constants, and generates as many instances of ρ as obtained by substituting $m_i(k_i)$ (wherever it occurs) by elements of L. A bridge rules will be potentially applicable whenever all contexts in its body are constants, i.e., whenever all context designators, if present, have been replaced by actual contexts' names.

(iv) *enable*(S, Q), which enables the application of a potentially applicable bridge rule ρ whose head matches with S and with associated trigger rule of the form Q **enables** S. It does so by generating its trigger, i.e., by adding Q as a new fact.

The combination of the introduction of both context designators and the *instantiate* actions extends the expressiveness of the bridge-rule approach: even allowing variables in place of contexts' names would not allow for the specific customization performed here. The purpose of defining context designators as terms is that of avoiding the requirement of the involved domains to be finite. In fact, context designators can denote values in an infinite domain, where, however, a finite number of *instantiate* actions generates a finite number of customized bridge rules. Notice that the computational complexity of the overall framework depends upon the computational complexity of the involved modules. In [8,9] significant sample cases are reported.

5   Case Study: Bridge Rules Customization and Application

In order to explain the features that we have introduced so far we apply them to the case study. The agent acting on behalf of a prospective college student would for instance include the following trigger rule:

$$wish\_to\_enroll(Universities, Budget) \textbf{ enables}$$
$$chooseU(Universities, Budget, Selected\_UniversitiesL)$$

The meaning is that the agent is supposed to be able to conclude at some stage of its operation $wish\_to\_enroll(Universities, Budget)$, where $Universities$ is the list of universities which are of interest for the student, and $Budget$ is the budget which is available for completing the application procedure. Whenever this conclusion is reached, the trigger rule is proactively activated, thus enabling a suitable bridge rule. This bridge rule exploits a quantitative reasoning module and might correspond to this simple bridge rule pattern, where however there is the relative context designator $qr\_mod(mymod)$ to be instantiated.

$$chooseU(Universities, Budget, Selected\_UniversitiesL) \leftarrow$$
$$qr\_mod(mymod) : chooseU(Universities, Budget, Selected\_UniversitiesL)$$

Let us assume that the agent somehow (dynamically) instantiates this designator, e.g., to the name of a RASP module $rasp\_mod$, thus obtaining:

$$chooseU(Universities, Budget, Selected\_UniversitiesL) \leftarrow$$
$$rasp\_mod : chooseU(Universities, Budget, Selected\_UniversitiesL)$$

The RASP module, invoked via a suitable plugin, will return its results in $Selected\_UniversitiesL$, that will be a list representing the potential options for sending applications while staying within the given budget. A relevant role is performed by the corresponding bridge-update rule, which may have the form:

upon $chooseU(Universities, Budget, Selected\_UniversitiesL)$ **then**
   $preferred\_subject(Subject),$
   $instantiate(apply(Univ, ResponseUniv), myuniv(u), Selected\_UniversitiesL),$
   $nearest\_sat\_center(Sc),$ $nearest\_toefl\_center(Tc),$
   $instantiate(general\_tests(Subject, R1, R2, R3), sat\_center(sc), [Sc]),$
   $instantiate(general\_tests(Subject, R1, R2, R3), language\_center(lc), [Tc]),$
   $enable(general\_tests(Subject, R1, R2, R3), enabledgentest)$

By evaluating the sub-queries from left to right, as it is usual in Prolog, this rule will determine the preferred subject *Subject*, and via an *instantiate* action it will create several copies of a bridge rule which finalizes the application (see below), namely one copy for each university included in *Selected_UniversitiesL*. Notice that such bridge rules are not enabled yet. Then, the bridge-update rule finds the contexts' names *Sc* and *Lc* of nearest SAT and language-test centers respectively, where the student may perform the tests. The subsequent two *instantiate* actions, together with the *enable* action, will instantiate and trigger a suitable bridge rule pattern (shown below). The trigger part is, in particular:

> *enabledgentest.*
> *enabledgentest* **enables** *general_tests(Subject, R1, R2, R3)*

which, as said, enables a bridge rule obtained by the following bridge rule pattern via its specialization to contexts' names *Sc* and *Lc*. This bridge rule will take care of performing the general tests (among which the language certification) and filling the general part of the application:

$$general\_tests(Subject, R1, R2, R3) \leftarrow sat\_center(sc) : general\_SAT\_test(R1),$$
$$sat\_center(sc) : specific\_SAT\_test(R2),$$
$$language\_center(lc) : language\_certification(R3),$$
$$collegeorg : fill\_application$$

Each test will return its results, which are then dynamically recorded, whenever available, by the bridge-update rule:

> **upon** *general_tests(Subject, R1, R2, R3)* **then** *record(test_res(R1, R2, R3))*

The recording of test results enables, via the following trigger rule, the application of the bridge rules, one for every selected university *Univ*, each of which will: send test the test results to that university; finalize the university-specific part of the application; wait for the response, returned in *ResponseUniv*.

> **upon** *test_res(R1, R2, R3)* **then** *apply(Univ, ResponseUniv)*

The bridge rule pattern from which such bridge rules are obtained is:

$$apply(Univ, ResponseUniv) \leftarrow test\_res(R1, R2, R3),$$
$$myuniv(u) : send\_test\_results(R1, R2, R3),$$
$$myuniv(u) : complete\_application(ResponseUniv)$$

The corresponding bridge-update rules, of the form

> **upon** *apply(Univ, ResponseUniv)* **then** *record(response(Univ, Response))*

will record the responses, to allow a choice to be made among the universities that have returned a positive answer. Finally, enrollment must be finalized (code not shown here). Notice that, in the above bridge rules, some elements in the body implicitly involve the execution of specific actions (such as the payment of fees) that may take time to be executed, and may also involve user intervention (e.g., the student must personally and practically go to perform the SAT and TOEFL tests). Such actions have to be specified in the internal definition of the involved module(s), while user interventions emerge from the interaction between the agent and the user. For lack of space we do not discuss plan revision strategies (that might be needed in case of failure of some of the above steps), to be implemented via agent's reactive and proactive features.

6   Semantics

In order to account for heterogeneity of composing modules, in MCSs and then in DACMACSs and in ACEs each module is supposed to be based upon a specific logic. Reporting from [8], a logic L is a triple $(KB_L; Cn_L; ACC_L)$, where KB_L is the set of admissible knowledge bases of L. A knowledge base is a set of KB-elements, or "formulas". Cn_L is the set of acceptable sets of consequences, whose elements are data items or "facts". Such sets can be called "belief sets" or simply "data sets". $ACC_L : KB_L \rightarrow 2^{Cn_L}$ is a function which defines the semantics of L by assigning to each knowledge-base a set of acceptable sets of consequences.

For any of the aforementioned frameworks, consider an instance $\mathcal{A} = \langle A_1, \ldots, A_h \rangle$ composed of h distinct modules, each of which can be either the basic agents, or an event-action module, or a reasoning module, or an external context. Each module is seen as $A_i = (L_i; kb_i; br_i)$ where L_i is a logic, $kb_i \in KB_{L_i}$ is the module's knowledge base and br_i is a set of bridge rules. A data state of $\mathcal{A}$ is a tuple $S = (S_1, \ldots, S_h)$ such that each of the S_is is an element of Cn_i, i.e. a set of consequences derived from A_i's knowledge base according to the logic in which module A_i is defined.

When modules are not considered separately, but rather they are connected via bridge rules, desirable data states, called *equilibria*, are those where bridge-rule application is considered. In MCSs, equilibria are those data states S where each S_i is acceptable according to function ACC_i associated to L_i, taking however bridge rules application into account. Technically, a data state S is an equilibrium iff, for $1 \leq i \leq n$, it holds that $S_i \in ACC_i(mng_i(app(S), kb_i))$. This means that if one takes the knowledge base kb_i associated to module A_i, considers all bridge rules which are applicable in data state S (i.e., S entails their body), applies the rules, applies the management function, it obtains exactly S_i (or at least S_i is one of the possible sets of consequences). Namely, an equilibrium is a data state that encompasses the application of bridge rules. In dynamic environments however, this does not in general imply that a bridge rule is applied only once, and that an equilibrium, once reached, lasts forever (conditions for reachability of equilibria are discussed in literature, see [23] and the references therein). In fact, contexts are in general able to incorporate new data items, e.g., as discussed in [10], the input provided by sensors. Therefore, a bridge rule is in principle re-evaluated whenever a new result can be obtained, thus leading to evolving equilibria.

As DACMACS and ACEs are frameworks for defining agents and multi-agent systems, the interaction with the external environment and with other agents goes beyond simple sensor input and must be explicitly considered. This is done by assuming, similarly to what is done in Linear Temporal Logic, a discrete, linear model of time where each state/time instant can be represented by an integer number. States $t_0, t_1, \ldots$ can be seen as time instants in abstract terms, though in practice we have $t_{i+1} - t_i = \delta$, where δ is the actual interval of time after which we assume a given system to have evolved.

Consider then a notion of *updates*: for $i > 0$, let $\Pi_i = \langle \Pi_{iA_1}, \ldots, \Pi_{iA_h} \rangle$ be a tuple composed of finite updates performed to each module and let $\Pi = \Pi_1, \Pi_2, \ldots$ be a sequence of such updates performed at time instants $t_1, t_2, \ldots$. Let $\mathcal{U}_E$, for $E \in \{A_1, \ldots, A_h\}$, be the *update operator* that each module employs for incorporating the new information, and let $\mathcal{U}$ be the tuple composed of all these operators. Notice that each $\mathcal{U}_E$, i.e., each module-specific operator, encompasses the treatment of both self-generated updated and updated coming from interaction with an external environment.

In this more general setting data states evolve in time, where a *timed* data state at time T is a tuple $S^T = (S_1^T, \ldots, S_h^T)$ such that each S_i^T is an element of Cn_i at time T. The timed data state S^0 is an equilibrium according the MCSs definition. Later on however, transition from a timed data state to the next one, and consequently the definition of an equilibrium, is determined both by the update operators and by the application of bridge rules. A bridge rule ρ occurring in each composing module is now *potentially applicable* in S^T iff S^T entails its body. However, in the basic agent a potentially applicable bridge rule is applied only when it has been triggered by a trigger rule of the form seen above, i.e., if for some $T' \leq T$ we have that $S^{T'} \models Q$. In any event-action module M instead, a potentially applicable bridge rule is applied only if the module is *active*, i.e., if $S^{T'} \models tr_M$, where tr_M is an *event expression* which triggers the module evaluation (cf. [13]). Therefore, a timed data state of M at time $T+1$ is an equilibrium iff, for $1 \leq i \leq n$, it holds that $S_i^{T+1} \in ACC_i(mng_i(App(S^T), kb_i^{T+1}))$, where $kb_i^{T+1} = \mathcal{U}_i(kb_i^T, \Pi_T^i)$ and App is the extended bridge-rule applicability evaluation function. The meaning is that an equilibrium is now a data state which encompasses bridge rules applicability (with the new criteria) on the updated knowledge base. So, contexts now evolve in time, where we may say that $A_i^0 = (L_i; kb_i; br_i)$ as before, while $A_i^T = (L_i; kb_i^T; br_i)$. As discussed in [14], if both the update operators and the management functions preserve consistency of modules, then conditions for existence of an equilibrium (at some time T) are unchanged w.r.t. MCSs and DACMACS.

Notice that, for each bridge rule which is triggered (and so is applicable) at time T' the state when it is actually applied is not necessarily T', nor $T' + 1$. In fact, a bridge rule becomes potentially applicable whenever a data state entail its body. So, the actual procedural sequence is the following:

- $S^{T'} \models Q$ for some trigger rule concerning bridge rule with conclusion $A(\hat{x})$, and then such a rule is executed at some time $T'' \geq T'$.
- At time $T \geq T''$ the results will be returned by the modules which are queried in the rule body; the case where $T' = T$, i.e., the bridge-rule body succeeds instantaneously, is an ideal extreme which is hardly the case in practice. In

fact, internal and external modules may take some (a priori unpredictable) amount of time for returning their results.

– At time T, bridge-rule results will be elaborated by the management function, in our case implemented by the bridge-update rule.

The important aspect that allows us to smoothly incorporate enhanced ACE features in this semantics is that knowledge base updates in an agent are not necessarily determined from the outside. Rather, (part of) an update can also be the result of proactive self-modification. So, the generality and flexibility of ACE's semantics allows us to introduce advanced features without needing substantial modifications.

In particular, we consider bridge rule patterns as elements of agent's knowledge base. A bridge rule pattern will produce new bridge rules only when its context designators will be instantiated. Such instantiation can be seen as a part of a self-modification, i.e., it can be seen as an update. Therefore, for the main agent we now have $A_i^0 = (L_i; kb_i; br_i)$ and $A_i^T = (L_i; kb_i^T; br_i^T)$, where at each subsequent time the set of bridge rule associated to the module can be augmented by newly generated instances. The other definitions remain unchanged. This limited though effective semantic modifications constitute, in our opinion, a successful result of the research work that we present here. In fact, we obtain more general and flexible systems without significantly departing from the original MCSs' semantics, and this grants our approach a fairly general applicability.

7   Case Study: RASP Implementation

Below we discuss how to represent in RASP the case study discussed in Sect. 2. We do not report the full code, that the reader can find on the web site http://www.dmi.unipg.it/formis/raspberry/ (section "Enrollment") where the solver Raspberry can also be obtained.[1] Our aim is to have a glance at how RASP works, and to demonstrate that the proposed approach is not only a more general architecture than basic ACE, but it has indeed a practical counterpart.

RASP code clearly must include a list of facts defining the universities to which the students is potentially interested, the SAT subjects (in general), and the SAT subjects corresponding to Courses (or Schools) available at each university.

```
% Universities
university(theBigUni).     university(theSmallUni).
university(thePinkUni).    university(theBlueUni).
university(theGreenUni).
% SAT subjects
sat_subject(literature).   sat_subject(mathematics).
sat_subject(chemistry).
```

---

[1] Raspberry, the grounder gringo (v.3.0.5), and the solver clasp (v.3.1.3) are used as follows: `raspberry_2.6.5 -pp -l3 -n 15000 -i enrollment_pref.rasp > enrollment_pref.asp` `gringo-3.0.5 enrollment_pref.asp | clasp-3.1.3 0.`

```
% SAT subjects in each University
availableSubject(theBigUni, S) :- sat_subject(S).
availableSubject(theGreenUni, S) :- sat_subject(S).
availableSubject(theSmallUni, mathematics).
availableSubject(thePinkUni,  mathematics).
availableSubject(thePinkUni,  literature).
availableSubject(theBlueUni,  mathematics).
availableSubject(theBlueUni,  chemistry).
```

Below we then list: the tuition fees and the maximum fee allowed; the university rankings and the minimum required; the basketball team ranking, as it constitutes an additional evaluation factor.

```
% Tuition fees
tuitionFee(theBigUni,    21000).  tuitionFee(theSmallUni, 16000).
tuitionFee(thePinkUni,   15000).  tuitionFee(theBlueUni,  25000).
tuitionFee(theGreenUni,  15000).
% Constraint C1: Tuition fee cannot exceed this threshold
maxTuition(22000).
% University reputation ranking R
reputation(theBigUni,    100).  reputation(theSmallUni, 90).
reputation(thePinkUni,    80).  reputation(theBlueUni,  75).
reputation(theGreenUni,   60).
% Constraint C2: R must be higher than this threshold
reputationThrs(70).
% BasketballTeam Ranking
extraRank(theSmallUni, 10).  extraRank(theBigUni,   10).
extraRank(thePinkUni,   8).  extraRank(theBlueUni,   8).
extraRank(theGreenUni,  6).
```

The RASP fact below states that we have 1500 dollars, sum intended here as the budget available for completing applications. In general, symbol '#' indicates that an atom represents a resource. The constant before '#', here 'dollar', indicates the (arbitrary) name of the resource. The number after the '#' indicates an amount. In case of a fact, this amount is available initially, and can be then (in general) either consumed or vice versa incremented, as in RASP resource production can also be modeled.

```
% Budget for the application procedure
dollar#1500.
```

Now, the subject of interest and (if applicable) the status as foreign prospective students are indicated. Concerning the English language, nothing needs to be done if the student is not foreign, otherwise the TOEFL fee must be payed for performing the required test (we remind the reader that this RASP program evaluates the necessary expenses, so it is concerned with fees).

```
% My_subject
my_subject(mathematics).
```

```
% Omit the following fact if not foreign:
foreign.
% Language prerequisite
languageReqOK :- not foreign.
languageReqOK :- testTOEFLfee, foreign.
```

The universities where to potentially apply are derived according to the preferred subject, and the constraints concerning the university ranking and tuition fee. The student can apply if some university meeting the required requisites is actually found.

```
% Filtering of Universities
canApply(U,S) :- university(U), my_subject(S), reputation(U, R),
    availableSubject(U, S), reputationThrs(Th), R > Th,
    maxTuition(M), tuitionFee(U, Tu), Tu < M.
canApplyForSubject(Subj) :- canApply(Univ,Subj).
canApply :- canApply(Univ,Subject).
```

We now introduce proper RASP rules that perform quantitative reasoning, specifically by considering the fees for the different kinds of tests. The reader can ignore the prefix [1-1] which means that whenever the rule is applied, or "fired", this is done only once. This specification is not significant here, whereas it is useful in the description of more complex resource production/consumption processes.

```
% 1) General SAT test, fee1 fixed
  [1-1]: testSATfeeGen :- dollar#300, canApply.
% 2) Disciplinary SAT test, fee2 fixed
  [1-1]: testSATfeeSbj(mathematics) :-
           dollar#170, canApplyForSubject(mathematics).
  [1-1]: testSATfeeSbj(literature) :-
           dollar#180, canApplyForSubject(literature).
  [1-1]: testSATfeeSbj(chemistry) :-
           dollar#150, canApplyForSubject(chemistry).
  [1-1]: testSATfeeSbj(physics) :-
           dollar#160, canApplyForSubject(physics).
% 3) For foreign student, TOEFL fee3 fixed
  [1-1]: testTOEFLfee :- dollar#200, foreign, canApply.
% 4) Collegeorg application, fee4 fixed
  [1-1]: testCollegeOrg :- dollar#130, canApply.
```

A general rule with head testGeneralDone then establishes whether all general tests have been considered. If the available budget is too low and so no applications can issued, then no money is actually spent. Otherwise, the costs related to potential applications and the remaining amount (if any) are computed. Clearly, this code (omitted here) performs a quantitative evaluation and does not execute actual actions, which are left to the agent.

At this point, the Raspberry RASP solver can compute all solutions which maximize the number of applications. Solutions can be further customized with respect to the constraints. For instance, the standard #maximize ASP statements allow one to prefer universities with the best ranking and, in case of equivalent solutions, the ones with the best basketball team ranking (see the full code in the web site mentioned earlier, for the details on how to optimize the solution and enforce student preferences).

With the given facts, the best preferred solution provided by Raspberry involves applying to thePinkUni and theBigUni, with a total rating (sum of the two rankings) of 180 for the universities and 18 for the basketball teams.

If omitting maximization, there is a second solution which involves applying to thePinkUni and theSmallUni, with a total rating (sum of the two rankings) of 170 for the universities and 18 for the basketball teams.

The RASP module always returns the remaining (not spent) amount which is 90 dollars in the former case and 120 dollars in the latter one. Then, the agent might in general choose the best solution. However, it might instead choose another one based upon other criteria not expressed in the RASP program, i.e., geographic location or acceptance rates or maybe lesser expense, in case there would be relevant differences.

8   Concluding Remarks

The contribution of this paper is twofold. First, we have demonstrated, also by means of a practical example, how quantitative reasoning can be performed in agent-based frameworks. Second, we have enhanced modular approaches inspired to MCSs with partially specified bridge rules, that can be dynamically customized and activated according to agent's reasoning results. The approach of this paper is fairly general, and can be thus adapted to several application domains and to different agent architectures. Since no significant related work exists, our approach to coping with the cost of knowledge and the cost of action is relevant in a variety of domains, from logistics to configuration to planning, which are particularly well-suited for agents and MAS. An important application that we envisage is planning in robotic environments, where agents are embodied in robots that have limited resources available (first of all energy) and must complete their tasks within those limits, while possibly giving priority to the most important/urgent objectives.

References

1. Alviano, M., Dodaro, C., Faber, W., Leone, N., Ricca, F.: WASP: a native ASP solver based on constraint learning. In: Cabalar, P., Son, T.C. (eds.) LPNMR 2013. LNCS, vol. 8148, pp. 54–66. Springer, Heidelberg (2013). doi:10.1007/978-3-642-40564-8_6
2. Bienvenu, M., Lang, J., Wilson, N.: From preference logics to preference languages, and back. In: Proceedings of KR 2010, pp. 414–424 (2010)
3. Bordini, R.H., Braubach, L., Dastani, M., Fallah-Seghrouchni, A.E., Gómez-Sanz, J.J., Leite, J., O'Hare, G.M.P., Pokahr, A., Ricci, A.: A survey of programming languages and platforms for multi-agent systems. Informatica (Slovenia) **30**(1), 33–44 (2006)

4. Bordini, R.H., Hübner, J.F.: BDI agent programming in agentspeak using *Jason*. In: Toni, F., Torroni, P. (eds.) CLIMA 2005. LNCS, vol. 3900, pp. 143–164. Springer, Heidelberg (2006). doi:10.1007/11750734_9

5. Bracciali, A., Demetriou, N., Endriss, U., Kakas, A., Lu, W., Mancarella, P., Sadri, F., Stathis, K., Terreni, G., Toni, F.: The KGP model of agency for global computing: computational model and prototype implementation. In: Priami, C., Quaglia, P. (eds.) GC 2004. LNCS (LNAI), vol. 3267, pp. 340–367. Springer, Heidelberg (2005). doi:10.1007/978-3-540-31794-4_18

6. Brewka, G., Delgrande, J.P., Romero, J., Schaub, T.: asprin: customizing answer set preferences without a headache. In: Bonet, B., Koenig, S. (eds.) Proceedings of AAAI 2015, pp. 1467–1474. AAAI Press (2015)

7. Brewka, G., Eiter, T.: Equilibria in heterogeneous nonmonotonic multi-context systems. In: Proceedings of AAAI 2007, pp. 385–390. AAAI Press (2007)

8. Brewka, G., Eiter, T., Fink, M.: Nonmonotonic multi-context systems: a flexible approach for integrating heterogeneous knowledge sources. In: Balduccini, M., Son, T.C. (eds.) Logic Programming, Knowledge Representation, and Nonmonotonic Reasoning. LNCS, vol. 6565, pp. 233–258. Springer, Heidelberg (2011). doi:10.1007/978-3-642-20832-4_16

9. Brewka, G., Eiter, T., Fink, M., Weinzierl, A.: Managed multi-context systems. In: Walsh, T. (ed.) Proceedings of IJCAI 2011, pp. 786–791. IJCAI/AAAI (2011)

10. Brewka, G., Ellmauthaler, S., Pührer, J.: Multi-context systems for reactive reasoning in dynamic environments. In: Schaub, T. (ed.) Proceedings of ECAI 2014. IJCAI/AAAI (2014)

11. Brewka, G., Niemelä, I., Truszczyński, M.: Preferences and nonmonotonic reasoning. AI Mag. **29**(4), 69–78 (2008)

12. Brik, A.: Extensions of answer set programming. Ph.D. thesis, University of California, San Diego (2012)

13. Costantini, S.: ACE: a flexible environment for complex event processing in logical agents. In: Baldoni, M., Baresi, L., Dastani, M. (eds.) EMAS 2015. LNCS, vol. 9318, pp. 70–91. Springer, Heidelberg (2015). doi:10.1007/978-3-319-26184-3_5

14. Costantini, S.: Knowledge acquisition via non-monotonic reasoning in distributed heterogeneous environments. In: Calimeri, F., Ianni, G., Truszczynski, M. (eds.) LPNMR 2015. LNCS, vol. 9345, pp. 228–241. Springer, Heidelberg (2015). doi:10.1007/978-3-319-23264-5_20

15. Costantini, S., De Gasperis, G.: Exchanging data and ontological definitions in multi-agent-contexts systems. In: Paschke, A., Fodor, P., Giurca, A., Kliegr, T. (eds.) Proceedings of RuleML 2015 Challenge, CEUR Workshop Proceedings. CEUR-WS.org (2015)

16. Costantini, S., Formisano, A.: Modeling preferences and conditional preferences on resource consumption and production in ASP. J. Algorithms Cogn. Inform. Logic **64**(1), 3–15 (2009)

17. Costantini, S., Formisano, A.: Answer set programming with resources. J. Logic Comput. **20**(2), 533–571 (2010)

18. Costantini, S., Formisano, A.: RASP and ASP as a fragment of linear logic. J. Appl. Non-class. Logics **23**(1–2), 49–74 (2013)

19. Costantini, S., Formisano, A., Petturiti, D.: Extending and implementing RASP. Fundam. Inform. **105**(1–2), 1–33 (2010)

20. Costantini, S., Tocchio, A.: A logic programming language for multi-agent systems. In: Flesca, S., Greco, S., Ianni, G., Leone, N. (eds.) JELIA 2002. LNCS (LNAI), vol. 2424, pp. 1–13. Springer, Heidelberg (2002). doi:10.1007/3-540-45757-7_1

21. Costantini, S., Tocchio, A.: The DALI logic programming agent-oriented language. In: Alferes, J.J., Leite, J. (eds.) JELIA 2004. LNCS (LNAI), vol. 3229, pp. 685–688. Springer, Heidelberg (2004). doi:10.1007/978-3-540-30227-8_57

22. Dal Palù, A., Dovier, A., Pontelli, E., Rossi, G.: GASP: answer set programming with lazy grounding. Fundam. Inform. **96**(3), 297–322 (2009)

23. Dao-Tran, M., Eiter, T., Fink, M., Krennwallner, T.: Distributed evaluation of nonmonotonic multi-context systems. JAIR **52**, 543–600 (2015)

24. Dastani, M., van Riemsdijk, M.B., Meyer, J.C.: Programming multi-agent systems in 3APL. In: Bordini, R.H., Dastani, M., Dix, J., Fallah-Seghrouchni, A.E. (eds.) Multi-agent Programming. Multiagent Systems, Artificial Societies, and Simulated Organizations, vol. 15, pp. 39–67. Springer, New York (2005)

25. Delgrande, J., Schaub, T., Tompits, H., Wang, K.: A classification and survey of preference handling approaches in nonmonotonic reasoning. Comput. Intell. **20**(12), 308–334 (2004)

26. Dovier, A., Formisano, A., Pontelli, E., Vella, F.: A GPU implementation of the ASP computation. In: Gavanelli, M., Reppy, J. (eds.) PADL 2016. LNCS, vol. 9585, pp. 30–47. Springer, Heidelberg (2016). doi:10.1007/978-3-319-28228-2_3

27. Fisher, M.: METATEM: the story so far. In: Bordini, R.H., Dastani, M.M., Dix, J., Fallah Seghrouchni, A. (eds.) ProMAS 2005. LNCS, vol. 3862, pp. 3–22. Springer, Heidelberg (2006). doi:10.1007/11678823_1

28. Gebser, M., Kaminski, R., Kaufmann, B., Romero, J., Schaub, T.: Progress in *clasp* series 3. In: Calimeri, F., Ianni, G., Truszczynski, M. (eds.) LPNMR 2015. LNCS, vol. 9345, pp. 368–383. Springer, Heidelberg (2015). doi:10.1007/978-3-319-23264-5_31

29. Gelfond, M.: Answer sets. In: Handbook of Knowledge Representation. Elsevier (2007)

30. Hindriks, K.V., Hoek, W., Meyer, J.-J.C.: GOAL agents instantiate intention logic. In: Artikis, A., Craven, R., Kesim Çiçekli, N., Sadighi, B., Stathis, K. (eds.) Logic Programs, Norms and Action. LNCS, vol. 7360, pp. 196–219. Springer, Heidelberg (2012). doi:10.1007/978-3-642-29414-3_11

31. Liu, G., Janhunen, T., Niemelä, I.: Answer set programming via mixed integer programming. In: Proceedings of KR 2012 (2012)

32. Maratea, M., Pulina, L., Ricca, F.: A multi-engine approach to answer-set programming. TPLP **14**(6), 841–868 (2014)

33. Naumov, P., Tao, J.: Budget-constrained knowledge in multiagent systems. In: Weiss, G., Yolum, P., Bordini, R.H., Elkind, E. (eds.) Proceedings of AAMAS 2015, pp. 219–226. ACM (2015)

34. Simons, P., Niemelä, I., Soininen, T.: Extending and implementing the stable model semantics. Artif. Intell. **138**(1–2), 181–234 (2002)

35. Web-references. Some ASP solvers. Clasp: http://potassco.sourceforge.net; Cmodels: http://www.cs.utexas.edu/users/tag/cmodels; DLV: http://www.dlvsystem.com; Smodels: http://www.tcs.hut.fi/Software/smodels

How Testable are BDI Agents? An Analysis of Branch Coverage

Michael Winikoff[(✉)]

University of Otago, Dunedin, New Zealand
michael.winikoff@otago.ac.nz

Abstract. Before deploying a software system, it is important to assure that it will function correctly. Traditionally, this assurance is obtained by testing the system with a collection of test cases. However, since agent systems exhibit complex behaviour, it is not clear whether testing is even feasible. In this paper we extend our understanding of the feasibility of testing BDI agent programs by analysing their testability with respect to the *all edges* test adequacy criterion, and comparing with previous work that considered the *all paths* criterion. Our findings include that the number of tests required with respect to the all edges criterion is much lower than for the all paths criterion. We also compare BDI program testability with testability of (abstract) procedural programs.

1 Introduction

When any software system is deployed, it is important to have assurance that it will function as required. Traditionally, this assurance, encompassing both validation and verification[1], is obtained by testing, and there has been work on tools and techniques for testing agent-based systems (e.g. [9,11,14,15,24]). However, there is a general intuition that agents exhibit behaviour that is complex. More precisely, due to the need to handle dynamic and challenging environments, agents need to be able to achieve their objectives flexibly and robustly, which requires richer and more complex possible behaviours than traditional software. Therefore, a key question is *whether agent systems are harder, and possibly even infeasible, to assure by testing.*

Before proceeding further we need to define what we mean by a program being testable. Rather than define testability as a binary property, we define it as a

---

This paper has originally been published in N. Osman and C. Sierra (Eds.), AAMAS 2016 Ws Best Papers, LNAI 10002, 2016.
© Springer International Publishing AG 2016
N. Osman and C. Sierra (Eds.): AAMAS 2016 Ws Best Papers, LNAI 10002, pp. 90–106, 2016.
DOI: 10.1007/978-3-319-46882-2_6

[1] More precisely: "software quality assurance (SQA) is a set of activities that define and assess the adequacy of software processes to provide evidence that establishes confidence that the software processes are appropriate and produce software products of suitable quality for their intended purposes." (ISO/IEC TR 19759:2015(E), pp. 10–15).

© Springer International Publishing AG 2016
M. Baldoni et al. (Eds.): EMAS 2016, LNAI 10093, pp. 210–226, 2016.
DOI: 10.1007/978-3-319-50983-9_12

numerical measure of the effort required to test a program[2]. Specifically, given a program and a *test adequacy criterion* [13], we consider the testability of a program to be the smallest number of tests that would be required to satisfy the criterion. For example, given the (very simple!) program "**if** c **then** s_1 **else** s_2", then we need two tests to cover all edges in the control-flow graph corresponding to this program, which satisfies the "all edges" test adequacy criterion (defined below),

The *all paths* and *all edges* test adequacy criteria are defined with respect to a control-flow graph. A given program P corresponds to a graph where nodes are statements (or, for agents, actions), and edges depict the flow of control: a node with multiple outgoing edges corresponds to a choice in the program. A single test corresponds to a path through the program's control-flow graph from its starting node to its final node (we assume that there is a unique start node S and a unique end node E, which can be easily ensured). The *all paths* criterion is satisfied iff the set of tests in the test suite T cover all *paths* in the control flow graph. The *all edges* criterion is satisfied iff the set of paths in the test suite T covers all *edges* in the control-flow graph [13]. The all edges criterion is also referred to as "branch coverage".

Given the importance of assurance, and the focus on testing as a means of obtaining assurance[3], there has been surprisingly little work that has considered whether testing agent systems is even feasible. In fact, the only work that we are aware of that considers this question is the recent work by myself & Cranefield[4] [20,21], which investigated the testability of Belief-Desire-Intention (BDI) agent programs with respect to the *all paths* test adequacy criterion. Winikoff & Cranefield concluded that BDI agent programs do indeed give rise to a very large number of possible paths (see left part of Table 1), and therefore they concluded that whole BDI programs are likely to be infeasible to assure via testing[5]. However, they do acknowledge that the all paths criterion is known to be overly conservative, i.e. it requires a very large number of tests. Specifically, all paths *subsumes* a wide range of other criteria, including all edges (e.g. see Fig. 7 of Zhu *et al.* [25] and Fig. 6.11 (p. 480) of Mathur [13]). This means that the question of whether (whole) BDI agent programs can be feasibly tested is still open. This paper aims to address this question by considering testability with respect to the *all edges* [13] test adequacy criterion. The all edges criterion is regarded as *"the generally accepted minimum"* [12]. In essence, previous work [20] has provided an *upper* bound ("if we

---

[2] We focus on system testing. See [20, Sect. 7] for a discussion of different forms of testing.

[3] There is also a body of work on formal methods (primarily model checking) as a means of assurance [3,6–8,10,16,23]. However, despite considerable progress, these are not yet ready to handle realistic programs (e.g. see [8]).

[4] To avoid confusion between this paper and the earlier work, I will refer to my earlier work with Stephen Cranefield as "Winikoff & Cranefield" in the remainder of this paper.

[5] They also compared BDI programs with procedural programs, and found that BDI programs are *harder* to test than equivalently sized procedural programs, with respect to the all paths criterion.

use a strong criterion, then it's this hard"). This paper provides a *lower bound* ("if we use a weaker criterion, than it's this hard").

The remainder of this paper is structured as follows. We (briefly) review BDI agent programs in Sect. 2. Section 3 is the core of the paper: it derives equations that compute for a given BDI program P the number of tests that are required to satisfy the all edges criterion. We then use these equations to compare testability (with respect to all edges) with testability with respect to all paths (Sect. 4). We also compare all edges testability for BDI programs with all edges testability for (abstract) procedural programs, in order to answer the question of whether BDI programs are *harder* to test than procedural programs with respect to the all edges criterion (Sect. 5). Finally, in Sect. 6 we conclude.

2   Belief-Desire-Intention (BDI) Agents

The Belief-Desire-Intention (BDI) model [4,5,18] is widely-used, and is realised in many agent-oriented programming languages (AOPLs) (e.g., [1,2]). It provides a human-inspired metaphor and mechanism for practical reasoning, in a way that is appropriate for achieving robust and flexible behaviour in dynamic environments.

A BDI agent program Π consists of a sequence of plans $\pi_1 \ldots \pi_n$ where each plan π_i consists of a triggering goal[6] g_i a context condition c_i and plan body b_i. The plan body is a sequence of steps $s_1^i \ldots s_{m_i}^i$ with each step being either an action or a sub-goal.

Due to space limitations, we give an informal summary of the semantics. Formal semantics can be easily defined following (e.g.) [17,19,22]. These semantics are common to the family of BDI programming languages (e.g. PRS, dMARS, JAM, AgentSpeak, JACK). A BDI program's execution begins with a goal g being posted. The first step is to determine the subset of *relevant* plans $\Pi_R \subseteq \Pi$ which is those plans π_i where the plan's trigger g_i can be unified with g. The second step is to determine the subset of *applicable* plans $\Pi_A \subseteq \Pi_R$ which is those plans π_i where the plan's context condition c_i holds with respect to the agent's current beliefs. The third step is to select one of the applicable plans $\pi_j \in \Pi_A$. The body b_j of the selected plan π_j is then executed. The execution is done step-by-step, interleaved with further processing of goals (and belief updates as information from the environment is received).

An important aspect of BDI execution is failure handling. A step in a plan body can fail. For an action, this can be because the action's preconditions do not hold, or due to the action simply not proceeding as planned (the environment is not always benign!). For a sub-goal, failure occurs when there is no applicable plan. When a plan step fails, the execution of the sequence of steps is terminated, and the plan is deemed to have failed.

A common way of dealing with the failure of a plan π_i which was triggered by goal g is to *repost* the goal g, and select another plan instance. More precisely, Π_A is re-computed (since the agent's beliefs might have changed in the interim), but

---

[6] For the purposes of this paper we ignore other possible plan triggers provided by some AOPLs, such as the addition/removal of belief, and the removal of goals.

with π_i excluded. A plan (instance) that has failed cannot be selected again when its triggering goal is reposted.

For the purposes of the analysis of this paper we consider a BDI agent program to be defined by the grammar below. This grammar simplifies from real BDI agent programs in a number of ways. Firstly, instead of a plan body having sub-goals g, with the relevant and applicable plan sets being derived from the plan library Π, we instead associate with each (sub-)goal g a set of plans[7] denoted $g^{\mathcal{P}}$ (where $\mathcal{P}$ is a set of plan instances). Because we have done this, we do not need to represent the plan library: a BDI program is simply a single (possibly quite complex) expression in the grammar below. Secondly, we follow CAN [22] in using an auxiliary "backup plan" construct to capture failure handling. Finally, we elide conditions: since the all edges criterion considers control-flow, we do not need to model the conditions that are used to decide which edge to take in the control flow graph.

We therefore define a BDI program P using the grammar:

$$ P ::= a \mid g^{\{P^*\}} \mid P_1 ; P_2 \mid P_1 \triangleright P_2 $$

where a is an action (and we use $a_1, a_2, a_3, \ldots$ to distinguish actions), $g^{\mathcal{P}}$ is a (sub-)goal with associated plans $\mathcal{P} = \{P_1, \ldots, P_n\}$ (a set of plans), $P_1 ; P_2$ is a sequence, and $P_1 \triangleright P_2$ represents a "backup plan": if P_1 succeeds, then nothing else is done (i.e. P_2 is ignored), but if P_1 fails, then P_2 is used. Any BDI program with given top-level goal can be mapped into a BDI program in this grammar. Note that this grammar does not capture some of the constraints of BDI programs (e.g. that a goal cannot directly post a sub-goal).

3   All-Edge Coverage Analysis

This section is the core of the paper. It derives equations that answer the question: "how many test cases (paths) are required to cover all edges in the control-flow graph corresponding to a given BDI program?".

Recall that a BDI agent program P can be either an action a, a sub-goal $g^{\mathcal{P}}$, a sequence (";"), or an alternative ("$\triangleright$"). We consider each of these cases in turn. For each case we consider how the construct is mapped to a control-flow graph, and then how many paths are required to cover all edges in the graph.

One important feature of BDI programs is that the execution of a BDI program (or sub-program) can either succeed or fail. A failed execution triggers failure handling. We represent this by mapping a program P to a graph (see right) where there is a start

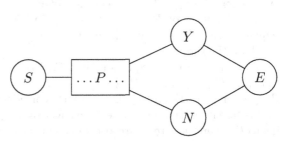

---

[7] For the moment we avoid specifying whether $\mathcal{P}$ is the set of relevant plans or applicable plans. The analysis in the next section considers both cases.

node S, the program P is mapped to a graph that is reachable from S, and that has *two* outgoing edges: to Y (corresponding to a successful execution) and N (corresponding to a failed execution). There are edges from Y and N to the end node E.

Note that there is an important difference between the notion of a test for a conventional program and for an agent system. In a conventional program a test corresponds to the setting up of initial conditions, and then the program is started and runs. However, in an agent system (or, more generally a reactive system), the running system continues to interact with its environment, and so a test is not just the initial conditions, but also comprises the ongoing interactions of the system with its environment. One consequence of this is that conditions are controllable. If an agent system tests condition c at a certain point in time, and then tests that condition again later, then in general the environment might have changed c, and so we assume that all conditions can be controlled by the test environment. This means that, for instance, if we have a test (i.e. path) that involves two subsequent parts of the graph, G_1 and G_2, then the specific path taken through G_2 can be treated as being independently controllable from that taken through G_1.

We now seek to derive equations that calculate the smallest number of paths from S to E required such that all edges appear at least once in the set of paths.

In order to do this, it turns out that we need to also capture how many of these paths correspond to successful executions (go via Y) and how many go via N. Notation[8]: we define $p(P)$ to be the number of paths required to cover all edges in the graph corresponding to program P. We also define $y(P)$ (respectively $n(P)$) to be the number of these paths that go via Y (respectively N). By construction we have that $p(P) = y(P) + n(P)$.

Let us now consider each case in turn. The base case of a single action a is straightforward. In the graph above it corresponds to the sub-graph P being a single node a. To cover all edges in the graph we need two test cases: one path S-a-Y-E and one S-a-N-E. This reflects that an action a can either succeed or fail, and therefore requires two tests to cover these possibilities. Formally we have that $p(a) = 2$, and that $y(a) = n(a) = 1$.

Next we consider $P_1; P_2$. Suppose that a sub-program P_1 requires $p(P_1)$ tests (i.e. paths) to cover all edges, with $n(P_1)$ of these tests leading to the failure of P_1, and the remaining $y(P_1)$ tests leading to successful execution of P_1. Since P_1 is put in sequence with P_2, we have the control flow graph on the right.

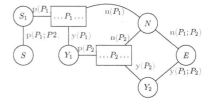

We seek to derive an equation for $p(P_1; P_2)$ (and for $y(P_1; P_2)$ and $n(P_1; P_2)$) in terms of the properties of P_1 and P_2. Let us firstly consider the case where $y(P_1) \leq p(P_2)$. In this case if we have enough tests to cover the edges of the sub-graph corresponding to P_2, then these tests are also sufficient to cover all edges of P_1 that result in a

---

[8] Colour is used to assist readability, but is not essential.

successful execution of P_1 (which lead to P_2). So to cover all edges of P_1 we need to add in enough tests to cover those executions that are failed, i.e. $n(P_1)$. Therefore we have that:

$$p(P_1; P_2) = n(P_1) + p(P_2) \tag{1}$$
$$y(P_1; P_2) = y(P_2) \tag{2}$$
$$n(P_1; P_2) = n(P_1) + n(P_2) \tag{3}$$

We now consider the case where $y(P_1) \geq p(P_2)$. In this case if we have enough tests (i.e. paths) to cover the edges of the sub-graph corresponding to P_1, then these tests are also sufficient to cover all edges of P_2. We therefore have that $p(P_1; P_2) = p(P_1) = n(P_1) + y(P_1)$.

However, when considering $y(P_1; P_2)$ and $n(P_1; P_2)$ things become a little more complex. Since $y(P_1) > p(P_2)$, the edge from the sub-graph corresponding to P_1 that goes to the sub-graph corresponding to P_2 has more tests traversing it than are required to cover all edges of P_2. In effect, this leaves us with "excess" tests (paths), and we need to work out how many of these excess paths should be allocated to successful executions of P_2 (i.e. $y(P_2)$), and how many to $n(P_2)$.

Consider the following example. Suppose that $P_1; P_2$ is such that[9] P_1 requires 5 tests to cover all edges (four successful, and hence available to test P_2, and one unsuccessful), and where P_2 only requires 2 tests to cover all edges. In this situation there are two additional tests that are required to test P_1 and which proceed to continue executing P_2. These two extra tests could correspond to failed executions of P_2, to successful executions of P_2, or to one successful and one failed execution. This means that, if we annotate each edge with the number of times that it is traversed by the set of tests[10], then the edge from Y_1 to the P_2 sub-graph is traversed 4 times, since the edge from P_1 to Y_1 traversed 4 times. The edge from P_2 to Y_2 could have either a 1, 2, or 3, and similarly the edge from P_2 to N could have either 3, 2, or 1 (see Fig. 1).

Returning to the analysis, in this case, where $y(P_1) > p(P_2)$, we define $\epsilon_1 + \epsilon_2 = y(P_1) - p(P_2)$. Then if we annotate each edge with the number of times that it is traversed by the tests, then the annotation on the edge from Y_1 to P_2 would be $p(P_2) + \epsilon_1 + \epsilon_2$. If we now consider the edges *from* the sub-graph corresponding to P_2, then the edge to N (the number of executions where P_2 failed) would be annotated with $n(P_2) + \epsilon_2$ and the edge to Y_2 would be annotated with $y(P_2) + \epsilon_1$. This gives us the following equations:

$$p(P_1; P_2) = n(P_1) + y(P_1) \tag{4}$$
$$y(P_1; P_2) = y(P_2) + \epsilon_1 \tag{5}$$
$$n(P_1; P_2) = n(P_1) + n(P_2) + \epsilon_2 \tag{6}$$
$$\text{where } \epsilon_1 + \epsilon_2 = y(P_1) - p(P_2)$$

---

[9] E.g. $P_1 = a_1 \triangleright a_2 \triangleright a_3 \triangleright a_4$ and $P_2 = a_5$.
[10] Note that for any internal node, the sum of annotations on incoming edges must equal the sum of annotations on outgoing edges, since all paths begin at S and terminate at E.

Merging these cases with Eqs. 1, 2 and 3, we obtain the following. Derivation: for y() and n() observe that Eqs. 2 and 3 are in the case where $y(P_1) \leq p(P_2)$ and hence $\epsilon_1 = \epsilon_2 = 0$, reducing the equations below to Eqs. 2 and 3, and if $y(P_1) > p(P_2)$ then the equations below are identical to Eqs. 5 and 6. For $p(P_1; P_2)$ observe that if $y(P_1) \leq p(P_2)$ then the equation below reduces to Eq. 1, and that if $y(P_1) > p(P_2)$ then the equation below reduces to Eq. 4.

$$p(P_1; P_2) = n(P_1) + \max(y(P_1), p(P_2))$$
$$y(P_1; P_2) = y(P_2) + \epsilon_1$$
$$n(P_1; P_2) = n(P_1) + n(P_2) + \epsilon_2$$
$$\text{where} \quad \epsilon_1 + \epsilon_2 = \max(0, y(P_1) - p(P_2))$$

Note that we don't have deterministic equations that compute $n(P_1; P_2)$ and $y(P_1; P_2)$. Instead, we have equations that permit a *range* of values, depending on how we choose to allocate the excess paths represented by $\epsilon_1 + \epsilon_2$ between the successful and unsuccessful executions of P_2.

Turning to $P_1 \triangleright P_2$ we perform a similar analysis. Note that the control glow graph for $P_1 \triangleright P_2$ has the same structure as that of $P_1; P_2$ except that N and Y are swapped (see Figure to the right). The simple case is when $n(P_1) \leq p(P_2)$, in which case the number of paths required to test (i.e. cover

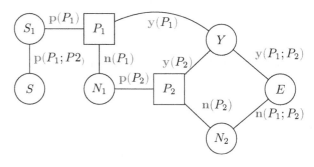

all edges of) P_2 also suffices to cover edges in P_1 when P_1 fails (for $P_1 \triangleright P_2$ it is when P_1 *fails* that P_2 is used). For this case we therefore have $p(P_1 \triangleright P_2) = y(P_1) + p(P_2)$

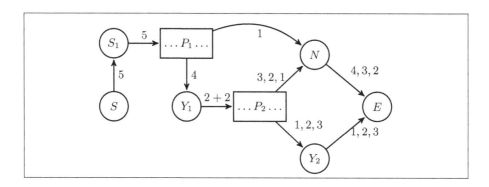

Fig. 1. Example for $P_1 = a_1 \triangleright a_2 \triangleright a_3 \triangleright a_4$ and $P_2 = a_5$.

$$\mathbf{p}(a) = 2 \qquad \mathbf{y}(a) = 1 \qquad \mathbf{n}(a) = 1$$

$$\mathbf{p}(P_1; P_2) = \mathbf{n}(P_1) + \max(\mathbf{y}(P_1), \mathbf{p}(P_2))$$

$$\mathbf{y}(P_1; P_2) = \mathbf{y}(P_2) + \epsilon_1$$

$$\mathbf{n}(P_1; P_2) = \mathbf{n}(P_1) + \mathbf{n}(P_2) + \epsilon_2$$

$$\text{where } \epsilon_1 + \epsilon_2 = \max(0, \mathbf{y}(P_1) - \mathbf{p}(P_2))$$

$$\mathbf{p}(P_1 \triangleright P_2) = \mathbf{y}(P_1) + \max(\mathbf{n}(P_1), \mathbf{p}(P_2))$$

$$\mathbf{y}(P_1 \triangleright P_2) = \mathbf{y}(P_1) + \mathbf{y}(P_2) + \epsilon_3$$

$$\mathbf{n}(P_1 \triangleright P_2) = \mathbf{n}(P_2) + \epsilon_4$$

$$\text{where } \epsilon_3 + \epsilon_4 = \max(0, \mathbf{n}(P_1) - \mathbf{p}(P_2))$$

$$\mathbf{p}(g^{\{P\}}) = \boxed{1+} \mathbf{p}(P) \qquad \mathbf{y}(g^{\{P\}}) = \mathbf{y}(P) \qquad \mathbf{n}(g^{\{P\}}) = \boxed{1+} \mathbf{n}(P)$$

$$\mathbf{p}(g^{\mathcal{P}}) = \boxed{1+} \sum_{P_i \in \mathcal{P}} \mathbf{y}(P_i) + \max(\mathbf{n}(P_i), \mathbf{p}(g^{\mathcal{P} \setminus \{P_i\}}))$$

$$\mathbf{y}(g^{\mathcal{P}}) = \sum_{P_i \in \mathcal{P}} \mathbf{y}(P_i) + \mathbf{y}(g^{\mathcal{P} \setminus \{P_i\}}) + \epsilon_i$$

$$\mathbf{n}(g^{\mathcal{P}}) = \boxed{1+} \sum_{P_i \in \mathcal{P}} \mathbf{n}(g^{\mathcal{P} \setminus \{P_i\}}) + \epsilon_i'$$

$$\text{where } \epsilon_i + \epsilon_i' = \max(0, \mathbf{n}(P_i) - \mathbf{p}(g^{\mathcal{P} \setminus \{P_i\}}))$$

$$\mathbf{p}(/^{\mathcal{P}}g) = \boxed{1+} \sum_{P \in \mathcal{P}} \mathbf{p}(P)$$

$$\mathbf{y}(/^{\mathcal{P}}g) = \sum_{P \in \mathcal{P}} \mathbf{y}(P)$$

$$\mathbf{n}(/^{\mathcal{P}}g) = \boxed{1+} \sum_{P \in \mathcal{P}} \mathbf{n}(P)$$

Fig. 2. Equations to calculate $p(P), y(P)$ and $n(P)$ when $\mathcal{P}$ is relevant plans. For applicable plans delete the grey shaded "$\boxed{1+}$".

and $y(P_1 \triangleright P_2) = y(P_1) + y(P_2)$ and $n(P_1 \triangleright P_2) = n(P_2)$. Similar analysis for the more complex case gives the equations in Fig. 2.

Finally, we consider goals. We begin with the simple case: a goal with a single *relevant* plan $g^{\{P_1\}}$. In this case either the goal immediately fails (due to the plan's context condition failing), or the plan is executed. If the plan is executed, then the goal succeeds exactly when the plan succeeds. Therefore we have: $n(g^{\{P_1\}}) = 1 + n(P_1)$, and $y(g^{\{P_1\}}) = y(P_1)$, and $p(g^{\{P_1\}}) = 1 + p(P_1)$. In the case where P_1 is *applicable*, then the context condition cannot fail, and we simply have $n(g^{\{P_1\}}) = n(P_1)$ and $p(g^{\{P_1\}}) = p(P_1)$.

For a goal with two *relevant* plans $g^{\{P_1, P_2\}}$ (henceforth abbreviated g^2), there are three non-overlapping possibilities: the plan fails immediately (neither context condition is true), or the first plan is selected, or the second plan is selected. If a plan is selected, then the plan is executed with the other plan as a (possible) backup option. Informally we can describe this as

$$g^2 = \text{fail or } P_1 \triangleright g^{P_2} \text{ or } P_2 \triangleright g^{P_1}$$

(where g^P is short hand for $g^{\{P\}}$). Which leads to the following equations.

$$\mathrm{p}(g^2) = 1 + \mathrm{p}(P_1 \triangleright g^{P_2}) + \mathrm{p}(P_2 \triangleright g^{P_1})$$
$$\mathrm{y}(g^2) = \mathrm{y}(P_1 \triangleright g^{P_2}) + \mathrm{y}(P_2 \triangleright g^{P_1})$$
$$\mathrm{n}(g^2) = 1 + \mathrm{n}(P_1 \triangleright g^{P_2}) + \mathrm{n}(P_2 \triangleright g^{P_1})$$

In the case where we are dealing with *applicable* plans, the only difference is that the "1+" in the equations for $\mathrm{p}(g)$ and $\mathrm{n}(g)$ is deleted, since the plan cannot fail. This can be generalised for a goal with k plans (details omitted) resulting in the equations in Fig. 2.

3.1   Removing Failure Handling

We now briefly consider what happens if we "turn off" failure handling, This is an interesting scenario to consider, because the all paths analysis of Winikoff & Cranefield [20] found that turning failure handling off reduced the number of tests required enormously. We use $\not{g}$ to denote a goal where failure handling is not used.

We firstly observe that without failure handling the equation for $\not{g}^{\{P\}}$ remains unchanged from $g^{\{P\}}$, since if the sole plan P fails, then there is no remaining plan available to recover.

However, for $\not{g}^{\{P_1,P_2\}}$ the equations are different. Instead of having (informally) $g^2 = \text{fail or } P_1 \triangleright g^{P_2} \text{ or } P_2 \triangleright g^{P_1}$, we have simply $\not{g}^2 = \text{fail or } P_1 \text{ or } P_2$. Therefore the corresponding equations are simply: $\mathrm{p}(\not{g}^2) = 1 + \mathrm{p}(P_1) + \mathrm{p}(P_2)$, and $\mathrm{y}(\not{g}^2) = \mathrm{y}(P_1) + \mathrm{y}(P_2)$, and $\mathrm{n}(\not{g}^2) = 1 + \mathrm{n}(P_1) + \mathrm{n}(P_2)$. These generalise for $\not{g}^P$ (where P denotes a set of plans), yielding the equations in Fig. 2. As before, for P being the *applicable* plans, remove the "$1 +$" from the equations.

3.2   Simplifying for Uniform Programs

In order to compare with the all paths analysis of Winikoff & Cranefield [20] we consider *uniform* BDI programs, as they did. A uniform BDI program is one where all plan bodies have j sub-goals, all goals have k plans, and the tree is uniformly deep.

Applying these assumptions allows the equations to be simplified, since all sub-goals of a plan (respectively plans of a goal) have identical structure, and are hence interchangeable.

For example, in the equation for $\mathrm{p}(P_1; P_2)$, P_1 and P_2 are identical, so instead of $\mathrm{p}(P_1; P_2) = \mathrm{n}(P_1) + \max(\mathrm{y}(P_1), \mathrm{p}(P_2))$ we have $\mathrm{p}(P; P) = \mathrm{n}(P) + \max(\mathrm{y}(P), \mathrm{p}(P))$.

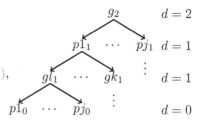

Now, since $p(P) > y(P)$, we can replace
$\max(y(P), p(P))$ with $p(P)$. Therefore, we have that $p(P; P) = n(P) + p(P)$.
Since $p(P) = y(P) + n(P)$ this is just $n(P) + y(P) + n(P) = y(P) + 2n(P)$. This
generalises to more than two sub-programs in sequence. Similar simplification can
be applied to the other cases, yielding the equations shown in Fig. 3 (ignore the
last four equations for the moment).

However, uniform programs (as used by the all paths analysis [20]) actually
have a mixture of actions and goals in plans, i.e. a plan (that is not a leaf) is of the
form $P = a; g; a; g; a$ (for $k = 2$), not $g; g$. This means we need to derive equations
for this form.

We begin by deriving $p(a; g), y(a; g)$ and $n(a; g)$, using the simplification that
$\epsilon_1 = \epsilon_2 = 0$, since $y(P_1) = y(a) = 1$ and hence $p(P_2) \geq 1$ so $\max(0, y(P_1) -$
$p(P_2)) = 0$.

$$
\begin{aligned}
p(a; g) &= n(a) + \max(y(a), p(g)) &= 1 + p(g) \quad (\text{since } p(g) > y(a) = 1) \\
y(a; g) &= y(g) \ (\text{since } p(g) > y(a) = 1) \\
n(a; g) &= 1 + n(g)
\end{aligned}
$$

We then define $p^1 = a; g; a$ and derive $p(p^1), y(p^1)$ and $n(p^1)$. In deriving $y(p^1)$
and $n(p^1)$ we derive the upper and lower bounds (recall that the equations in Fig. 2
specify a range, depending on how we split "excess" $(y(P_1) - p(P_2))$ between ϵ_1
and ϵ_2). We work out the upper bound for $y(P_1)$ (respectively $n(P_1)$) by assigning
all the excess to ϵ_1 (respectively ϵ_2). We derive equations under the assumption
that $y(a; g) > 1$, and hence $y(a; g) \geq p(a) = 2$. This assumption holds when goals
have more than one plan (i.e. $j > 1$), which is the case in Table 1.

$$
\begin{aligned}
p((a; g); a) &= n(a; g) + \max(y(a; g), p(a)) \\
&= n(a; g) + y(a; g) &= p(a; g) &= 1 + p(g) \\
y((a; g); a) &\leq y(a) + \max(0, y(a; g) - p(a)) \\
&= 1 + y(a; g) - 2 &= y(g) - 1 \\
y((a; g); a) &\geq y(a) &= 1 \\
n((a; g); a) &\leq n(a; g) + n(a) + \max(0, y(a; g) - p(a)) \\
&= (1 + n(g)) + 1 + (y(a; g) - 2) &= n(g) + y(g) &= p(g) \\
n((a; g); a) &\geq n(a; g) + n(a) &= (1 + n(g)) + 1 &= 2 + n(g)
\end{aligned}
$$

We then note that $p^2 = a; g; a; g; a$ can be defined as $p^2 = (a; g); p^1$, and, more
generally, $p^{k+1} = (a; g); p^k$.

$$
\begin{aligned}
p(p^{k+1}) &= n(a; g) + \max(y(a; g), p(p^k)) \\
&= n(a; g) + p(p^k) \ (\text{since } p(p^k) \geq y(a; g)) \\
&= 1 + n(g) + p(p^k) \\
&\text{which can be generalised to} \\
&= k \times (1 + n(g)) + 1 + p(g) \\
y(p^{k+1}) &\leq y(p^k) + \max(0, y(a; g) - p(p^k)) \\
&= y(p^k) \ (\text{since } p(p^k) \geq y(a; g)) \\
&\text{so eventually we just get } y(p^1) \text{ which is } \ldots \\
&= y(g) - 1
\end{aligned}
$$

$$\begin{aligned}
y(p^{k+1}) \quad &\geq \quad y(p^k) \quad \geq y(p^{k-1}) \quad \geq 1 \\
n(p^{k+1}) \quad &= \quad n(a;g) + n(p^k) + \max(0, y(a;g) - p(p^k)) \\
&= \quad (1 + n(g)) + n(p^k) \text{ (since } p(p^k) \geq y(a;g)) \\
&= \quad k \times (1 + n(g)) + n(p^1)
\end{aligned}$$

The yields the last four equations of Fig. 3, which are required to calculate the testability of uniform BDI programs. Note that in the last equation, since $n(p^1) \geq 2 + n(g)$ and $n(p^1) \leq p(g)$, we also have a range for $n(p^k)$.

4   All-edges vs. All-paths

In the previous section we derived equations that tell us how many tests (paths) are required to ensure adequate coverage of a BDI program with respect to the all *edges* criterion. We now use these equations to compare the all edges criterion against the all paths criterion. We know that the all paths criterion requires more tests to be satisfied, but how many more? Since comparing (complex) formulae is not easy, we follow the approach of Winikoff & Cranefield, and instantiate the formulae with a number of plausible values, to obtain actual numbers that can be compared. We use the same scenarios (i.e. parameters) that they used.

In order to derive the All Edges numbers in Table 1 the equations of Fig. 2 were implemented as a Prolog program that computed (non-deterministically) the values of $p(P), y(P)$ and $n(P)$ for any given BDI program P. Additionally, code was written to generate a uniform BDI program P, given values for j, k, and d. This was used to generate the full uniform program P for the first three cases in Table 1, and then compute $p(P)$ for the generated BDI program. The last case exhausted Prolog's stack.

Additionally, the equations of Fig. 3 were implemented as a Scheme program that computed $p(), y()$, and $n()$ for given values of j, k, and d. These were used to calculate values of $p()$. These values matches those computed by the Prolog program for the first three cases, and provided the values for the fourth case ($d = 3$, $j = 3$, $k = 4$ for which Prolog ran out of stack space).

Table 1 contains the results for these illustrative comparison cases (ignore the rightmost column for now). The left part of the Table (Parameters, Number of goals, plans, and actions, and All Paths) are taken from the all paths analysis of Winikoff & Cranefield [20]. The right part (All Edges) is the new numbers from this work.

Comparing the results we make a number of observations. Firstly, as expected, the number of tests required to adequately test a given BDI program P with respect to the all edges test adequacy criterion is lower than the number of tests required with respect to the all paths criterion. However, what is interesting is that the numbers are very much lower (e.g. a few thousand compared with more than 2×10^{107}). Specifically, the number of tests required with respect to the all edges criterion is sufficiently small to be feasible. For instance, in the third case ($j = 2$, $k = 3$, $d = 4$) where the (uniform) BDI program has 259 goals and 518

$$\mathbf{p}(P_1; \ldots; P_j) = \mathbf{y}(P) + j \times \mathbf{n}(P)$$
$$\mathbf{y}(P_1; \ldots; P_j) = \mathbf{y}(P)$$
$$\mathbf{n}(P_1; \ldots; P_j) = j \times \mathbf{n}(P)$$
$$\mathbf{p}(P_1 \triangleright \ldots \triangleright P_k) = \mathbf{n}(P) + k \times \mathbf{y}(P)$$
$$\mathbf{y}(P_1 \triangleright \ldots \triangleright P_k) = k \times \mathbf{y}(P)$$
$$\mathbf{n}(P_1 \triangleright \ldots \triangleright P_k) = \mathbf{n}(P)$$
$$\mathbf{p}(g^{\{P\}}) = 1 + \mathbf{p}(P)$$
$$\mathbf{y}(g^{\{P\}}) = \mathbf{y}(P)$$
$$\mathbf{n}(g^{\{P\}}) = 1 + \mathbf{n}(P)$$
$$\mathbf{p}(g^{\mathcal{P}}) = 1 + |\mathcal{P}| \times (\mathbf{y}(P) + \mathbf{p}(g^{\mathcal{P} \setminus \{P_i\}}))$$
$$\mathbf{y}(g^{\mathcal{P}}) = |\mathcal{P}| \times (\mathbf{y}(P) + \mathbf{y}(g^{\mathcal{P} \setminus \{P_i\}}))$$
$$\mathbf{n}(g^{\mathcal{P}}) = 1 + |\mathcal{P}| \times \mathbf{n}(g^{\mathcal{P} \setminus \{P_i\}})$$
$$\mathbf{p}(/^{\mathcal{P}}\!g) = 1 + |\mathcal{P}| \times \mathbf{p}(P)$$
$$\mathbf{y}(/^{\mathcal{P}}\!g) = |\mathcal{P}| \times \mathbf{y}(P)$$
$$\mathbf{n}(/^{\mathcal{P}}\!g) = 1 + |\mathcal{P}| \times \mathbf{n}(P)$$
$$\mathbf{p}(p^{k+1}) = k \times (1 + \mathbf{n}(g)) + 1 + \mathbf{p}(g)$$
$$\mathbf{y}(p^{k+1}) \leq \mathbf{y}(g) - 1$$
$$\mathbf{y}(p^{k+1}) \geq 1$$
$$\mathbf{n}(p^{k+1}) = k \times (1 + \mathbf{n}(g)) + \mathbf{n}(p^1)$$

Fig. 3. Equations to calculate $\mathbf{p}(P), \mathbf{y}(P)$ and $\mathbf{n}(P)$, simplified for uniform programs, where p^{k+1} denotes a program of the form $a; g; a; \ldots a; g; a$ with $k + 1$ goals ($k \geq 0$).

plans, corresponding to a non-trivial agent program, the number of required test cases is less than 1600.

However, it is worth emphasising that the all edges criterion, even for traditional software, is regarded as a *minimum*. Additionally, it can be argued that agents, which are situated in an environment that is typically non-episodic, might be more likely than traditional software to be affected by the history of their interaction with the environment [20, Sect. 1.1], which means that the all paths criterion is more relevant (since a path includes history, and requiring all paths insists that different histories are covered when testing).

We now turn to consider the four cases under All Edges, i.e. the effects of disabling failure handling, and allowing goals to fail even when there are remaining plans. Whereas a key finding of Winikoff & Cranefield was that failure handling made an enormous difference, in our analysis we found the opposite. This does not reflect a disagreement with their analysis, but a difference in the characteristics of all paths vs. all edges. Adding failure handling has the effect of extending paths that would otherwise fail. This means that enabling failure handling increases the number of paths. However, for the all edges criterion, we do not need to cover all paths, only all edges, so the additional paths created by enabling failure handling do not require a commensurate increase in the number of tests required to cover all edges.

Finally, we consider the difference between the set of plans associated with a goal being the *relevant* and being the *applicable* plan set. Interestingly, this makes a difference, and surprisingly, in some cases it makes more of a difference than enabling failure handling! For example, in the third example case ($j = 2$, $k = 3$, $d = 4$) where *more* tests are required without failure handling (1037) than with failure handling, but where the plans are the applicable plan set (808). Note that the all paths analysis considered the j plans associated with each goal to be *applicable*.

Table 1. Comparison of All Paths and All Edges analyses. The first number under "actions" (e.g. 62) is the number of actions in the tree, the second (e.g. 13) is the number of actions in a single execution where no failures occur. For All Edges there are four numbers: the first two are the (normal) case where failure handling is used to re-post a goal in the event that a plan fails. The next two are the case where failure handling is disabled, so if a plan fails, the parent goal fails as well. The columns labelled "relev." and "applic." are where the plans associated with a goal are respectively the *relevant* plans (so a goal can fail even though there are still untried plans), and the *applicable* plans.

Params			Number of ...			All Paths		All Edges				All Edges $q(Q)$
								$\mathsf{p}(g)$		$\mathsf{p}(\cancel{g})$		
j	k	d	Goals	Plans	Actions	$n^{\checkmark}(g)$	$n^{\times}(g)$	Relev.	Applic.	Relev.	Applic.	
2	2	3	21	42	62 (13)	6.33×10^{12}	1.82×10^{13}	141	78	85	64	62
3	3	3	91	273	363 (25)	1.02×10^{107}	2.56×10^{107}	6,391	2,961	469	378	363
2	3	4	259	518	776 (79)	1.82×10^{157}	7.23×10^{157}	1,585	808	1,037	778	776
3	4	3	157	471	627 (41)	3.13×10^{184}	7.82×10^{184}	10,777	4,767	799	642	627

5   BDI vs. Procedural

The previous section considered the question of whether testing BDI agent programs was *hard*. We now consider the question of whether it is *harder*, i.e. we compare the number of tests required to adequately test a BDI agent program (with respect to the all edges criterion) with the number of tests required to adequately test an equivalent-sized (abstract) procedural program.

We choose to compare equivalently-sized programs for the simple reason that, in general, a larger program (procedural or BDI) will require more tests. So in order to compare procedural and BDI programs we need to keep the size fixed. The particular measure of size that we use is the number of primitive elements, actions for BDI programs, primitive statements for procedural programs.

Following Winikoff & Cranefield [20] we define an abstract procedural program as (we use Q to avoid confusion with BDI programs P):

$$Q ::= s \mid Q + Q \mid Q; Q$$

In other words, the base case is a statement s, and a compound program can be a combination of programs either in sequence $(Q_1; Q_2)$, or as an alternative choice $(Q_1 + Q_2)$. Note that for our analysis we do not need to model the condition on the choice, so the program "if c then Q_1 else Q_2" is simply represented as a choice between Q_1 and Q_2, i.e. $Q_1 + Q_2$. Note that loops are modelled as a choice between looping and not looping (following standard practice [13, p. 408] we only consider loops to be executed once, or zero times). Mapping these programs to control-flow graphs is straightforward, and a program is mapped to a single-entry and single-exit graph.

We now consider how many tests (i.e. paths) are required to cover all edges in the graph corresponding to a procedural program Q. We denote this number (i.e. the testability of program Q with respect to the all edges criterion) by $\mathbf{q}(Q)$. There are three cases. In the base case, a single statement, a single path suffices to cover both edges. In the case of an alternative, each path either traverses the sub-graph corresponding to Q_1, or the sub-graph corresponding to Q_2. Therefore the number of paths required to cover all edges in the graph corresponding to $Q_1 + Q_2$ is the *sum* of the number of paths required for each of the two sub-graphs, i.e. $\mathbf{q}(Q_1 + Q_2) = \mathbf{q}(Q_1) + \mathbf{q}(Q_2)$. Turning to a sequence $Q_1; Q_2$, suppose that we require $\mathbf{q}(Q_1)$ tests to cover all edges in Q_1, and, respectively, $\mathbf{q}(Q_2)$ paths to cover all edges in Q_2. Note that each path traverses the sub-graph corresponding to Q_1, and then continues to traverse the sub-graph corresponding to Q_2. This means that each path "counts" towards both Q_1 and Q_2, so the smallest number of paths that might be able to cover all edges is just the maximum of the number of paths required to test each of the two sub-graphs ($\mathbf{q}(Q_1; Q_2) = \max(\mathbf{q}(Q_1), \mathbf{q}(Q_2))$).

However, this assumes that paths used to cover the part of the control-flow graph corresponding to Q_1 can be "reused" effectively to cover the Q_2 part of the graph. This may not be the case, and since conditions are not controllable (the environment cannot change conditions while the program is running), we cannot make this assumption. So although it might be possible that only $\max(\mathbf{q}(Q_1), \mathbf{q}(Q_2))$ tests (i.e. paths) would suffice to cover all edges in the control flow graph corresponding to $Q_1; Q_2$, it may also be the case that more tests are required. In the worse case it might be that the set of tests designed to cover all edges of Q_1 all take the same path through Q_2, in which case we would require an additional $\mathbf{q}(Q_2) - 1$ tests to cover the rest of the sub-graph corresponding to Q_2. This yields the following definition:

$$\mathbf{q}(s) = 1$$
$$\mathbf{q}(Q_1; Q_2) \geq \max(\mathbf{q}(Q_1), \mathbf{q}(Q_2))$$
$$\mathbf{q}(Q_1; Q_2) \leq \mathbf{q}(Q_1) + \mathbf{q}(Q_2) - 1$$
$$\mathbf{q}(Q_1 + Q_2) = \mathbf{q}(Q_1) + \mathbf{q}(Q_2)$$

We define the *size* of a program Q (denoted by $|Q|$) as being the number of statements. It can then be shown that for a procedural program Q of size m it is the case that $\mathbf{q}(Q) \leq m$.

Lemma 1. $\mathbf{q}(Q) \leq |Q|$.

Proof by induction: *Base case: size 1, so $Q = s$, and $\mathbf{q}(s) = 1 \leq 1$. Induction: suppose $\mathbf{q}(Q) \leq |Q|$ for $|Q| < m$, need to show it also holds for $|Q| = m$. Observe that $\mathbf{q}(Q_1; Q_2) < \mathbf{q}(Q_1 + Q_2)$, so we only need to show that $\mathbf{q}(Q_1 + Q_2) \leq |Q_1| + |Q_2|$, and the case for $\mathbf{q}(Q_1; Q_2)$ then follows. So, consider the case where $Q = Q_1 + Q_2$, hence $\mathbf{q}(Q) = \mathbf{q}(Q_1) + \mathbf{q}(Q_2)$. By the induction hypothesis we have that $\mathbf{q}(Q_1) \leq |Q_1|$ and $\mathbf{q}(Q_2) \leq |Q_2|$ and so $\mathbf{q}(Q_1 + Q_2) = \mathbf{q}(Q_1) + \mathbf{q}(Q_2) \leq |Q_1| + |Q_2| = |Q|$.* □

In other words, the number of paths (tests) required to cover all edges is at most the number of statements in the program. By contrast, to cover all paths, the number of tests required is approximately $3^{m/3}$ [20, p. 109].

The rightmost column of Table 1 shows the number of tests (paths) required to test a procedural program Q of the same size as the BDI program in question for that row. Following Winikoff & Cranefield, we define size in terms of the number of actions (BDI) and statements (procedural), so, for example, the first row of Table 1 concerns a BDI goal-plan tree containing 62 actions (with $j = k = 2$ and $d = 3$), and a procedural program containing 62 statements.

We observe that the case with no failure handling and where $\mathcal{P}$ is *applicable* plans (i.e. the rightmost of the four numbers) is very close to $\mathbf{q}(Q)$. On the other hand, enabling failure handling does, for some cases, result in significantly more tests being required to adequately test the program. For example, 6,391 vs. 363, or 10,777 vs. 627. Both these cases have $j = 3$, whereas for the other two cases where $j = 2$ the difference is smaller. So we conclude that, especially where failure handling exists (which is the case for most BDI agent programming languages), and where goals have multiple plans available, then testing a BDI agent program is indeed harder than testing an equivalently-sized procedural program.

6   Conclusion

We considered the question of whether testing of BDI agent programs is feasible by quantifying the number of tests required to adequately test a given BDI agent program with respect to the all edges criterion. Our findings extend the earlier analysis of this question with respect to the all paths criterion to give a more nuanced understanding of the difficulty of testing BDI agents.

One key conclusion is that the number of tests required to satisfy the all edges criterion is not just lower (as expected) but very much lower (e.g. $> 2 \times 10^{107}$ vs. around $6,400$). Indeed, the number of tests required is sufficiently small to be feasible, although we do need to emphasise that all edges is generally considered to be a *minimal* requirement, and that there are arguments for why it is less appropriate for agent systems.

We also found that the introduction of failure handling did not make as large a difference for the all edges criterion, as it did for the all paths analysis.

When comparing BDI programs to procedural programs, our conclusion lends strength to the earlier result of Winikoff & Cranefield. They found that BDI agent programs were *harder* to test than equivalently sized procedural programs (with respect to the all paths criterion). We found that this is also the case for the all edges criterion, but only where goals had more than two plans.

Our overall conclusion is that BDI programs do indeed seem to be *harder* to test than procedural programs of equivalent size. However, whether it is feasible to test (whole) BDI programs remains unsettled. The all paths analysis (which is known to be pessimistic) concluded that BDI programs could not be feasibly tested. On the other hand, the all edges analysis (known to be optimistic) concluded that BDI programs could be feasibly tested. Further work is required.

Other future work includes applying these calculations to real programs, and continuing the development of formal methods for assuring the behaviour of agent-based systems [3, 6–8, 10, 16, 23].

References

1. Bordini, R.H., Dastani, M., Dix, J., El Fallah Seghrouchni, A. (eds.) Multi-Agent Programming: Languages, Platforms and Applications. Springer, Berlin (2005)
2. Bordini, R.H., Dastani, M., Dix, J., El Fallah Seghrouchni, A. (eds.) Multi-Agent Programming: Languages, Tools and Applications. Springer, Berlin (2009)
3. Bordini, R.H., Fisher, M., Pardavila, C., Wooldridge, M.: Model checking AgentSpeak. In: Autonomous Agents and Multiagent Systems (AAMAS), pp. 409–416 (2003)
4. Bratman, M.E.: Intentions, Plans, and Practical Reason. Harvard University Press, Cambridge (1987)
5. Bratman, M.E., Israel, D.J., Pollack, M.E.: Plans and resource-bounded practical reasoning. Comput. Intell. **4**, 349–355 (1988)
6. Dastani, M., Hindriks, K.V., Meyer, J.-J.C. (eds.): Specification and Verification of Multi-agent Systems. Springer, Heidelberg (2010)
7. Dennis, L.A., Fisher, M., Lincoln, N.K., Lisitsa, A., Veres, S.M.: Practical verification of decision-making in agent-based autonomous systems. Automated Software Engineering, 55 pages (2014)
8. Dennis, L.A., Fisher, M., Webster, M.P., Bordini, R.H.: Model checking agent programming languages. Autom. Softw. Eng. J. **19**(1), 3–63 (2012)
9. Ekinci, E.E., Tiryaki, A.M., Çetin, Ö., Dikenelli, O.: Goal-oriented agent testing revisited. In: Luck, M., Gomez-Sanz, J.J. (eds.) AOSE 2008. LNCS, vol. 5386, pp. 173–186. Springer Berlin Heidelberg, Berlin, Heidelberg (2009). doi:10.1007/978-3-642-01338-6_13
10. Fisher, M., Dennis, L., Webster, M.: Verifying autonomous systems. Commun. ACM **56**(9), 84–93 (2013)
11. Gómez-Sanz, J.J., Botía, J., Serrano, E., Pavón, J.: Testing and debugging of MAS interactions with INGENIAS. In: Luck, M., Gomez-Sanz, J.J. (eds.) AOSE 2008. LNCS, vol. 5386, pp. 199–212. Springer, Heidelberg (2009). doi:10.1007/978-3-642-01338-6_15
12. Jorgensen, P., Testing, S.: A Craftsman's Approach, 2nd edn. CRC Press, Boca Raton (2002)
13. Mathur, A.P.: Foundations of Software Testing. Pearson (2008). ISBN 978-81-317-1660-1

14. Nguyen, C.D., Perini, A., Tonella, P.: Experimental evaluation of ontology-based test generation for multi-agent systems. In: Luck, M., Gomez-Sanz, J.J. (eds.) AOSE 2008. LNCS, vol. 5386, pp. 187–198. Springer, Heidelberg (2009). doi:10.1007/978-3-642-01338-6_14

15. Padgham, L., Zhang, Z., Thangarajah, J., Miller, T.: Model-based test oracle generation for automated unit testing of agent systems. IEEE Trans. Softw. Eng. **39**, 1230–1244 (2013)

16. Raimondi, F., Lomuscio, A.: Automatic verification of multi-agent systems by model checking via ordered binary decision diagrams. J. Appl. Logic **5**(2), 235–251 (2007)

17. Rao, A.S.: AgentSpeak(L): BDI agents speak out in a logical computable language. In: Velde, W., Perram, J.W. (eds.) MAAMAW 1996. LNCS, vol. 1038, pp. 42–55. Springer Berlin Heidelberg, Berlin, Heidelberg (1996). doi:10.1007/BFb0031845

18. Rao, A.S., Georgeff, M.P.: Modeling rational agents within a BDI-architecture. In: Allen, J., Fikes, R., Sandewall, E. (eds.) Proceedings of the Second International Conference on Principles of Knowledge Representation and Reasoning, pp. 473–484. Morgan Kaufmann (1991)

19. Vieira, R., Moreira, Á., Wooldridge, M., Bordini, R.H.: On the formal semantics of speech-act based communication in an agent-oriented programming language. J. Artif. Intell. Res. (JAIR) **29**, 221–267 (2007)

20. Winikoff, M., Cranefield, S.: On the testability of BDI agent systems. J. Artif. Intell. Res. (JAIR) **51**, 71–131 (2014)

21. Winikoff, M., Cranefield, S.: On the testability of BDI agent systems (extended abstract). In: Journal Track of the International Joint Conference on Artificial Intelligence (IJCAI), pp. 4217–4221 (2015)

22. Winikoff, M., Padgham, L., Harland, J., Thangarajah, J.: Declarative & procedural goals in intelligent agent systems. In: Proceedings of the Eighth International Conference on Principles of Knowledge Representation and Reasoning (KR), Toulouse, France, pp. 470–481. Morgan Kaufmann (2002)

23. Wooldridge, M., Fisher, M., Huget, M.-P., Parsons, S.: Model checking multi-agent systems with MABLE. In: Autonomous Agents and Multi-Agent Systems (AAMAS), pp. 952–959 (2002)

24. Zhang, Z., Thangarajah, J., Padgham, L.: Automated unit testing for agent systems. In: Second International Working Conference on Evaluation of Novel Approaches to Software Engineering (ENASE), pp. 10–18 (2007)

25. Zhu, H., Hall, P.A.V., May, J.H.R.: Software unit test coverage and adequacy. ACM Comput. Surv. **29**(4), 366–427 (1997)

Author Index

Printed in the United States
By Bookmasters